Those About Him Remained Silent

Those About Him Remained Silent

THE BATTLE OVER W. E. B. DU BOIS

Amy Bass

University of Minnesota Press
Minneapolis
London

This book is published with assistance from the Margaret S. Harding Memorial Endowment honoring the first director of the University of Minnesota Press.

The first nine plates in the photography gallery are reprinted by permission of the *Berkshire Eagle*. The photograph of Walter Wilson from 1973 was taken by Joel Librizzi for the *Berkshire Eagle*. The five contemporary photographs in the gallery were taken by Ruth Bass in July 2008.

Published by the University of Minnesota Press
111 Third Avenue South, Suite 290
Minneapolis, MN 55401-2520
http://www.upress.umn.edu

Library of Congress Cataloging-in-Publication Data

Bass, Amy.
    Those about him remained silent : the battle over W.E.B. Du Bois / Amy Bass.
        p. cm.
    Includes bibliographical references and index.
    ISBN 978-0-8166-4495-7 (acid-free paper) — ISBN 978-0-8166-4496-4 (pbk. : acid-free paper)
    1. Du Bois, W. E. B. (William Edward Burghardt), 1868–1963—Homes and haunts—Massachusetts—Great Barrington. 2. Du Bois, W. E. B. (William Edward Burghardt), 1868–1963—Birthplace. 3. Great Barrington (Mass.)—History—20th century. 4. Great Barrington (Mass.)—Biography. 5. African American intellectuals—Biography. 6. African American civil rights workers—Biography. I. Title.

    E185.97.D73B37 2009
    303.48′4092—dc22

                                                    2009023610

Printed in the United States of America on acid-free paper

The University of Minnesota is an equal-opportunity educator and employer.

15 14 13 12 11 10 09   10 9 8 7 6 5 4 3 2 1

It is in the early days of rollicking boyhood that the revelation first bursts upon one, all in a day, as it were. I remember well when the shadow swept across me. I was a little thing, away up in the hills of New England, where the dark Housatonic winds between Hoosac and Taghkanic to the sea. . . . Then it dawned upon me with a certain suddenness that I was different from the others; or like, mayhap, in heart and life and longing, but shut out from their world by a vast veil. I had thereafter no desire to tear down that veil, to creep through; I held all beyond it in common contempt, and lived above it in a region of blue sky and great wandering shadows. . . . Alas, with the years all this fine contempt began to fade; for the words I longed for, and all their dazzling opportunities, were theirs, not mine. But they should not keep these prizes, I said; some, all, I would wrest from them.

—**W. E. B. Du Bois,** *The Souls of Black Folk*

Contents

The Shadow of the Veil

The black children of America will cease to hear my name.
—W. E. B. Du Bois, 1951

I DID NOT KNOW that I grew up approximately sixteen miles from W. E. B. Du Bois's birthplace and childhood home until my second year of graduate school. This fact is remarkable to me, not because the majority of residents of the beautiful Berkshire Hills in Massachusetts have no idea that Du Bois was born in Great Barrington in 1868 but because *I* did not know. Given that anyone who graduated from the public school systems of the Berkshires boasts a healthy knowledge of their famous surroundings, I thought there was little that I—the daughter of two noted local journalists and culture gurus—did not know about this westernmost county of the Bay State. I understood the preeminence of the local music, theater, and art scenes; I attended concerts at Tanglewood and plays in Williamstown; and I knew everything there was to know about Norman Rockwell and Edith Wharton and Herman Melville. But not until I read a random mention of Great Barrington as Du Bois's birthplace in Paul Gilroy's book *The Black Atlantic* did I know of Du Bois's location in Berkshire history. I then asked my parents, only to find that yes, they knew. In fact, there was a terrible controversy over Du Bois in the late 1960s.

As my parents offered me their memories of the controversy, I began to realize that this battle over Du Bois not only created a rift within the local community but also struck right at the heart of Cold War–era politics, the anxieties over civil rights movements and the Vietnam War, and racial unrest in America writ large.[1] They told me about their friends who were supporters of a project to create a memorial—a national land-mark—to Du Bois at the site of his childhood home. They mentioned often a fellow named Walter Wilson as someone they knew, a friend, who was particularly involved. They thought the movement had been success-ful, that a national landmark designation had been granted to Du Bois's home, but they were not sure of the details.

I filed away this information, devoting myself to my doctoral work, my first book, and some kind of career track. But when I finally began to research it, I found it a fascinating gambit of study, not only for its larger historical implications but also because I was learning about my child-hood surroundings; talking daily with my parents about the figures that I unearthed in my research; asking my mother to keep a watchful eye on the local newspaper, the *Berkshire Eagle,* for which both my parents still write weekly columns, for tidbits about Du Bois; and tracking down ran-dom bits of information from local sources. And the more I learned, the more disturbing it became to me that it had taken some twenty-five years to find out that one of *the* founding voices of my life's work was born just a stone's throw away from my childhood home. My own unawareness, I thought, was likely important to some bigger picture.

Yet I was not alone in this ignorance. Among the stacks of research and file folders on my desk is the story of Philip Pettijohn, who grew up in Pittsfield, Massachusetts, where I attended high school. In 1987, Petti-john wrote his senior thesis for Simon's Rock of Bard College, noting that although he—like me—had heard lots about Rockwell in school, it was not until his second year at the University of Massachusetts that he dis-covered Du Bois as a local. "He's at least on a par with Norman Rockwell," submitted Pettijohn. "He's our kin, our brother, our home boy."[2]

Philip Pettijohn is one up on me. He began his senior thesis project with the wish to bring Du Bois the same sort of attention that figures such as Rockwell and Melville reap in the Berkshires. Two years after he wrote the thesis, he found out he was distantly related to Du Bois. Pettijohn learned from the family documents of a cousin—Denise Williams, of New Jersey—that his mother, Virginia Frye, could be traced back to Du Bois: Du Bois's great-aunt Maria M. Burghardt was Pettijohn's great-great-great-grandmother. Initially, Pettijohn said, he was "skeptical" about the genealogy. "There had always been rumors," he said, "but [a relation to Du Bois has] been said about any black family that has been in Berkshire County for a long time." Pettijohn hoped that his discovery would help spur more interest in Du Bois locally. "Giving recognition to Du Bois in Berkshire County will give something to the young black people here," he said. "It will give motivation and inspiration to break the cycle of going nowhere."[3]

While Pettijohn reveled in his newfound discovery regarding his blood relation to one of his academic interests, most others in the area continued to ignore the legacy of arguably its most famous native son. Local civil rights activist Elaine Gunn found this to be true when she returned to the Berkshires in the 1950s. Gunn had grown up in the segregated community of Hagerstown, Maryland, but moved to Stockbridge, Massachusetts, for the last three years of high school. She left the Berkshires for New York University but returned to Great Barrington to marry, raise her family, and eventually work as a teacher at Bryant Elementary School. Gunn remembers there being no black history in the high school curriculum in Stockbridge, just as there had been little in Maryland. "I remember hearing about Du Bois, but not much," she says. "During Negro History Week, most of the black folks that we studied were [Booker T.] Washington and [Harriet] Tubman—Du Bois was lesser known, and I didn't pay much attention to it." However, this began to change after her time at NYU: "After I graduated [from high school] and went to school in New York and returned, I thought, 'Golly—Du Bois from the town of Great Barrington? I should look into this.'" In the early 1950s, Gunn remembers that she made a trip to the Great Barrington library to begin her exploration. "I was a mother, I was home during the day, and I lived downtown near the library, so I looked into Du Bois," she remembers. "I heard about *The Souls of Black Folk,* and I went to the library and I told the head librarian what I wanted, and she said, 'You know, I think we have a book, it's probably in a box somewhere—you come back and I'll find it for you.'" Gunn returned a few days later. "I went back and got the book," she recalls. "It was very old, quite almost tattered, and I borrowed it and read it, and I found Great Barrington in it." For Gunn, reading *The Souls of Black Folk* was a turning point. "It was not easy reading," she remembers, "and it took me a long time to get through it, but my eyes were open."[4]

As Gunn recalls, the timing of her introduction to Du Bois was critical in her understanding of his importance. She read *The Souls of Black
Folk* while civil rights movements were becoming increasingly visible in
the South, such as the lunch counter sit-ins at the Woolworth's in Greens-
boro, North Carolina. At the same time, Du Bois—as well as many other
vocal opponents to segregation and inequality, and advocates of anything
else deemed "socialist" in nature—was coming under increased scrutiny
from the U.S. State Department. "That was my introduction," Gunn says
of reading *The Souls of Black Folk* at that particular time. "It happened
when things started happening down south in the 1950s and, of course,
when he [Du Bois] was in the news with the State Department, and with
the rise of [Martin Luther] King."[5]

But as Gunn became more interested in Du Bois and his work, finding herself inspired by him and framing her increased interest in civil
rights accordingly, many others were finding cause for concern over the
nature of his politics, which would have a tremendous influence on why
he has been seemingly absent from Berkshire history. The Berkshires, of
course, and Great Barrington in particular, were not alone in abandoning
Du Bois. For many, his most enduring legacy has been his numerous publications, which include, in addition to *The Souls of Black Folk* (1903),
The Philadelphia Negro (1896), *Darkwater* (1920), *The Gifts of Black Folk*
(1924), *Black Reconstruction* (1935), *Dusk of Dawn* (1940), *Color and
Democracy* (1945), *The Encyclopedia of the Negro* (1946), and *The Autobiography of W. E. Burghardt Du Bois* (1968). Revolutionary from the
very start of his extensive and prolific career, he is perhaps best known
for his public disagreements with Booker T. Washington and his central
involvement, in 1905, in the creation of the Niagara Movement, an organization founded to target racial discrimination that led to the founding of
the NAACP (the National Association for the Advancement of Colored
People), in 1909. As the only African American in the NAACP's inaugu-
ral administration, Du Bois served as editor of the organization's famous
publication, *The Crisis,* for twenty-five years, during which time he became
one of the most important voices on issues of race, politics, and equality
in both the United States and the world at large. Du Bois, who held a variety of academic posts throughout his life, left the NAACP in 1934, after a
series of disputes with the organization's board of directors, and returned

to Atlanta University in Georgia, where he had previously taught. At this point he increased his global travels, including to China, becoming one of the critical framers of the ideology of Pan-Africanism, which espoused an ardent belief that members of the African diaspora, holding much in common with one another, should work in solidarity against the inequalities they faced.

Du Bois's shift into increasingly leftist politics did not, however, mean that he left his distinctly New England character behind him, a fact that would become critical in terms of how those in Great Barrington would negotiate his memory. Even among fellow travelers, Du Bois was continually criticized for his assumption of an upper-middle-class to somewhat elite self-perception, a feature that could be attributed to his education in late nineteenth-century New England. For example, in a discussion of the role of the United States in establishing black sovereignty in Liberia, Cedric J. Robinson, a leading voice on black political radicalism, goes so far as to argue that Du Bois was "blinded by the elitism characteristic of his class prerogative," thus greatly complicating Du Bois's criticism of U.S. imperialism and skewing his assumption to regard Liberia as a nation-state.[6]

However, it was for Du Bois's ideologies and understandings, which continued on both Pan-African and socialist tracts, rather than his attitude and sense of self, that he became disfavored by colleagues and enemies alike. First arrested for his leftist leanings in 1951, he lost his passport to the U.S. State Department for extended periods. At the height of the postwar "red scare," his writings were trashed from public libraries and he became a focal point of the Federal Bureau of Investigation. Yet it was his decision to officially become a member of the Communist Party that cemented his outsider position, ideologically expatriating him before he physically left the country, in a move to Ghana not long before his death, in 1963.

Indeed, it is in Ghana that the legacy of Du Bois fully enjoys honored recognition. On August 27, 1986, in Accra, the dedication of a national monument honoring the life's work of Du Bois took place, including the opening of the W. E. B. Du Bois Memorial Centre for Pan-African Culture, located on the property where he lived the last two years of his life and is now buried alongside his wife, Shirley Graham Du Bois. According to the

Ghanaian Embassy in Washington, D.C., the residents of Ghana wanted "to show our special appreciation and special gratitude. He dedicated himself to Africans and to blacks. He was a great man."[7] Today, the memorial center, which welcomes visitors with a plaque inscribed with Du Bois's poem "Children of the Moon," includes a research library, portraits of notable Africans, and a gallery of manuscripts. Located at 22 First Circular Road, the house, according to the Ghana Department of Tourism, "has been dedicated and consecrated to the memory of a man who loved Africa . . . a modest man, but whose life and works raised him above ordinary men and placed him among the great men of all time."[8]

People in the Berkshires, conversely, have been unable to decide upon Du Bois's place in local history, choosing to focus largely on his Communist Party membership and eventual Ghanaian residency rather than his local, national, and Pan-African achievements and legacies, and choosing to vilify one of the region's most notable native sons, as well as those who tried to pay tribute to him. The death of Du Bois, however, cannot merely be marked by sharp descriptions that solely address his expatriation. His passing in Ghana, at the age of ninety-five, came at a remarkable moment in history, far from both the pastoral splendor of New England and the political passion stirring in the nation's capital: Du Bois died on the eve of the March on Washington, just two years after officially joining the Communist Party, and more than half a century after cofounding the NAACP. On Thursday afternoon, August 29, 1963, the Republic of Ghana held its state funeral for Du Bois, as prescribed by President Kwame Nkrumah, while thousands stood on the mall of the capital of the United States of America listening to Martin Luther King Jr. offer one of the most important speeches in U.S. history. In the days that followed, a striking collection of condolences arrived via telegram from a veritable who's who of the leftist world, including members of the American Communist Party, African leaders, North Korea's Kim Il Sung, China's Mao Tse-tung, and Soviet premier Nikita Khrushchev.[9]

Although Nkrumah used the funeral of Du Bois as an event to both memorialize one he called a friend and simultaneously proclaim ownership for Ghana of a Pan-African leadership, and others recognized his death as that of a great Marxist leader, and despite a lifetime—a very long one—of demonstrating his brilliance, Du Bois died in relative obscurity in a faraway land rather than next to his grandfather Alexander, in New Haven, Connecticut, as he once predicted would happen in one of his many autobiographies.[10] Thus, as a host of civil rights activists assembled in the U.S. capital to produce the most visible stance for civil rights yet taken, one of the movement's creators died an outcast, exiled by many as a communist turncoat who had committed treason against democracy.

In striking comparison to the state funeral in Ghana, the residents of Great Barrington, Massachusetts, paid little, if any, attention to the passing of one of their own. If David Levering Lewis, unquestionably Du Bois's greatest biographer to date, is to be believed, Du Bois felt similarly about Great Barrington. Although Lewis acknowledges the importance of the town in shaping Du Bois, he also finds it to be a precarious part of Du Bois's past, one that as a writer Du Bois carefully crafted throughout the various versions of his autobiographies to suit his own needs:

> His sense of identity or belonging was spun out between the poles of two distinct racial groups—black and white—and two dissimilar social classes—lower and upper—to form that double consciousness of being he would famously describe at age thirty-five in *The Souls of Black Folk*. Because he sedulously invented, molded, and masked this village world to suit his egocentric, if inspired, purposes of personal and racial affirmation, a sojourn there needs to be leisurely and probing enough to recover the Great Barrington that its most famous citizen knew and yet did not wish to know or have known. There were family matters of which he was deeply ashamed, others that made him angrier than he could admit to himself. For Willie Du Bois, the Berkshire period was variously Edenic fable, racial definition, and psychic trapdoor.[11]

What Lewis does not consider (as it was not the focus of his magnificent two-volume biographic tome) is the lack of interest in Great Barrington's "most famous citizen" by others who also called it home. Du Bois was not part of Great Barrington's distant past but had maintained his connections to his hometown in a variety of ways. As he details in his autobiography, "a group of friends," including Jane Addams and Clarence Darrow, purchased his old homestead in 1928 and gave it to him as a gift for his sixtieth birthday. "I planned eventually to make it my country home," Du Bois writes, "but the old home was dilapidated; the boundaries of the land had been encroached upon by neighbors, and the cost of restoration was beyond my means."[12] According to local Great Barrington historian Bernard Drew, Du Bois went so far as to have blueprints made by local architect Joseph McArthur Vance to renovate the property, but, after he moved to Atlanta, interest in the project waned.[13] Du Bois sold the land in 1955, a few years before his death, but kept something from the house that stood there: "There was a great fireplace, whose wrought-iron tongs stand now before my fireplace as I write."[14]

Du Bois's early years in Great Barrington had a profound impact on his political leanings and insights. According to his own memory, Du Bois first learned of democracy by witnessing the New England tradition of a town meeting, in which a "ragged old man came down from the hills and for an hour or more reviled the high school and demanded its discontinuance." He watched the town listen to the man, a "citizen and property-holder," and then witnessed the town vote to give the high school its annual budget. "I began to see that this was the essence of democracy: listening to the other man's opinion and then voting your own, honestly and intelligently."[15]

According to his adopted son, David Graham Du Bois, Du Bois "always remembered and treasured his boyhood in Great Barrington," and loved to spend time there in his later years during the summer.[16] Great Barrington, however, did not always hold Du Bois in the same favorable regard. Within a few years of Du Bois's death, residents of the Berkshires, both full time and summer only, engaged in a heated debate over the legacy of the famed civil rights forefather in Great Barrington's history. At question, most directly, was whether or not a memorial park should be established on the site of his childhood home. Nestled in the heart of the bucolic yet culturally sophisticated Berkshires, Great Barrington is part of an internationally recognized regional summer culture that has encompassed a wide array of veritable national treasures. As a local journalist observed, "In Ashley Falls, one can visit the home of Col. John Ashley. In Stockbridge, there is the Norman Rockwell Museum. But in Great Barrington, there is little more than a small metal plaque hidden in the weeds."[17]

Indeed, whereas many figures enjoy substantial commemoration from the various museums and historical groups in the areas that exalt them, little notice is paid to the fact that the most important voice on American race relations of the twentieth century began his life in Great Barrington, making clear that discussions regarding public memory are also implicitly about public forgetting. Great Barrington greeted the small movement that emerged in the 1960s to memorialize Du Bois with a hostility bred by a Cold War worldview that reduced complicated global politics to a vehement hatred of communism (or anything else deemed even faintly critical of U.S. democracy). This view was further tainted by a racist discourse regarding the man and what he espoused. The debate over Du Bois raged through the small community in the late 1960s and 1970s, chiefly orchestrated by Walter Wilson, a prominent yet controversial real estate broker and former Communist labor organizer from the South who, after moving to the Berkshires, took on the Du Bois commemoration campaign as his own. Wilson received support from the *Berkshire Eagle,* a nationally recognized family-owned daily newspaper, as well as prominent national figures such as Harry Belafonte, Norman Rockwell, Julian Bond, and Sidney Poitier. Opposed to the movement to memorialize Du Bois were the local weekly newspapers, the *Berkshire Record* and the *Berkshire Courier,* and a wide array of "patriots" who defined themselves by their devout anticommunist beliefs, including members of the American Legion, the Daughters of the American Revolution, and the John Birch Society. Perhaps most vocal were members of a local chapter of the Veterans of Foreign Wars. "[Memorializing Du Bois is] like building a statue of Adolph Hitler," said Harold J. Beckwith, a past commander of the James A. Modolo Post of the VFW in Great Barrington. "The man was a Marxist as far back as 1922 and we oppose a monument to a Communist any place in the United States."[18]

The comparison of Du Bois to Hitler is, without question, a startling one. It reveals much about the racial shades that Cold War battles took, and provides the incentive to look further into this seemingly impossibly local moment in history in order to unpack the national political debates over race and Cold War politics at a troublesome time in American civic life. Within the controversy, members of the Great Barrington community had to choose sides regarding what the legacy of Du Bois in his hometown was to be. This debate brought with it a torrent of questions: What was the image of Du Bois in the community where he spent the first eighteen years or so of his life? How did the red-baiting encompassed within the Cold War affect the ability of the Great Barrington community to accept him? How did general attitudes compare to those of the community in which Du Bois lived? What does the battle over the memorial to Du Bois reveal about the racialized mind-set of the Cold War, most broadly, and about the mind-set and motivations of the people of Great Barrington, most specifically? Why could they not, as a whole, honor their own—if indeed they ever accepted him as such?

The process of finding answers delves into the most complicated realms of civil rights, national identity, and concepts of collective memory. In many ways, the battle that took place in Great Barrington over the figure of Du Bois was one of the first encounters in the United States to grapple with civil rights as a legacy, rather than as a series of ongoing political and social movements. To repeat, Du Bois's death took place the night before the March on Washington, arguably the most iconic of the many civil rights spectacles. Wilson's efforts to memorialize Du Bois began to take form almost a full year before the assassination of Martin Luther King Jr., almost inarguably the most iconic of the many civil rights leaders. The debate that Great Barrington was thrown into, then—that of how to commemorate, if at all, one of the founding voices of a still-thriving and controversial social movement—would prove to be among the first of its kind, as it asked, How should civil rights be remembered? That it should take place in New England, where the abolitionist movement emerged in full force in the nineteenth century, only further complicates the story. New Englanders are supposed to be the good guys, so to speak. These are the townsfolk who were egalitarian enough to "allow" someone like Du Bois to flourish in their public space. Yet, fast-forwarding almost a century after abolitionism, we find that ideologies of northern apathy and complacence—a feeling of "Why should *we* be the ones to deal with this, given that *we* never had *legalized* segregation?"—largely dominate the public discourse, making it difficult to figure out who, if anyone, really are the good guys anymore.

The landscape of the Cold War is critical to how this dialogue has played out, as issues of racial politics became seemingly irretrievably entangled with Cold War rhetoric, rhetoric that was often employed to mask racist sensibilities. Although there is some wonderful scholarship on the relationship between Cold War ideologies and civil rights movements, it is always difficult to unpack the racist under- and overtones of Cold War politics. The battle over Du Bois that the Berkshires endured in a small space in western Massachusetts reveals much about the racial shades embedded in the Cold War battle against communism. After years of Du Bois's demonstrating his socialist leanings in his vast array of writings, speaking engagements, and political activities, and after suffering personally and professionally from living under the watchful eye of the U.S. State Department, his decision late in his life to become a Communist enabled folks, such as those who belonged to the VFW in the Berkshires, to refuse to accept him as a member of their community, whether at the local, national, or global level. For them, Du Bois's official endorsement of communism branded him forever unpatriotic, forever anti-American. And even though the movement to commemorate Du Bois eventually succeeded in making the Du Bois homestead site a National Historic Landmark, in 1979, indicated by an unremarkable roadside sign, today his legacy in Great Barrington remains controversial, with many people resurrecting Cold War postures to oppose those who continue to want to elevate Du Bois's historical visibility in the community, including members of the newly revamped Du Bois Memorial Committee. Thus, what to do with the five-acre plot of land—the site of much of Du Bois's boyhood and earliest memories—has been up for grabs for the last forty years or so, demonstrating a common problem in creating anything of note in a public space.

Of course, such debates are widespread, as the act of *remembering* also involves the act of *forgetting*. Things become contentious when the public engages in decisions about which moments and figures to create monuments to, and which to erase. Without the latter, the former would have little, if any, meaning.[19] Yet even when it is decided that a monument should be created, that someone or something should be remembered, there is still disagreement. For example, the plans for the artistically and historically revolutionary wall that Maya Lin created for the Vietnam Veterans Memorial on the mall in Washington, D.C., which she originated while still a student at Yale University, raised vicious eyebrows about the wall's worth and relevance, bringing both the design of the project and her Asian heritage under fire. One Vietnam veteran described the memorial to the U.S. Commission of Fine Arts as a "black scar," concluding that he found it "insulting and demeaning" to the memory of those who served in the war.[20] A part of the same complex Cold War political framework as the public memory of Du Bois, recollections of Vietnam, as observed by historian Marilyn Young, are complicated by the fact that they are located within the broad emotional sweep of civil rights politics, ensuring that the war "came . . . to threaten the integrity of the narrative [of American history] itself."[21] Vietnam escalated in a moment when the nation's morality and allegiance to citizenship for all were already under fire from civil rights activists, making clear the contradictions embedded in the attempts of the United States to ensure democracy in Southeast Asia while simultaneously denying it at home. Lin, as scholar David Simpson observes, "had to respond to a mandate against making any political statement about the Vietnam War, which was (and indeed remains) a very divisive component of the national culture, indeed so divisive as to call into question what the 'nation' is and who gets to be included in it and to benefit from it."[22]

More recently, a debate regarding the footprint of the World Trade Center and how best to re-create the space in terms of corporate profit and strength (to ensure that terrorism had, indeed, not "won") filled the pages of newspapers even before the dust of the 9/11 attacks had settled and the so-called healing began. Those people dedicated to the rebuilding effort quickly butted heads with those who focused on ideas of somber remembrance and urged New York to maintain a sensitive understanding that regardless of what might be built upward, the site served as a grave for many below. Thus, the resurrection faced the complicated task of both catering to the friends and families of those lost and symbolizing capitalist growth and, therefore, national might and victory.

According to Marita Sturken, these conversations regarding how to remember 9/11 operated from the perspective of "the cultures of fear and paranoia," exemplified by the controversy that arose over the International Freedom Center planned for the "Ground Zero" site.[23] The center looked to transform the location from a place of mourning to "a site of pedagogy about world events," locating the events of 9/11 in a broader international context.[24] However, as the Bush administration's escalation of the war in Iraq increasingly mandated that any critique of the United States or its policies was labeled an act of disloyalty, governor George Pataki canceled the project, as it became manufactured as yet another so-called leftist attempt at America bashing.

That history—or what Sturken calls "the practices of remembrance"— can be so publicly controversial is not, of course, surprising. It has to be so, as it relies on an assemblage of memories and representations. Some are constructed by scholars via archival materials, creating what historian Edward Linethal has called the "historical voice." Others are created by people using their own experiences, as well as those of their friends, family, and neighbors, creating the "commemorative voice."[25] In the mid-1990s, the curators of the National Air and Space Museum of the Smithsonian Institution found this to be true in their attempt to display the *Enola Gay,* the plane used in the bombing of Hiroshima in World War II. The protests against the exhibit came from many sides, but particularly from veterans and antiwar activists, and they perhaps best correlate to the debate that raged over Du Bois in the Berkshires in the late 1960s. Summarizing the overall problem that his organization had with the *Enola Gay* project, the executive director of the Air Force Association, General Monroe W. Hatch Jr., wrote NASM director Martin Harwit, "Balance is owed to all Americans, particularly those who come to the exhibition to learn. What they will get from the program as described is not history or fact but a partisan interpretation."[26] Others had problems with what the plane itself represented. Upon its arrival at the Smithsonian, for example, nuclear-arms protesters lined the street singing peace songs and issuing calls to "disarm."[27]

Like the figure of Du Bois, the *Enola Gay* signified many things to many people, showing just how complicated the politics and culture of memory can be, and how public space can serve as the front line for battles regarding how various social groups are represented and defined. Memory is "not a transhistorical phenomenon, a single definable practice that has remained the same over time," observes scholar Alison Landsberg. "Rather, like all modalities, memory is historically and culturally specific; it has meant different things to people and cultures at different times and has been instrumentalized in the service of diverse cultural practices."[28] Although the commemoration of Du Bois in Great Barrington differs from the examples of the Vietnam Veterans Memorial, Ground Zero, and the *Enola Gay* in significant ways, any public debate in which there are vilified aspects proves useful, whether discussing a war memorial, a terrorist attack, a warplane, or a figure of historical consequence.

All help to determine how decisions regarding facets of public space and memory are made, and where the power lies in determining the outcome. Commemoration does not ever mean the creation of an official or definitive history but, rather, the version that eventually wins over the public, becoming a competition of sorts for a history that works for the people who had to live it.[29]

It is always, of course, at least to some degree about power—about who or what is structuring the conversation regarding what is being commemorated. With the Cold War as its framework, the controversy over Du Bois's legacy demonstrates an underlying rage regarding race relations and ideas of communism held within a community. But why? Why did residents in Great Barrington fear the legacy of a man? Was it simply that they were afraid of what he represented?

Historians too often forget the power of fear within history, dismissing it as a viable emotion that ensured people behaved in the past in a way that we hope no one will behave in the present. But, of course, this does not work. Did the events of September 11, 2001, for example, and the federally sponsored fearmongering that continues to take place in its wake make historians better understand the actions of A. Mitchell Palmer during the red scare after World War I? Do Americans now better understand what it is like to be afraid, and what people seem to be willing to accept from one another and from their government in times of great, and sometimes absolutely legitimate, fear? Regardless of the answers to these questions, a historical hypocrisy is evident, exemplified by how Americans turned their collective head away from the prisons in Guantanamo while continuing to historically speak of shame and regret over the Japanese internment camps, so similar in nature. How do we accept the circumstances of one action while historically despising and condemning the other?

In many ways, understanding the role of Du Bois in Great Barrington's collective soul is a difficult task, because public opinion is a seemingly impossible thing to corral and, perhaps even more important, because the roles of the personal, the local, and the public in the act of making history remain so difficult to gauge. Yet the nature of the controversy needs to be examined within its broader historical contexts: the figure of Du Bois himself, the Cold War, rural New England life, and civil rights. At the bottom of all of this lie seemingly straightforward questions for the residents of Great Barrington: Why did Du Bois make you all so mad? What values did you find compromised at the thought of remembering Du Bois, and what kinds of power did you have in order to make your noise, your opposition, so public?

Defining the public is, of course, critical to this kind of exploration, questioning whether it constitutes anyone with an expressed opinion or includes those who might have an opinion but do not have the means or will to make it public. Some people argue that public space needs to be for everyone. However, another way to think about public space is to see it as a part of the public sphere, one that, despite its open access, is intended for the few that will appreciate and find it useful, despite the fact that many others also will have right of entry. What defines the interpretation of public space, then, is the time frame in which people inhabit it, making its meaning either conflict or accord with the principal thoughts and opinions.

Thus, public space can be articulated in different ways. Whereas the contemporary moment is undoubtedly subjugated by what has been dubbed the "war on terror," for example, in the 1980s the so-called culture wars dictated the perception of how public space should be utilized. So, though the particular words of any given public controversy may differ, the song remains the same. For those in Great Barrington contemplating the legacy of Du Bois in the 1960s and 1970s, the frameworks of civil rights and the Cold War ensured that his reception was recognized as questionable at best, and that it would remain so because, when remembered within the combating contexts of capitalism *or* communism, totalitarianism *or* democracy, Du Bois proved to be an alienating figure, one who could not be positively reconstructed in the quaint, bucolic, very New England space of Great Barrington. He simply was too foreign a presence, whether because of the color of his skin, because of his political affiliations, or because of his chosen resting place in Africa, which ensured his status as a decidedly nonlocal entity. Such a figure does not make for a simple process of commemoration. As historian Kirk Savage has argued in his pathbreaking study of the racial politics of Civil War statues,

> Public monuments were meant to yield resolution and consensus, not to
> prolong conflict. The impulse behind the public monument was an
> impulse to mold history into its rightful pattern. And history was
> supposed to be a chronicle of heroic accomplishments, not a series of

messy disputes with unresolved outcomes. Even now, to commemorate is to seek historical closure, to draw together the various strands of meaning in a historical event or personage and condense its significance for the present in a speech or a monument. It is true that the process of commemoration often leads to conflict, not closure, because in defining the past we define our present. Yet in choosing to remember "historical" events or heroes we still hope to plunge them into a past secured against the vicissitudes of the present.[30]

Regardless of the meticulous historical research that continues to revolve around him, the long and prolific life of Du Bois remains a hard thing for most anyone to capture. David Levering Lewis certainly comes closest, yet he concludes his research by explaining just why Du Bois is so difficult: "W. E. B. Du Bois attempted virtually every possible solution to the problem of twentieth-century racism—scholarship, propaganda, integration, cultural and economic separatism, politics, international communism, expatriation, [and] third-world solidarity." His was, Lewis concludes, "an extraordinary mind of color in a racialized century."[31]

So while scholars such as Lewis continue to frame Du Bois and his legacy in terms of the broadest of historical questions, a grasp of the local, public perceptions on Du Bois remains undefined, leaving us with bigger questions regarding the gambles, politics, and workings of memory. In similar fashion, debates over history that continually and consistently unfold take place in classrooms, at local and national parks, over museum exhibits, around art installations, and elsewhere. They are competitions with much at stake, because once the public conversation ends and a monument or memorial is erected, it will, as Savage points out, "become a kind of natural fact, as if it had always been meant to be."[32] In the 1960s, a figure such as Du Bois comprised a problematic piece of the historical landscape, ensuring that conflicting portrayals of him virtually erased his legacy from the Berkshires, a place where cultural figures and festivals generally reign supreme. It is, as James Williams, a spokesman for the NAACP, observed of Great Barrington in 1988, on the twenty-fifth anniversary of Du Bois's death, "a heck of a way for [a] town to treat its most distinguished citizen."[33]

CHAPTER ONE

Du Bois in Great Barrington and Beyond

In general thought and conduct I became quite thoroughly New England.
—*The Autobiography of W. E. B. Du Bois*

SUMMER 2004. The bright, colorful images that extend along the side of the Carr Hardware building on Railroad Street in Great Barrington end with an intricate image of a black left hand, raised high in a familiar stance of protest. The mural, designed and executed by the Railroad Street Youth Project, coordinated by then assistant director Anna Phelan, serves as yet another tribute to Great Barrington native son W. E. B. Du Bois. This resurrection of Du Bois in the town of his birth came on the heels of the centennial celebration of his most decisive work, *The Souls of Black Folk,* along with the debut of a course focusing on Du Bois at Great Barrington's Monument Mountain High School; a series of lectures and historical walks given by the regrouped and increasingly present Du Bois Historical Society; Berkshire Country Day School's various activities devoted to teaching about the civil rights leader to its flock of elite students; and the creation of the W. E. B. Du Bois River Park and Garden along the banks of the Housatonic River.

The Berkshires, one might cautiously hope, a region that prides itself as "America's premier cultural resort,"[1] has let Du Bois come home. In the hills of western Massachusetts, the Berkshires offer tourists a range of activities. Pittsfield, for example, the so-called urban center of the area, boasts Arrowhead, the home of Herman Melville, operated by the

Berkshire County Historical Society. At Arrowhead, Melville wrote *Moby-Dick*, among other works, and many claim that the view from his study of frozen Mount Greylock (the state's highest peak) and Saddleback Mountain influenced his decision to make the great whale white. In Hancock, visitors of the Hancock Shaker Village, which features twenty-one historic buildings filled with Shaker furniture, can sample foods, watch "heritage" animals, and purchase unique Shaker offerings, and in Lenox, visitors at the Mount, Edith Wharton's estate and gardens, can prowl through the 1902 mansion in awe of the writer's space. Quaint Stockbridge offers both Chesterwood, the home of sculptor Daniel Chester French, whose hands created the Lincoln Memorial; and the Norman Rockwell Museum, which includes both a gallery and Rockwell's studio, a fitting space for the artist who spent his last twenty-five years in the Berkshires, and the most popular year-round cultural attraction in the Berkshires, housing the largest collection of Rockwell's work in the world.

In terms of culture, the Berkshires, indeed, have some serious bragging rights. The crown jewel, Tanglewood, lies on the Stockbridge-Lenox border. As the summer home of the Boston Symphony Orchestra since 1936, some three hundred thousand music lovers enjoy the world's most famous summer music festival each July and August. Theater lovers have the daunting task of choosing among several internationally recognized stages, such as the Berkshire Theatre Festival, Shakespeare and Company, and the Tony Award–winning Williamstown Theatre Festival. The best of the dance world can be found at the Jacob's Pillow Dance Festival, in Becket. And among the numerous antique shops, small art galleries, and area museums sits the Sterling and Francine Clark Art Institute in Williamstown, with works from masters such as Pierre-Auguste Renoir, Claude Monet, Camille Pissarro, Winslow Homer, John Singer Sargent, Paul Gauguin, Pierre Bonnard, Edgar Degas, Henri de Toulouse-Lautrec, Goya, Frederic Remington, and Mary Cassatt, as well as one of the most important collections of decorative arts in the world. For those interested in the modern, Mass MoCA (the Massachusetts Museum of Contemporary Art), built on the site of a nineteenth-century industrial factory, stands as one of the largest cultural institutions in the country with more than 300,000 square feet of developed space.

The role of Great Barrington within this cultural extravaganza varies. First inhabited by Indians, the area was settled by the Dutch and English in 1730, and in 1761 the Great and General Court of Massachusetts established Great Barrington as a town, named for British prime minister William Pitt's war minister, Lord Barrington. In 1786, the courthouse became one of those targeted by Daniel Shays and his rebellious group of farmers, in an attempt to prevent the court from prosecuting debtors. According to the first history of Berkshire County, collected in 1829, early nineteenth-century Great Barrington emerged as somewhat of a manufacturing center, with a population of 2,264 people and featuring two taverns, four merchant stores, two tanneries, a grist mill, a plaster mill, and a variety of mechanic shops, as well as many businesses that thrived in the surrounding hamlets.[2]

Today, Great Barrington serves, among other things, as somewhat of a weekend and summer bedroom community for Manhattan. As Du Bois once offered about those he called "a quiet and rather stodgy set,"[3]

> One class of rich folk with whom I came in contact were summer boarders who made yearly incursions from New York. I think I was mostly impressed by their clothes. Outside of that there was little reason so far as I could see to envy them. The children were not very strong and rather too well dressed to have a good time playing. I think I probably surprised them more than they me, for I was easily at home with them and happy. They looked to me just like ordinary people, while my brown face and frizzled hair must have seemed strange to them. (77)

The invasion of "summer people" or "second-homers" to the Berkshires began in the post–Civil War era, when the fruits of the Gilded Age brought to Lenox and Stockbridge, primarily, droves of the so-called nouveau riche, alongside artists searching for that rare combination of culture and solitude (Melville, Wharton, Nathaniel Hawthorne, Catherine Sedgwick, Fanny Kemble, Henry Wadsworth Longfellow, Henry David Thoreau), fueling an architectural explosion throughout the rolling hills. The "Berkshire cottages," as they are now called, exhibited the desire of an era eager to demonstrate its wealth, with marbled mansions such as Ventfort Hall, which served as a summer escape for the powerful Morgan family, and Bellefontaine, built in 1897 as a reproduction of

Louis XV's Petite Trianon and now the home of the exclusive Canyon Ranch Spa. The Berkshires "arrived" within this period, as the lives that took place within some seventy-five "cottages" appeared regularly in society columns throughout the nation.[4]

Lenox and Stockbridge continue to exhibit the most celebrated cultural agendas, whereas Great Barrington, it seems, with a year-round population of approximately 7,500 people, is where those who vacation in the Berkshires opt to hang out, eat, and buy property. With some forty restaurants dotting its streets, the largest town in the south Berkshire area is of relatively equal distance from Boston and Manhattan, but it is largely ignored by the Brahmin sort, who flee eastward to Cape Cod and its islands for refuge from summer city heat rather than head west. The absence of Bostonians from Berkshire society somewhat alters what should be a quintessential New England character. Du Bois, for one, recognized that in many ways he had not grown up in a New England town. "Physically and socially our community belonged to the Dutch valley of the Hudson rather than to Puritan New England," he wrote, "and travel went south to New York more often and more easily than east to Boston" (80).

For New Yorkers, who, as Du Bois observed, are likely to enter the Berkshires from the south, Great Barrington is a cultural gateway. According to the Massachusetts Department of Housing and Community Development, "Second-home owners and transplants from large, metropolitan areas are discovering what longtime residents have known for many years; Great Barrington is a great community to raise a family, run a business, and enjoy the pleasures of small town living."[5] Michael Ballon, chef-owner of the trendy Castle Street Café and its next-door jazz club, the Celestial Bar, describes it as a geographical displacement of sorts. "In summer, Manhattan's entire Upper West Side is empty," he says. "Everyone is here."[6] According to *New York* magazine, the appeal of Great Barrington, just like the appeal of the Berkshires in general, is fairly obvious to sophisticated city folk. "We love that we can dress down in jeans and sneakers yet still get our fill of Manhattan-worthy arts," confesses one vacationing couple; another professes that "some of the galleries—and many of the restaurants—are as good as those in the city. . . . But minus the attitude."[7]

Yet amid the restaurants and the galleries and the construction of vast second homes sits a sign near the Great Barrington–Egremont border noting a place of historical importance. Such signs dot the sides of many highways throughout the United States, pointing out some of the most intriguing local aspects of history, such as the Mitchell Corn Palace in Mitchell, South Dakota. This sign, situated next to a small parking lot on the side of Route 23 heading out of Great Barrington, marks a place that W. E. B. Du Bois once vividly recalled: "If one slips out the northern neck of Manhattan and flies to the left of the silver Sound, one swoops in time onto the Golden River; and dodging its shining beauty, now right, now left, comes after a hundred miles of lake, hill and mountain, in the Old Bay State. Then at the foot of high Mt. Everett one takes a solemn decision; left is sweet, old Sheffield; but pass it by stolidly and slip gently into tiny South Egremont which always sleeps. Then wheel right again and come to Egremont Plain and the House of the Black Burghardts."[8] The site is the boyhood home of W. E. B. Du Bois.

GROWING UP DU BOIS

W. E. B. Du Bois was born in the Jefferson McKinley cottage on Church Street in Great Barrington on February 23, 1868, to Mary Burghardt and Alfred Du Bois.[9] His birth, as he locates it, took place days after Congress impeached Andrew Johnson and the day after the townsfolk of Great Barrington gathered to celebrate the birth of George Washington (61). According to the *Berkshire Courier,* his birth certificate named him William E. Duboise, the "colored" son of Alfred and Mary Duboise. The couple had married two years earlier in the Great Barrington enclave of Housatonic, and Alfred's birthplace was listed as San Domingo, Haiti. According to David Levering Lewis, the Great Barrington town clerk likely spelled the family's name as heard.[10]

Aside from these kinds of facts from the town register and census, most of what is known about Du Bois's family and his years growing up in Great Barrington comes from his own autobiographical writings, from which David Levering Lewis culled the majority of his material. According to Lewis, in what is inarguably the most thorough biographic treatment of Du Bois's youth,

Most of what is known about these years comes from Du Bois himself, whose compelling prose re-creations of the town, the times, the races, and of his own family and himself are landmarks in American letters. He was to leave his hometown at age seventeen, returning during the following fourscore years only infrequently, and always for brief stays. Fifteen years after leaving, the village prodigy had transformed himself, almost beyond recognition, into a cosmopolitan traveler and distinguished scholar. But the importance of the Great Barrington period, its imprint upon all that Willie Du Bois grew to be, was deep, and certainly singular. His sense of identity or belonging was spun out between the two poles of two distinct racial groups—black and white—and two dissimilar social classes—lower and upper—to form that double consciousness of being he would famously describe at age thirty-five in *The Souls of Black Folk*. Because he sedulously invented, molded, and masked this village world to suit his egocentric, if inspired, purposes of personal and racial affirmation, a sojourn there needs to be leisurely and probing enough to recover the Great Barrington that its most famous citizen knew and yet did not wish to know or have known. There were family matters of which he was deeply ashamed, others that made him angrier than he could admit to himself. For Willie Du Bois, the Berkshire period was variously Edenic fable, racial definition, and psychic trapdoor.[11]

Although Lewis emphasizes the difficulties in dealing with the multiple legacies of "the Great Barrington period," he underscores, again, that its impact upon Du Bois cannot be underestimated. His family, for sure, was a complicated lot, one that undoubtedly plagued his increasingly genteel self as he progressed through life. His pedigree originated with some of the earliest peoples to arrive in western Massachusetts, a group of Hudson Valley Dutch families, of which the Burghardts were one. Coenraet "Borghardt," for example, filed a petition in 1741 regarding a land dispute, some twenty years before Great Barrington became incorporated.[12] Burghardt had gotten a slave, Tom, sometime in the 1730s from West Africa. In 1780, Tom served under Captain John Spoor in the Revolution, and likely received his freedom for his efforts. Of Tom's many offspring, his son Jacob, the father of Du Bois's maternal grandfather, Othello, whom Du Bois remembered as "very dark," is thought to have taken part in Shays's Rebellion (64). More importantly, Jacob's second wife, after first wife Violet died, was Elizabeth Freeman.

Freeman served as a slave in the house of Col. John Ashley, under whose authority Captain Spoor's company operated in the Revolution. A veteran of the French and Indian War, Ashley is credited for drafting the Sheffield Declaration, a series of grievances against the British that is considered a forerunner to the Declaration of Independence, in 1773 at his house in Sheffield, Massachusetts, just south of Great Barrington.[13] Now owned by the Trustees of Reservations, which owns and protects more than 50,000 acres in the state of Massachusetts, and open to the public, the Ashley house is famous for its representative eighteenth-century architecture, for its social and political importance in its time, and—most importantly—as a symbol of the abolishment of slavery. While Ashley worked with his colleagues upstairs to draft the Sheffield Declaration, legend says that his wife Hannah's slave, Elizabeth "Mum Bett" Freeman, overheard some of his ideas regarding individual liberty. After a particularly abusive encounter with Hannah, Mum Bett sought out Theodore Sedgwick in Stockbridge, a member of a prominent New England family with abolitionist leanings. On behalf of Mum Bett and another of Ashley's slaves, Brom, Sedgwick brought *Brom & Bett v. Ashley* to court. The jury's ruling in their favor made them the first slaves to be freed via an American court. The court mandated that Colonel Ashley pay them thirty shillings each, as well as court costs, setting a precedent that eventually led to the abolition of slavery in Massachusetts.

Mum Bett refused Ashley's offer that she work for his family for wages, and instead moved to Stockbridge and worked for the Sedgwicks, making a name for herself as a nurse and midwife. Her loyalty to the illustrious Sedgwick band was renowned, particularly evident when she hid their silver from Daniel Shays's followers and passed them off when they knocked on the door of the home during the famous rebellion.[14]

Elizabeth Freeman died in 1829, and the Sedgwick family, considering her one of its own, buried her in the famous Sedgwick pie. The pie lies at the corner of the graveyard in Stockbridge, with Theodore in the center next to his wife, Pamela. They are surrounded, in concentric circles, by their descendants (except for Edie Sedgwick, the actress), buried with their feet pointing inward and their heads outward, in the hope that when Judgment Day arrived, they would arise and face no one else but Sedgwicks. Freeman's grave reads: "She was born a slave and remained a slave for nearly thirty years: She could neither read nor write; yet in her own sphere she had neither superior nor equal: She neither wasted time, or property. She never violated a trust, nor failed to perform a duty. In every situation of domestic trial she was the most efficient helper and the tenderest friend. Good mother, farewell!"

Du Bois refers to his great-grandmother as "the celebrated Mom Bett" in his final autobiography, and mistakes that she was Jacob's first wife and Violet was the second (62). His mistake illustrates why autobiography is a problematic historical source. Although it often offers unique insight and information, it also inflicts upon history numerous challenges, largely because of its reliance on a single person's memory about his or her self. Further, autobiography often becomes more about the time in which the author is writing than about the one he or she is remembering. Case in point: Du Bois produced several versions of his life, using each autobiographical tome to represent a different stage of his political evolution. According to literary scholar Jodi Melamed, for example, in *Dusk of Dawn* (1940) Du Bois "offered his life story as an example of how the meaning of race is lived in the world"; David Levering Lewis has called *Darkwater* (1920) "the most passionate but least candid of his autobiographical writings"; and historian Manning Marable finds that *Darkwater* "best represents Du Bois's ideas at the height of his political influence and intellectual maturity."[15]

In his final autobiography, entitled simply *The Autobiography of W. E. B. Du Bois* (1968) and subtitled *A Soliloquy on Viewing My Life from the Last Decade of Its First Century,* Du Bois not only offers his most profound statement regarding the global politics of race in the post–World War II period but also gives the most thorough version of his time in Great Barrington. And even though *Darkwater* provides a viewpoint that is perhaps "least candid," as Lewis finds, it also is most revealing in terms of the strong feelings Du Bois imparts upon his reader regarding a variety of subjects, including his childhood. It is not mere autobiography, as Marable argues, but rather "part autobiography, part poetry," designed to take "the reader on a spiritual journey."[16]

Du Bois was keenly aware of the historical difficulty inherent in autobiography and memoir, which is one of many reasons that he wrote so many versions of his own, making strategic political use of each one: "Autobiographies do not form indisputable authorities. They are always incomplete, and often unreliable. Eager as I am to put down the truth, there are difficulties; memory fails especially in small details, so that it becomes finally but a theory of my life, with much forgotten and mis-conceived, with valuable testimony but often less than absolutely true, despite my intention to be frank and fair" (12).

Du Bois's writing on his boyhood home comes across, quite as Lewis argues, as "Edenic," as he describes what seems to be an almost utopian place. Of course the Berkshires are renowned for their beauty. Herman Melville, for example, wrote of escaping "the Babylonish brick-kiln of New York" for the "sea feeling" of the country, and sculptor Daniel Chester French spent his summers in an "ecstasy of delight over the loveliness" of the Berkshires. (*"That* is heaven," he wrote. "New York is—well, New York.")[17] In this vein, and like so many other autobiog-raphers, Du Bois begins one autobiography with an idyllic vision of his hometown, demonstrating a grasp of both the local and the national moment into which he entered:

> I was born by a golden river and in the shadow of two great hills, five
> years after the Emancipation Proclamation, which began the freeing
> of American Negro slaves. The valley was wreathed in grass and trees
> and crowned to the eastward by the huge bulk of East Mountain, with
> crag and cave and dark forests. Westward the hill was gentler, rolling
> up to gorgeous sunsets and cloud-swept storms. The town of Great
> Barrington, which lay between these mountains in Berkshire County,
> Western Massachusetts, had a broad Main Street, lined with maples
> and elms, with white picket fences before the homes. The climate was
> to our thought quite perfect. (61)[18]

From the house on Church Street, which he describes as "quaint," Du Bois and his mother moved "to live on the lands of [her] clan on South Egremont Plain in the southern part of our town," while his father traveled to Connecticut to try to "build a life and home" for the family (62). This plot of land, which included a farmhouse, a barn, and two waste areas, is now considered to be an archaeological site by the University of

Massachusetts, which took the title for the land from the Du Bois Foundation in 1988. In the cellar hole that remains, as well as the farmyard, a range of material artifacts has been found, including ceramics, liquor bottles, a chamber pot, shoes, a comb, lamps, and ink bottles. According to UMass anthropologist Robert Paynter, the Burghardt farm was one of many that African Americans created along one road beginning early in the nineteenth century. Regarding the Burghardt property, Paynter suggests that between 1820 and 1873 the family farmed the land and also took in some boarders.[19]

Du Bois remembers the house on this land to have been "sturdy, small and old-fashioned" (64). His mother's family had lived in this section of town, according to Du Bois, for almost two hundred years when the "black Burghardts," which he describes as "a group of African Negroes descended from Tom," arrived in Great Barrington after being brought to the nearby Hudson Valley by Dutch slave traders (62). Although Du Bois claims to recall the farmstead quite well, his writings on it indicate that he also did some research:

> I remember three of those houses and a small pond. These were
> homes of Harlow and Ira; and of my own grandfather, Othello, which
> he had inherited from his sister, Lucinda. There were 21 persons in
> these three families by the Census of 1830. Here as farmers they long
> earned a comfortable living, consorting usually with each other, but
> also with some of their white neighbors. The living to be earned on
> the farms gradually became less satisfying, and the group began to
> disintegrate; some went to the Connecticut Valley, some went West;
> many moved to town and city and found work as laborers and
> servants. Usually their children went to school long enough to learn
> to read and write, but few went further. I was the first of the clan to
> finish high school. (63)

The course his family took as they left their plot of land in the southern reaches of Great Barrington indicated much to Du Bois about the difficulty of being black, as he understood it to be "not solely race prejudice" but also a lack of education and what he calls a "fear of a land still strange to family mores which pictured travel as disaster." His family wanted to stay close, and thus assumed positions within familiar fields in African American history: domestic work, physical labor, and service industries. Not all fared badly. He proudly recalls that his "cousins, the Crispels of West Stockbridge, owned one of the best homes in town, and had the only barber shop." Other relatives, working in the hotel and restaurant industry in the Berkshires, "were in charge of dining rooms, did well and were held in esteem." Another cousin served as "a sexton in the most prominent church" in Lenox, where his wife and daughters successfully "ran an exclusive laundry." Cousin Ned Gardner, a "well-bred man," worked as a waiter at the Berkshire Hotel, and Du Bois's uncle served the Kellogg family, who failed to pay him until a Kellogg daughter married into the prominent Hopkins family. "She was left a rich widow and returned to Great Barrington in 1880," Du Bois recalls. "This circumstance helped me enter the profession of teaching" (63–64).

Du Bois's mother, Mary Silvina, was among the youngest of his grandparents'—Othello and Sally's—"ten or more children."[20] Du Bois describes his mother, who was born in 1831 and died in 1885, as "dark shining bronze, with smooth skin and lovely eyes; there was a tiny ripple in her black hair, and she had a heavy, kind face." An affair between her and John Burghardt, a first cousin, bore Idelbert, a son. Du Bois writes that the incident was one not spoken of in his family, speculating that "the mating was broken up on account of the consanguinity of the cousins." It did, however, change his mother into "a silent, repressed woman." Mary eventually began working in town as a maid, and it was there, at age thirty-five, that she met Alfred Du Bois (64–65).

In his autobiography, Du Bois appears both taken with and skeptical of his father's heritage. He seems to write of it far more formally than that of his mother's lineage, yet he also throws doubt on claims that "the white American family," which migrated in the seventeenth century from Flanders, was of an aristocratic social class. According to Du Bois, James Du Bois, born in 1750, worked as a physician in Poughkeepsie until he migrated to the Bahamas to oversee a series of plantations after Lord Dunmore, New York State governor, gave land grants to the family to thank them for their service as loyalists. In the Bahamas, Du Bois speculates, James Du Bois had an affair with a plantation slave or married "a free Negro woman." Regardless, by means of his union with a black woman, in the early nineteenth century James Du Bois fathered two sons, Alexander—Du Bois's grandfather—and John, whom he moved to New York in 1810 upon the death of their mother. Light-skinned enough to "pass," both boys enrolled in the Cheshire School in Connecticut, but in 1820, after the sudden death of James Du Bois, "the white New York family removed the boys from school and took charge of their father's property" (65–66).

Du Bois met his grandfather, Alexander, only once, when he was fifteen years old. "Always he held his head high, took no insults, made few friends," he remembers. "He was not a 'Negro'; he was a man!" (71). Alexander Du Bois became a shoemaker's apprentice. His early upbringing as a gentleman had a large impact on him (Du Bois described him as being "of stern character"), and, refusing to learn the shoemaking trade, he fled to Haiti. Although details of his years in Haiti are vague, he married there and fathered Alfred, who was born in 1825. In 1830, Alexander Du Bois left Haiti for New Haven, Connecticut, where he established himself in business by launching his own grocery and eventually assuming the position of steward on the New Haven–New York ferry. He achieved both financial stability and social respect in New Haven, but he moved to Springfield, Massachusetts, in 1856 after deciding that it was a more racially open landscape. He continued working on the New Haven–New York passenger line in the warmer months. "He lived well," remembers Du Bois, who amply quotes his grandfather's diary in order to make sense of his family history (68).

In 1861, Alexander Du Bois briefly returned to Haiti, for reasons that Du Bois can only speculate about, but perhaps because he had left Alfred behind when he initially moved to New Haven. Alfred was one of Alexander's four children. "As a father," Du Bois writes of his grandfather," he was naturally a failure—hard, domineering, unyielding." A daughter "passed over into the white world, and her children's children are now white, with no knowledge of their Negro blood"; Alfred took a different course, according to Du Bois, and "married my brown mother" (71).

Despite his attempts to piece together his father's lineage and his obvious respect for his grandfather, Du Bois indicates that he never knew much about his father's upbringing, writing, "I really know very little of my father" (71). He does offer, however, remarkable insight from the perspective of his mother's family:

> When my father came to Great Barrington in 1867, the black
> Burghardts did not like him. He was too good-looking, too white. He
> had apparently no property and no job, so far as they knew; and they
> had never heard of the Du Bois family in New York. Then suddenly
> in a runaway marriage, but one duly attested and published in the
> *Berkshire Courier*, Alfred married Mary Burghardt and they went to
> live in the house of Jefferson McKinley. Here they lived for a year or
> two and against them the black Burghardt family carried on a more
> or less open feud, until my birth. (72)

Much of this disdain emanated from Alfred's apparent desertion of Mary.
Although the couple planned that Mary would join Alfred once he settled in New Milford, Connecticut, some forty miles south of Great Barrington, Du Bois indicates that she had qualms about leaving both her
home and her family, who continued to oppose her joining her husband.
"The result was in the end that mother never went and my father never
came back to Great Barrington. . . ." Du Bois writes. "I never saw him,
and know not where or when he died" (73).

　　Although his mother fell into a state of melancholy over her husband's
departure, Du Bois found that the Burghardts' distaste for Alfred failed to
prejudice them against him. He remembers the curiosity he encountered
from his mother's family and, seemingly, all of Great Barrington. "I was
of great interest to the whole town," he writes. "The whites waited to see
'when my hair was going to curl,' and all my Burghardt relatives admired
me extravagantly" (72). Although his father's mixed racial heritage obviously fed a great deal of this interest, it is likely his mother's apparent
depression from the dissolution of her marriage helped create a protective
relationship of the town toward the young Du Bois. "The town folk who
knew the Burghardts took her and me into a sort of overseeing custody,"
he remembers. "We lived in simple comfort, and living was cheap" (73).

　　After his grandfather's death, Du Bois and his mother left the house
on Egremont Plain and moved into town. This coincided with shifts in
the Great Barrington economy alongside national trends of industrial-
ization in the 1870s. For the small community as a whole, the increased
presence of New Yorkers visiting for vacations demanded an augmented
commercialization. For those on farms on the outskirts of the town, it
meant the rethinking of their lifestyle. As Robert Paynter describes,

A farm living was less satisfying. Blacks moved to town and took jobs. There were clear color lines in the professions and the factories. So the people at the [Burghardt] home site worked on other farms, they took in laundry and they worked at hotels. The men seemed to stop working so much on their own land, and more on white farms. So the agricultural fields were used more for gardening, the barn for storage. It eventually collapsed. Women still brought in boarders. Some Burghardts [men] left Great Barrington, [whereas] the women were more rooted to town.[21]

Du Bois and his mother first lived in a group of rooms over the stable at the Sumner estate, which he thinks his mother chose because of its proximity to the school, and then moved, after his grandmother's death, to a house with a "poor white family, kindly," next to the train station on Railroad Street. As Du Bois entered high school, he and his mother, increasingly ill, moved in with the Cass family on Church Street (74). The vested interest of the community in the obviously talented young Du Bois was evidenced in its continued support of his well-being. Though he describes his youth as comfortable, he also admits, in a bit of reevaluation, that he and his mother likely lived "near the edge of poverty," supported both by his mother's family and, occasionally, by "white families, long closely connected with the Burghardts." Such support strengthened his relationship with the residents of Great Barrington. At the Cass house, for example, his mother missed rent payments—which he estimates were four dollars per month—but the balance of what they owed was regarded as a "gift when I went to college," making Mrs. Cass an important supporter of his education and, as a result, his future (73).

THE PATH TO HARVARD: EDUCATION AND THE VEIL

For the most part, then, Du Bois felt he fit into life quite well in Great Barrington. He had a supportive religious life at the Congregational Church, which was closer to where he and his mother lived than the Episcopal Church that the majority of his family attended. At church, where he thinks he and his mother were likely the only "colored communicants," they "felt absolutely no discrimination, and I do not think there was any, or any thought of it" (89). Indeed, there was little that

Great Barrington did not offer to Du Bois. "In the ordinary social affairs of the village—the Sunday School with its picnics and festivals; the temporary skating rink in the Town Hall; the coasting in crowds on all the hills—in all of these, I took part with no thought of discrimination on the part of my fellows, for that I would have been the first to notice" (94).

Beyond acceptance in social affairs, specific individuals, particularly, supported the young Du Bois. Du Bois remembers Johnny Morgan, for example, who owned a bookstore in town that Du Bois often visited. "He became interested in me and very sympathetic," Du Bois remembers. Morgan let Du Bois look at the wares of his store, and allowed him to purchase Thomas Macauley's *History of England*—all five volumes—on an installment plan, not a usual practice. Morgan also helped Du Bois become the local correspondent for the *Springfield Republican,* the most significant publication in western Massachusetts at that time, which issued Du Bois's first published works (88–89).

Like the inhabitants of most towns of a similar size in New England, the residents of Great Barrington put a great deal of emphasis on education. As he showed academic ability early on, the town's interest in Du Bois grew proportionately to his scholarly achievement, with widespread attempts to secure his success regardless of his financial resources or his racial heritage. For Du Bois, however, the seeming racial ease of the town became relative, and despite the support he acquired from neighbors and teachers and classmates, it was within the walls of Great Barrington's schools, which he describes as "simple but good, well-taught," that he began to first understand what he eventually articulated in *The Souls of Black Folk* as "the Veil"—that which he saw as separating and concealing black America from white, blocking insight into the problems of race in the United States, and creating a symbolic wall that denied full citizenship (77). Of his education, he remembers this:

> In the public schools of this town, I was trained from the age of six
> to 16, and in the town schools, churches, and general social life, I
> learned my patterns of living. I had, as a child, almost no experience
> of segregation or color discrimination. My schoolmates were
> invariably white; I joined quite naturally all games, excursions,
> church festivals; recreations like coasting, swimming, hiking and
> games. I was in and out of the homes of nearly all my mates, and ate

and played with them. I was as a boy long unconscious of color
discrimination in any obvious and specific way. I knew nevertheless
that I was exceptional in appearance and that this riveted attention
upon me. Less clearly, I early realized that most of the colored
persons I saw, including my own folks, were poorer than the well-to-
do whites; lived in humbler houses, and did not own stores. (75)

To combat his increasing awareness of difference, Du Bois maintains
that he focused on academic excellence; his merit ensured that he sur-
passed his peers academically. For a time, there was "another dark boy"
in his high school, but he remembers being "very much ashamed of him
because he did not excel the whites as I was quite used to doing" (99).
His mother, he claims, believed that such attention to formal education
remained the key to "equal whites," reassuring herself that the rest of her
family could have been equally accomplished had they simply finished
school: "There was no real discrimination on account of color—it was
all a matter of ability and hard work" (75).

This philosophy, Du Bois admits, "doubtless cloaked some half-
conscious misgivings," reassuring him that if his "brown face" was the
first thing noticed, his abilities soon overshadowed it (75–76). To some
degree, perhaps, he was correct. In many ways, the generosity of Great
Barrington to Du Bois and his mother seems out of the ordinary. He
notes, for example, C. C. Taylor, "a little white-haired man who was
writing a history of the town." Taylor, a banker, owned a herd of milking
cows just off Main Street and offered unlimited milk to Du Bois and his
mother whenever they wanted. "I remember those morning walks up to
the great elm on our corner . . . ," Du Bois writes, "up to the Taylor home
and the delicious fresh milk" (81).

However, race relations, as Du Bois remembers them, were complicated in Great Barrington:

> Over against this general basic community of white Americans were
> two groups. One was composed of a mass of Irish peasants who began
> to reach this town in the early 50's after the well-known famine. They
> were Catholics and came in increasing numbers as house servants
> and workers in the local woolen mills. The older Irish families
> became laborers on the railroads and artisans of various sorts. They
> formed a group of the respectable poor. They were followed by poorer

and more ignorant peasants, ill-trained and ragged and given to drink. . . . As a boy, I was afraid of the Irish and kept away from their part of town as much as possible. Sometimes they called me "nigger" or tried to attack me. On the other hand, the older and better class of them had children in school whom I knew quite well. (82)

In Great Barrington, the Irish lived separately from others because of their religion, not to mention their poverty; Du Bois remembers how "the Irish became the basis of jokes and ridicule in town and throughout New England." He recognized, for example, that "two Irishmen" replaced the "'nigger' jokes of Tennessee" when he returned to New England after a stint in the South, but saw his "own attitude toward this hard-working Irish minority" as "naturally complicated" (82). The Irish, like his "own colored people," were a minority population in Great Barrington, and two Irish children, Mike Gibbons and Ned Kelly, were friends and school-mates of his. Indeed, when reflecting upon his high school years, in which he recalls there being "some rather puzzling distinctions" that he concluded were "social and racial," he found that "the racial angle was more clearly defined against the Irish than against me" (94).

By Du Bois's estimates, "in Great Barrington there were perhaps 25, certainly not more than 50, colored folk in a population of 5,000." The differences reflected within this population—intermarriage, "infiltra-tion of white blood," and "intermingling with local Indians," as well as the presence of African migrants, Indians, and "freed Negroes from the South"—were many, exacerbated, perhaps, by the fact that some of the Southern migrants formed their own Methodist Zion church to the aston-ishment of townsfolk. However, in terms of the perceptions regarding this diverse population of "colored," the famous "Veil" did not make such distinctions. Du Bois's recognition of perhaps his most famous symbol did not seem to plague his early adolescence, but with age and familiarity his understandings of race and community intensified, and his observations of the small town that he so admired in those early years began to take on the cynicism of experience. "After I entered high school, I began to feel the pressure of the 'Veil of color'; in little matters at first and then in larger," he recalls. "There were always certain com-pensations" (83). These compensations, according to Du Bois, were dealt with by a balance that he and his chosen playmates created—some were white, had money, and were "rather dumb in class," whereas Du Bois was "colored" and "certainly not in current style" but did well in school (84). Because of this kind of trade-off, Du Bois had a substantial circle of friends with whom he played, visited, and ate meals.

At school, the most significant figure in Du Bois's life was Frank Hosmer, principal of Great Barrington High School from 1879 to 1888. Hosmer had graduated from Amherst College in 1875 and worked at schools in Brimfield and Palmer, both located in central Massachusetts. After his stint as principal, he went on to become editor of the local newspaper, the *Berkshire Courier,* and then moved to Hawaii in 1890, where he became president of Oahu College, in Honolulu. A supporter and leader in the move for the annexation of the territory by the United States—to the point where Queen Liliuokalani called for his head— he served on the advisory council of the provisional government after Sanford B. Dole became provisional president, in 1893.[22]

Initially, as Du Bois remembered, Hosmer got off to a rocky start at the school. His introduction to the student body was his proposal to mandate a school uniform of a hat inscribed in gold with G.B.H.S., the school's initials. The students hated the idea, deeming it "the Great Big Hosmer Speculation." Du Bois, of course, could not have afforded such a hat anyway (85).

Hosmer encouraged Du Bois's studies and relied on other members of the Great Barrington community to help him. For example, when Hosmer wanted Du Bois to begin the study of Greek, which his mother could not afford because of the price of books, Hosmer turned to Mrs. Russell, the second wife of Farley Russell, who owned the mill. Mrs. Russell paid for Du Bois's Greek books. At her encouragement, he also became close friends with the couple's son, Louis Russell, who was "frail, good-hearted, but slow-witted, and did not go to public school." Mrs. Russell welcomed Du Bois into their home, where he was waited upon by Irish servants and able to borrow a range of toys.[23]

Du Bois graduated from high school in 1884, the first in the Burghardt family to do so, and, as he described, "of course the only colored student." The ceremony required a speech from each of the thirteen graduates. Du Bois gave his, which was the valedictory address, on Wendell Phillips, the Boston abolitionist, who had died a few months before the graduation. Of his study of Phillips for the speech, Du Bois writes, "I was fascinated by his life and his work and took a long step toward a wider conception of what I was going to do" (99). The speech, as he remembered it, was well received, and indicative of Great Barrington's perspective on the young black man who graduated with such distinction: "My own essay brought loud applause from the audience because of my race and subject. I was born in a community which conceived itself as having helped put down a wicked rebellion for the purpose of freeing four million slaves. They deeply admired Phillips despite the fact that recently he had adopted socialism. My mother was in the audience and was filled with pride" (100). Du Bois's mother was not the only one proud of his performance. For many in the town, it was a turning point in their understanding of the young scholar—a direct example of just what he might achieve. In an item marking the ten-year anniversary of the speech, the *Berkshire Courier* wrote, "Many remember him as a bright-faced, active, mischief-loving boy. It was not until the delivery of his oration on Wendell Phillips at the time of his graduation as valedictorian from the high school in 1884 that people began to regard him as one possessing marked abilities."[24]

After graduation, Du Bois found that Frank Hosmer had set him on a path equal to his talents. As Du Bois remembers, Hosmer was instrumental in determining that his high school career would focus on a college-preparatory sequence, including advanced math courses and, of course, Greek. "If Hosmer had been another sort of man," Du Bois recalls early in his autobiography, "with definite ideas as to a Negro's 'place,' and had recommended agriculture or domestic economy, I would doubtless have followed his advice. . . . I did not then realize that Hosmer was quietly opening college doors to me, for in those days they were barred with ancient tongues" (101). Later, he credits Hosmer more forcefully, wondering what his future would have held if his principal had indeed been a different sort of man: "*Suppose* Principal Hosmer had been born with no faith in 'darkies,' and instead of sending me to college had had me taught carpentry and the making of tin pans?" (183; emphasis in original).

Although the esteemed walls of Williams and Amherst colleges stood nearby, Du Bois set his sights on Harvard. His life, however, took a bit of a turn, for a range of reasons. For one, his mother died suddenly of a stroke, which somewhat stalled his plans yet also created somewhat of a smoother path toward them. "Whatever her death really meant to him," David Levering Lewis observes, "the timing was perfect. One more obstacle to Harvard College had fallen. Finally, he was free from familial obligation to begin redefining himself."[25]

With the death of Du Bois's mother, according to Lewis, "the African-American community, about which he says always as little as possible, came to his rescue."[26] After moving in with one of his mother's sisters, Minerva, his future began to crystallize. As Du Bois tells it, he decided, on the advice of "a sort of guardianship of family and white friends," (102) to work and study for a year at Fisk University, in Nashville, Tennessee, because of his age and because the town's high school was likely below the range of Harvard's requirements.

Because of this focus on college, which few of his classmates considered, Du Bois found that he "occupied an unusual position among whites in the town" (101). Many townsfolk likely understood their relationship to Du Bois as a way of understanding their own values and worth; how they treated an exceptional young black man reflected well upon them and their New England ideals, making for a benevolent rapport that bordered on fetish, in that they saw him as "our Negro." His teachers undoubtedly had recognized the tremendous potential Du Bois demonstrated, yet college was an exceptional pursuit for anyone from Great Barrington, never mind a black youth raised primarily by a single mother and her expansive family.

As Lewis posits, it was the death of Du Bois's mother that set him free from his emotional ties to Great Barrington. Even so, he had little means by which he could sustain himself, never mind his education. However, "the town in its quiet and unemotional way was satisfied with my record and silently began to plan" (192). According to Du Bois, while his family helped house him and find jobs, there were three central (white) figures who collaborated on and financially contributed to his future: Hosmer, his principal; Edward Van Lennep, the principal of a local private school and the superintendent of Sunday school at Du Bois's church; and C. C. Painter, a Congregationalist minister, who was the father of one of Du Bois's classmates. According to Du Bois, Hosmer was likely the one that brought his situation to the attention of the other two. Years later, upon receiving best wishes at his fiftieth birthday party from his former principal, Du Bois declared that he owed to Hosmer, "more than to any single person, the fact that I got started toward the higher training in my youth."[27]

Yet although Du Bois remained forever grateful to Hosmer, he admits it was Painter who put together what eventually became a scholarship for Du Bois, getting a series of area churches to commit twenty-five dollars each, per year, to him for as long as he was in college, and it was likely Painter who plotted for Du Bois to go south before returning for Harvard (he entered as a junior in 1888). Du Bois recalled that Painter, who had once worked for the Federal Indian Bureau, was interested in Reconstruction projects in the South, and he speculated, particularly after he arrived at Harvard, that his special circumstances in Great Barrington likely contributed to the Fisk University plan (103). "Had I gone from Great Barrington high school directly to Harvard," he writes, "I would have sought companionship with my white fellows and been disappointed and embittered by a discovery of social limitations to which I had not been used. But I came by way of Fisk, and the South and there I had accepted color caste and embraced eagerly the companionship of those of my own color" (135). But for Du Bois, his understanding of color—and its consequence—was only beginning its long and imperative evolution.

CHAPTER TWO

Evolution of a Progressive Mind

I hope that soon you will see in Socialism and communism, not a threat or a crime, but a difference of opinion. . . . I have just returned from living eight months behind the iron curtain. My whole attitude toward life has been changed.
—W. E. B. Du Bois to William M. Brewer, 1959

D U B O I S ' S   V E R S I O N of the period in which he left Great Barrington for Nashville and Fisk gives an impression that it was his first immersion in black community and culture. For David Levering Lewis, this is both problematic and somewhat correct. "Even though he always minimized the role that Great Barrington's African-American community had played in his growing up," Lewis writes, "Willie's knowledge of the larger world of black people—and especially of southern black people—was as indirect and negligible as he said it was." Du Bois may have discovered "the Veil" within the racial workings of Great Barrington's schoolyards, but without question, as Lewis continues, "Western Massachusetts was an incomparably kinder place, racially, in which to grow up than the lynch-law backwaters and scabrous townships that were home to most young men and women who came to Fisk University."[1] From Du Bois's perspective, he was more than ready to leave behind what he increasingly saw as the confines of New England life, which Fisk would provide and Harvard would not, regardless of how relatively good it had been to him.

> My family and colored friends rather resented the idea [of moving to the South]. Their Northern free Negro prejudice naturally revolted at

the idea of sending me to the former land of slavery, either for
education or for living. I am rather proud of myself that I did not
agree with them. Whether or not I should always live and work in the
South, I did not then stop to decide; that I would give up the idea of
graduating from Harvard, did not occur to me. But I wanted to go to
Fisk, not simply because it was at least a beginning of my dream of
college, but also, I suspect, because I was beginning to feel lonesome
in New England.[2]

From his family and friends' "unromantic view of the situation," as
Du Bois remembers, Fisk did not present an opportunity but, rather,
served as an insult. They felt that while white classmates were able to
settle into occupations in town, Du Bois was being sent away—and to
the South, no less—rather than, say, becoming a teacher or a store
owner at home. Du Bois recognized degrees of truth in this perspective.
"Great Barrington was not able to conceive of me in such local positions," he writes. "It was not so much that they were opposed to it, but
it did not occur to them as a possibility."[3]

So, as history has well documented, Du Bois left Great Barrington
for Nashville. In the process, he left behind one identity and assumed
another. As he writes, upon entering Fisk, "I was a Negro."[4] He did not,
however, forget Great Barrington, writing letters to his church: "I have
not forgotten to love my New England hills, and I often wish I could join
some of your pleasant meetings in person as I do in spirit."[5] Although
such letters were likely written because many members of the Congregationalist communities of Great Barrington were helping him foot the
bills, they also convey an affection for the place of his youth.[6] Thus,
despite the eagerness with which Du Bois describes his impending first
year at Fisk, Great Barrington remained an important part of his life. As
he made his way through his life, it became subtly apparent just how
important the small rural community was to him. Indeed, Lewis conjec-
tures that when Du Bois finally arrived at Harvard, where he would
become the storied institution's first black PhD recipient, Frank Hosmer
had probably rounded up further funds to help him along the way.[7]

However, beyond the funds that the Great Barrington community
continued to provide to him, and his correspondences with his relatives
there, it is perhaps his decision to use the New England community as

a safe haven that speaks most directly to his need and appreciation for it. In 1887, for example, his first wife, Nina, gave birth to their son in Great Barrington, in the home of his uncle, James Burghardt. Du Bois was not there for the birth, and he visited only briefly before returning to finish his work on his second book, *The Philadelphia Negro*, which had consumed him.[8] Two years later, when his son died of diphtheria, he chose Mahaiwe Cemetery, in Great Barrington, for the burial, and left Nina there shortly afterward to head to Atlanta to supervise a conference entitled "The Negro in Business," the first of the Atlanta conferences.[9] The birth of the couple's daughter, Nina Yolande, in 1899, also took place in Great Barrington, where Nina had spent the final weeks of her pregnancy.[10]

In 1903, with the publication of *The Souls of Black Folk*, the importance of Great Barrington became clearer. In the mournful essay entitled "Of the Passing of the First-Born," the birth and death of his son is situated within geographic references specific to Du Bois's childhood, describing the birth as having taken place "away from the flickering sea into my own Berkshire Hills that sit all sadly guarding the gates of Massachusetts," and the death having occurred "above the western hills." Of his son's life, he writes, "A perfect life was his, all joy and love, with tears to make it bright,—sweet as a summer's day beside the Housatonic."[11]

Conversely, it is also in *The Souls of Black Folk* where Du Bois reveals that it was in Great Barrington that he first found the "the Veil":

It is in the early days of rollicking boyhood that the revelation first bursts upon one, all in a day, as it were. I remember well when the shadow swept across me. I was a little thing, away up in the hills of New England, where the dark Housatonic winds between Hoosac and Taghkanic to the sea. In a wee wooden schoolhouse, something put it into the boys' and girls' heads to buy gorgeous visiting-cards—ten cents a package—and exchange. The exchange was merry, till one girl, a tall newcomer, refused my card,—refused it peremptorily, with a glance. Then it dawned upon me with a certain suddenness that I was different from the others; or like, mayhap, in heart and life and longing, but shut out from their world by a vast veil. I had thereafter no desire to tear down that veil, to creep through; I held all beyond it in common contempt, and lived above it in a region of blue sky and

great wandering shadows. That sky was bluest when I could beat my
mates at examination-time, or beat them at a foot-race, or even beat
their stringy heads. Alas, with the years all this fine contempt began
to fade; for the words I longed for, and all their dazzling opportunities,
were theirs, not mine. But they should not keep these prizes, I said;
some, all, I would wrest from them.[12]

Du Bois, then, grants Great Barrington a dual identity of its own. He
posits it as the space in which he learned about his difference from his
peers and learned what kinds of devastating ramifications that difference might hold. Yet even after publishing the story of "the Veil," he
continued to use Great Barrington as a refuge. After the 1906 Atlanta
race riot, for example, which he wrote about in "A Litany of Atlanta,"
Du Bois sent Nina and Yolande to Great Barrington, in part so that he
could focus on the burgeoning Niagara Movement but also because he
felt they would be safer there.[13] Great Barrington also became Nina's
final resting place. When she died, in 1950, Du Bois took her body to the
Mahaiwe Cemetery, where she lies next to their young son, Burghardt.[14]
In a piece in the *Chicago Globe,* he explained why he chose to bury her
in the "town where I was born . . . under the great and beautiful elms."
He wrote, "So it seemed fitting that at the end of her life, she should go
back to the hills of Berkshire, where the boy had been borne [*sic*] and
be buried beside him, in soil where my fathers for more than two centuries lived and died. I feel that here she will lie in peace."[15]

That Du Bois chose Great Barrington for these burials assures some
locals, such as Elaine Gunn, that his hometown really meant something
to him. "Here was this guy from Great Barrington who had gone off—to
Fisk, to Harvard—but he still had this very soft, warm spot for Great
Barrington," Gunn affirms, "even when he said the turning point was
the visiting cards, when he was rebuffed and turned down. He went off
to Tennessee and really found out what it was like—he hadn't really ex-
perienced that kind of racism and discrimination in Great Barrington—
it was there, obviously, but it wasn't that severe. So he still came back
from time to time."[16]

The gravestones of Nina and Burghardt Du Bois remain in the
Mahaiwe Cemetery today, surrounded by the always growing south Berkshire community. The cemetery sits across busy Route 7 from the hillside

that a tornado ravaged on May 29, 1995, downing trees and creating a gigantic swath of a scar on the mountainside. The funnel cloud that took the lives of three people and injured twenty-seven spared the headstones of the cemetery. The graves of Nina and Burghardt are marked by a signpost, erected by the Great Barrington Historical Society in 1994, with a plaque quoting Du Bois, described as the "premier architect of the American civil rights movement." His words read, "In 1950 the month of February had for me special meaning. I was a widower. The wife of 53 years lay buried in the New England hills beside her firstborn boy."

A COLD WAR WORLD

The body of Du Bois himself, of course, rests far away in Ghana, where he exiled himself from a country that told him he was no longer welcome because of the wars that raged throughout his lifetime between democracy and totalitarianism, capitalism and communism, the United States and the Soviet Union, and most other binary oppositions that could create an "us" versus a "them." In Great Barrington, the Cold War context created a landscape filled with this political polarization, a polarization largely driven by fear, and responses to fear, in terms of America's place in the world, and Great Barrington's place within America.

Because these fears often easily translated into racial terms, the context of the Cold War, perhaps more than anything else, largely determined what Du Bois's legacy was to be in the place of his birth. For so many reasons, Du Bois could have been heralded by his hometown as the poster child of an American success story, one who had been supported by his mostly white, rural community to the highest levels of education, becoming an important intellectual with an unquestionable legacy to pass on. Du Bois, for his part, somewhat maintained his ties to his rural upbringing; when he left Great Barrington, he continually maintained just how New England he remained, regardless of where he was. When he found himself in Nashville at Fisk, for example, he found he had brought his New England decorum with him, whether in being "very quiet and subdued" in church or in how he would, because of what he called his "New England training," raise his hat to a woman.[17]

But the Great Barrington—and the United States, and the world—of Du Bois's youth differed greatly from that of his death, in 1963. As civil rights campaigns became increasingly national in scope, exemplified by the tens of thousands who gathered on the mall in the nation's capital that August for the March on Washington, and by the assassination of President John F. Kennedy that November, heralding what many consider to be the unofficial dawn of the 1960s, the social, cultural, and political landscape of the United States reached new heights of instability. It was a period that meant different things to different people, whether on the very local or the national level: some people considered needed social change to finally be within reach, and others found that their cherished ways of life were being pulled apart at the seams.

A critical underpinning of the volatility of the period was the sweeping global landscape of the ever-escalating Cold War. It is critical to understand the history of the national and international landscapes of this period in order to grasp the actions that the residents of Great Barrington took—and failed to take—in remembering Du Bois. The politics of the Cold War had immeasurable effects on civil rights movements that dominated the shifts toward social change that permeated the post–World War II period, meaning, as historian Carol Anderson asserts, that "the tenuous unity that characterized African Americans' postwar plans was rapidly fracturing along the U.S.-Soviet fault line."[18] Although ideologies of equality and human rights continued to expand with the increasing influence of established organizations such as the Southern Christian Leadership Conference (SCLC) and figures such as Martin Luther King Jr. in the decade or so that followed the war, as well as the eventual emergence of groups such as the Student Nonviolent Coordinating Committee (SNCC), the intensifying specter of the Cold War saturated American life, creating binaries of "right" and "wrong" on every level. Increasingly, the battle against communism replaced the World War II battle against totalitarianism, ensuring that democracy and capitalism became one and the same, and that communism and its advocates, including Du Bois, were beyond salvation, never mind commemoration. The production of this false dualism affected anyone engaged in a critique of the American way of life, as it became clear that securing conformity to democratic, capitalist ideals was the only way to defeat ideas that the Soviet Union espoused. As Anderson summarizes, "The Cold War, McCarthyism, the Soviets' atomic explosion, and the Korean War unleashed a maelstrom of fear, xenophobia, and conformity that wreaked havoc across America's political and progressive landscape."[19]

Of course, the early victims of Cold War warriors such as the House Un-American Activities Committee (HUAC), which had been created to find Americans with connections to the Communist Party, seemed to be obvious choices, far more obvious than an intellectual such as Du Bois. Perhaps the most famous target of HUAC was the blacklisted "Hollywood Ten," charged with using mass media such as film to convey leftist, subversive messages, including negative imagery of the United States and its democratic political system.[20] But while HUAC dominated Cold War headlines in the 1950s at home, and the United States became increasingly involved in the Korean conflict abroad, civil rights engaged in its most public battles to date in the decade that followed the conclusion of World War II. Turning points such as the landmark *Brown v. Board of Education* decision, in 1954, and the Montgomery bus boycotts, in 1955, established civil rights activists as forces to be reckoned with, particularly as the latter established the SCLC and King as the dominant powers in the battle for racial equality. But such spectacles also created dividing lines, exemplified when the Dixiecrats in the South put forth their Southern Manifesto, signed in 1956 by eighty-one U.S. representatives and nineteen senators, in order to reassure those who believed devoutly that racial integration in American society was a bad thing.

But regardless of the political chaos civil rights created on the domestic front, these dividing lines did not pit the United States against other political systems or other forms of state. Rather, they fueled a struggle regarding how the ideologies of American democracy were to be fulfilled, what the definitions of American citizenship were, and who, exactly, was allowed to take part. This conversation, of course, did not begin in the aftermath of the Allied victories in Europe and Asia, just as the strategies of the Cold War did not begin with HUAC. Both civil rights and the Cold War had substantial origins that far preceded World War II, but it was in the postwar period that both began to take their more familiar and modern forms. World War II was, in so many ways, a "race war," both domestically, in terms of policy such as Japanese internment and segregated army units, and globally, in terms of moments such as the Rape of Nanking and Nazi strategies of extermination.[21] But with its defeat of fascism, it was also a war that redefined global understandings of democracy and capitalism, especially in terms of the global visibility of communism and the explosion of anticolonial battles in Africa.[22] For civil rights activists and Cold War warriors alike, World War II presented unparalleled opportunities to move forward utopian democratic agendas, using the victory of the Allies over fascism—in terms of both the Nazi regime in Germany and the imperial regime in Japan—as proof positive that they were on the "right" side.

Yet the heightening of the Cold War in the lines drawn between the United States and the Soviet Union also created tensions over how best to achieve these agendas, both at home and abroad. The philosophy that seemed clearly defined in the years that immediately followed the conclusion of World War II—that democracy (and capitalism) must prevail over totalitarianism (and communism)—became blurred with other battles globally dominated by the Soviet Union and the United States, enabling a devastating game of finger-pointing to take place at home among Americans who seemed to want the same things: democracy and equality for all. "The Cold War identified in stark, pejorative terms entire categories of rights as antithetical to basic American freedoms," Anderson argues. "It punished mercilessly those who advocated a more expansive definition and a more concrete commitment to those rights. And it demanded unconditional loyalty."[23]

Thus, although the Cold War created numerous—and bloody—conflicts around the world and spurred an arms race that continues on many levels today, one of its greatest impacts was the way in which it turned the eyes of Americans, including those living in Great Barrington, on themselves, who carefully ensured that the country's global image was one of example, rather than shame. The United States focused a great deal of attention on how the rest of the world viewed its policies regarding citizenship, equity, and race, culminating, as historian Mary Dudziak argues in *Cold War Civil Rights*, her definitive work on civil rights and the Cold War, in "organized U.S. government efforts to disseminate favorable information about the United States to other countries."[24] The United States Information Agency (USIA), for example, produced propaganda campaigns designed to present the most fair-minded of faces, one that would enable the United States to argue for the fruits of democracy in a manner that would have global appeal, especially in the newly forged African nations that emerged as a product of the postcolonial efforts that flooded the postwar period.

For its part, the Soviet Union engaged in its own operation, seeking, as Jodi Melamed summarizes, "to undermine consent for U.S. influence and involvement in Asia and Africa by publicizing racial violence and segregation in the United States, claiming these as evidence that white supremacist doctrine suffused the world-ordering ambitions of the United States and the social relations of capitalism."[25] The concept that young independent African nations might forge relationships with the Soviet Union worried the U.S. government, particularly as the vision of African sovereignty played an ever-more-significant role in domestic civil rights movements and as intellectuals such as Paul Robeson and Du Bois became increasingly interested in a more global understanding of civil liberty. Rather than exist as a symbolic refuge for African Americans, in the postcolonial period Africa became a collaborator that underpinned black national identity. As historian Manning Marable observes, "In the 1950s, the image of Africa as a cultural and political entity began to reassert its impact upon African American intellectuals and artists." Marable is careful to recognize that the trend was not new in the postwar period but, rather, had roots in both the nineteenth and early twentieth centuries, such as in missionary tours to Liberia and in the symbolic use of Africa as a homeland by influential leaders such as Marcus Garvey and his Universal Negro Improvement Association.[26]

World War II had provided a critical juncture for the way in which successful decolonization campaigns in Africa influenced civil rights movements in the United States. In 1941, A. Philip Randolph, head of the powerful Brotherhood of Sleeping Car Porters, threatened a march on Washington to demand the desegregation of wartime manufacturing, providing the foundations for the famous Double V campaign ("Victory abroad, victory at home"), an insistence that a triumph over European and Asian totalitarian regimes must be met with the triumph over Jim Crow at home. Given the burgeoning civil rights movements in this international context, the consequences for segregation in the United

States became global. As the NAACP's Walter White warned in his landmark book *A Rising Wind*, published in 1945, an American refusal to acknowledge its own racial tyranny would have dire—and global—consequences:

> World War II has given to the Negro a sense of kinship with other colored—and also oppressed—peoples of the world. Where he has not thought through or informed himself on the racial angles of colonial policy and master-race theories, he senses that the struggle of the Negro in the United States is part and parcel of the struggle against imperialism and exploitation in India, China, Burma, Africa, the Philippines, Malaya, the West Indies, and South America. The Negro soldier is convinced that as time proceeds that identification of interest will spread even among some brown and yellow peoples who today refuse to see the connection between their exploitation by white nations and discrimination against the Negro in the United States.[27]

This development increased understanding of a "black internationalism" in the Cold War, exhibited by the formation of groups such as the Organization of African Unity (1963), events such as the First International Congress of Negro Writers and Artists (1956), and the publication of the review *Présence Africaine*,[28] all of which pushed the United States to concentrate on how the overt policies of segregation that permeated the American South and the covert strategies of racism that blanketed the nation played abroad. With the Allied victories of World War II, the United States found itself in a hypocritical situation because it did not practice the universal mission of liberation and democracy that it had preached throughout the war years. Thus, desegregation, as Dudziak articulates, became "a Cold War imperative."[29]

As Melamed argues, America's postwar strategy of "racial liberalism" became clear in Gunnar Myrdal's *An American Dilemma: The Negro Problem and American Democracy* (1944). Myrdal argued, according to Melamed, that "the key to the nation's achievement of its international manifest destiny was to be the visible integration of African Americans into American democracy, through the extension of formal equality and the recognition of African American cultural citizenship."[30] Much of such strategy focused on areas that easily conveyed the riches offered by the United States to its citizens—especially its black ones—in order to persuade newer nations, such as those in Africa, that the best choice for their own citizenries was to align with the West and its policies of democracy, rather than with the Eastern bloc of the world and its policies of communism. American propaganda efforts placed much emphasis on exemplars of domestic integration, such as sports. The *Sporting News,* for example, with details of Jackie Robinson's professional debut, in 1946, circulated around the globe, giving visible, if superficial, evidence as to just how easily whites and blacks played together in the United States.

These efforts also, as Dudziak argues, aired the past dirty laundry of the country, giving proof to "sins that were purposefully exposed," in order to demonstrate just how rigorously the United States had worked to create a better life for all of its citizens. The best example, according to Dudziak, was *The Negro in American Life,* a pamphlet published by the USIA in the early 1950s. *The Negro in American Life* incorporated tales of past mistakes in order to demonstrate how the United States had made amends in accordance with the foundations and benefits of a democratic political and ideological system. Its thesis, as Dudziak interprets, argued that "given how bad things were in the past . . . isn't it amazing how far we've come?"[31]

Yet such campaigns were often ineffectual, forcing propaganda officials to recognize that the difficulties of positioning American racial struggles within the promotion of global democracy required tools more dynamic than mere pamphlets. Efforts were begun to put a range of faces abroad, in connection with U.S. embassies, in order to directly speak to questions about American race relations.[32] The U.S. State Department sponsored cultural tours that put black figures on display in order to confirm that equal opportunity was a critical feature of a democratic system of government. Many of these tours sent musicians to perform as cultural ambassadors, most famously Duke Ellington, who traveled throughout the world in the 1960s and 1970s, making stops in the Soviet Union and taking three separate trips to Africa. Alongside artists, athletes, too, worked on behalf of U.S. foreign policy, with legendary figures such as Jesse Owens, Althea Gibson, and Wilma Rudolph, and groups such as the Harlem Globetrotters, traveling around the world to substantiate America's declared devotion to racial equality. Although artists and athletes clashed, at times, with the goals of the State Department, as would Du Bois, because they often brought the civil rights agenda abroad with them, the efforts to put black faces on the road on behalf of the nation had a commanding impact. When the SNCC, for example, went on an African tour in 1964, members saw the effects of the U.S. diplomatic missions on African perceptions of African American life. "There were all these pictures of Negroes doing things, Negro judges, Negro policemen," remembers Julian Bond of the trip, "and if you didn't know anything about America . . . you would think these were really commonplace things. That's the worst kind of deceit."[33]

The urgency of American efforts magnified as the Soviet Union proffered similar (and far more organized) programs in the hope that it would make its own impact—politically, economically, and culturally—on Africa and would curtail Western—especially American—power. The Soviet program for African sport included sending Soviet coaches to Africa and bringing African athletes into the Soviet Union to train. In 1961, the Soviet Union took its agenda to the next level, recommending that the International Olympic Committee pass a resolution to help with the development of sports in Latin America and Asia, as well as Africa. For the United States, the contact between the Soviets and newly independent African nations posed a serious threat, creating the possibility, according to historian Penny Von Eschen, that "resentment of American racism might cause Asian and African peoples to seek closer relations with the Soviet Union."[34]

Thus, as civil rights movements blossomed in the 1960s, organizations such as the SCLC and SNCC continued to connect domestic politics and policies with those of the international arena. They added oppositional stances to the war in Vietnam, for example, to their agendas of racial equality at home. In more aggressive fashion, organizations further out on the fringe of militancy, such as the Black Panthers, added unflagging anti-imperialist avowals to their agendas of Black Power.[35]

In terms of Du Bois, whose death occurred on the eve of the March on Washington, the increasing fervor of the Cold War greatly complicated how he was to be remembered, regardless of the increasingly national attention toward civil rights and his status as one of the key builders of the movement. The various paths that he chose in his pursuit of global equality allowed many people—from the U.S. State Department to his hometown—to find his legacy to be a counternarrative to postwar American life; his was a story that bordered on treason, rather than a tale of exemplary citizenship and American-forged success. As historians Edward T. Linethal and Tom Engelhardt have observed, "The act of challenging sacred historical narratives is a thankless task at any time, but especially in periods of great uncertainty," as the very act of remembrance comes under fire. When this occurs, history becomes "material for editorialists to condemn, politicians to denounce, and citizens to complain about or protest," and those who are trying to do the remembering—whether community activists or professional historians—must determine "what Americans can and cannot bear to look at or consider at any moment, and why."[36]

The narrative of Du Bois has two tracks: some write his history as that of a founder of modern civil rights, Pan-Africanism, and the NAACP, as well as a prolific voice on global egalitarianism and human rights; others have chosen to remember him chiefly as the author of political ideologies that worked against democracy and, particularly, on behalf of communism. For the latter set, many of whom proved to be the most vocal in the years that followed his death, his legacy as an intellectual quickly became synonymous—and not in a positive manner—with his studied and passionate beliefs in Marxist foundations for global solutions. And for a terribly vocal few, including those who now occupied the streets of Great Barrington, the only part of his long biography worth knowing was that he had joined the Communist Party in 1961, reducing him to an anticapitalist, pro-Soviet agent, one whom the community may have helped in the past but no longer felt any connection to.

The double-stranded narrative of Du Bois exemplified just how easily things could be angled for political use during the height of the Cold War period. The "right" black faces, such as musicians and athletes, used as tools of American foreign-affairs propaganda campaigns, were heralded by citizens and government alike, whereas others, particularly vocal black intellectuals, were denied their constitutional rights in an attempt to silence their critiques of U.S. racial policies. But it was a terribly tricky path for the U.S. State Department to tread, as it tried to figure out which African Americans would deliver messages that would serve the greater good of the nation, and which articulated ideas that should be curtailed. Ellington, for example, considered one of the great ambassadors of the propaganda efforts, began to use his goodwill tours to go beyond the authorized narrative supplied by the government and focus more on black culture and American life. As Von Eschen argues, the visibility given to Ellington and others and the agency that these Cold War ambassadors employed ensured that the state-sponsored tours inadvertently proved just how central a role black culture played in United States history.[37]

A RED TIDE TURNS

Of course, such efforts had mixed results because they, like the State Department, were engaged in a thorny balance of beliefs, particularly when they attempted to bolster civil rights campaigns while simultaneously disassociating them from communism and communists. Early on, Walter White, for example, traveled to Europe on behalf of the U.S. government to quell problems among black soldiers during World War II, making him a favorite in the Roosevelt administration. His support of the NAACP resolution that expelled Communists from membership further raised his state clout, giving him a platform to work domestically against racial oppression provided he continue to argue the merits of U.S. democracy abroad.[38] Contempt for communism on the part of the NAACP was not new, of course, but had come of age during the Scottsboro trials in the 1930s, as the organization fought with the Communist Party USA over the defense of nine young men who had wrongly been accused of rape.[39] But as Cold War fervor continued in the postwar period, the NAACP increasingly felt its own influence to be in peril because of assumed associations with communists, illustrated by the assertion of Arthur Schlesinger Jr. that the Communist Party was "sinking tentacles" into the NAACP, a claim that few had any evidence to support but was inflammatory enough to make waves.[40]

Max Yergan, too, exemplified the effort to detach the United States from the image of the radical "Negro." Once a key adviser of Paul Robeson, Yergan founded the Council on African Affairs (CAA), which the FBI identified as "active in creating considerable unrest among the negroes [*sic*] by stressing racial discrimination" in order to support decolonization efforts in Africa.[41] In 1948, Yergan took the reins of the group and steered it powerfully toward the right, making, according to Von Eschen, "perhaps the most pronounced political about-face among African American activists and intellectuals of the Cold War era."[42] Yergan traveled to Nigeria in 1952, where he gave a high-profile lecture that promoted American race relations while simultaneously condemning communism, arguing that African Americans had collectively denounced it. According to one report, Yergan stated, "Every communist is a potential traitor to his country, . . . and my people in America have chosen to cast their lot with democracy, because they believe it offers them the opportunity to achieve full equality."[43]

The American embassy in Lagos proclaimed Yergan's appearance a success, but many criticized his statements. Two members in the audience at the lecture, for example, asked Yergan whether communists continued to be civil rights leaders in the United States and theorized that perhaps the U.S. Constitution had broken as many promises to African Americans as Yergan claimed the communists had done. Yergan responded in the negative to both questions, yet editorials in local newspapers continued such queries. The *West African Pilot,* for example, wrote, "Any honest inquirer after truth pondering over the motivations of Dr. Max Yergan urging the African to shun the vices of 'Communism and its agents as one shuns poison' will only surmise, 'We have heard this before.' For, in the grim days of the battle against the forces of Nazism and Fascism, Africans were warned too to shun Nazism and Fascism as one shuns poison all because at the time we were—all lovers of freedom—engaged in a battle to guarantee freedom in order that free men may continue to learn freedom." The American embassy in Lagos dismissed the editorial, claiming that its author had a "personal axe to grind" with Yergan, illustrated by the photo the paper published of Yergan with, among others, "the controversial Dr. W.E.B. Du Bois."[44]

The use of the language of communism in civil rights struggles helped seal the perception of many civil rights activists as anti-American. Although Robeson and Du Bois joined forces to return the CAA's focus to where it once had been, it became clear that the issue of communism could not be cleared from the political landscape of civil rights. A central tenet of the Cold War, of course, was to restrain, confiscate, and condemn those who threatened the strength of the state, a strategy that argued that the larger battle to "contain" communism took priority over any other struggles.[45] In an era of increasing decolonization, in which both Soviet and American ideologies wooed newly independent African nations, the United States had to ensure that its own house—at least in the public image—was clean, particularly in terms of the role of race and equity in democracy, meaning that what had begun as an international battle between communism and democracy had a progressively more domestic presence.

But this was an effort that the United States increasingly saw itself as losing, as it realized that its anticommunism propaganda programs were largely ineffectual. A 1952 report on the anticommunist agenda surmised that "efforts to counteract communist exploitation of the race relations problem in the United States have not been fully successful."[46] Even as the embassies continued to sponsor the speaking tours of a variety of African Americans whose lives served as noticeable examples of social change, the State Department began to finally realize that some who traveled abroad were working to establish a counternarrative to the agreed-upon story of how America worked. Particularly suspicious were those who equated racism with imperial and capitalist practices, a stance considered akin to directly subscribing to the tenets of the Soviet Union.

While the government targeted many figures, including Richard Wright, Josephine Baker, and Louis Armstrong (a one-time State Department goodwill-tour favorite), it was the celebrated Paul Robeson who bore much of the brunt, beginning with his service as chair of the Council on African Affairs, which ended in 1946. Famously, Robeson endured a series of hearings for remarks that he made while in Paris in 1949 at the Congress of World Partisans for Peace. In the speech, Robeson compared U.S. government policy to that of Nazi Germany and declared it "unthinkable" that African Americans would ever fight against the Soviets. Although Robeson biographer Martin Duberman has argued that Robeson's speech was largely misquoted, many reviled him for it. The press largely condemned him and riots broke out at his once-popular concerts, but perhaps most disturbing was the breaking of ranks by those who had once stood beside him in his political and social quest, including the NAACP's Roy Wilkins, Adam Clayton Powell, Jackie Robinson, and Lester Grange.[47] Rather than join in censuring Robeson, Du Bois, in his own speech in Paris, took the opportunity to deem the United States "drunk with power" in policies that would lead to "a Third World War which will ruin the world." As a consequence, Morgan State College revoked its invitation to Du Bois to give that year's commencement address, criticizing his failure "to condemn [Robeson's] treasonable statement."[48]

Despite the criticism, Robeson continued to voice his opinion. In 1950, he spoke out against U.S. participation in the Korea conflict, which proved to be the last straw for the government. The U.S. State Department issued notice to all U.S. ports that Robeson was not to leave the country, and J. Edgar Hoover delivered orders that the FBI was to bring Robeson in. When Robeson refused to relinquish his passport, the State Department declared that it was invalid, stating that Robeson's "travel abroad at this time would be contrary to the best interests of the United States." Robeson posed a threat because of his international critiques of U.S. policy regarding the treatment of African Americans. Rather than speak of such things in public and, no less, abroad, Robeson must be silenced because such matters were, according to the State Department, "a family affair."[49]

TARGET DU BOIS

Although much of the attention in this period focused on Robeson, largely due to the former athlete and singer's international celebrity, the State Department targeted others, too, including Du Bois. His civil rights work, in general, had always caught the attention of government officials. But with his affiliation with William Patterson, chair of the Civil Rights Congress, the spotlight widened upon him, particularly after Patterson accused the United States of genocide. Patterson articulated his controversial stance in a petition to the United Nations Committee on Human Rights in 1951, arguing that "history has shown that the racist theory of government of the U.S.A. is not the private affair of Americans, but the concern of mankind everywhere."[50]

Labor groups around the world—especially the many with ideologically Marxist foundations—came out in favor of Patterson's efforts, but the U.S. State Department asked for his passport, claiming, just as it did with Robeson, that his travels were not in the "best interest of the United States."[51] As one of ninety-four people who signed Patterson's petition, Du Bois stood out especially because he himself had orchestrated and helped write a petition for the NAACP, entitled "An Appeal to the World: A Statement on the Denial of Human Rights to Minorities in the Case of Citizens of Negro Descent in the United States of America," four years earlier, in 1947. According to the *Afro-American*, the piece accused the United States of "failing to practice what it preached," deeming the American South a far greater threat to U.S. democracy than the Soviet Union.[52]

For Du Bois, it was yet another turning point in his relationship with the NAACP, which he had left in 1934 and returned to in 1944 after retiring from Atlanta University. Seeing Walter White delay that petition when it was initially written, for an array of reasons, including the fact that Eleanor Roosevelt declared that the document embarrassed both her and the country, Du Bois began to further question the organization's commitment to achieving the goals he considered paramount.[53] The tense relationship between Du Bois and White continued to deteriorate on issues of foreign policy, particularly after Du Bois condemned the Truman Doctrine in a piece he wrote in the *Defender*, in which he declared "Truman's pleas to arm Greece against Russia" to be the "most stupid and dangerous proposal ever made by the leader of a great modern nation" and then decided to back third-party candidate Henry Wallace for president.[54] Du Bois wrote a memo to White, dated September 7, 1948, expressing his disdain of White's support of the Truman administration's foreign policy, among other things. When the memo became public, Du Bois vehemently denied having anything to do with its leaking, yet the NAACP board informed Du Bois that "at the expiration of his present term," his services would no longer be needed.[55]

It was a difficult departure to many people, because, in NAACP cofounder Arthur B. Spingarn's words, Du Bois remained the "voice of this organization" and "one of the greatest leaders of his race."[56] Although Du Bois was certainly no easy hero, many agreed with Spingarn and withdrew from the NAACP in protest of his dismissal. However, the damage was done. As Cold War fury escalated on the domestic political landscape, views such as those held by Du Bois went from controversial to treasonous. Thus, Du Bois left the NAACP for the last time in September 1948.

"Three years after exiting the NAACP his reputation would lie in ruins and his freedom to work and walk among his compatriots would hang in the balance of Cold War justice," David Levering Lewis poignantly writes. "He would be but one victim among the many accused, censured, and convicted, yet the humiliation to be visited upon him, as with his friend Paul Robeson, was meant as an express warning to his people and their leaders—a message that their long struggle for equality must continue to exemplify commendable patience, conventional patriotism, and indifference to radical economic ideas."[57] Du Bois was about to set out on the last phase of his ideological evolution of influence.

THE LEGACY THAT IS LEFT

Of course, Du Bois continued to write, speak, and serve as a figurehead, although to a smaller audience. In 1948, the *Defender* dropped him as a contributor, based on his support of Wallace for the presidency. After Truman's election, Du Bois increasingly made his way further left, but his central viewpoints, rather than finding spheres of influence, put him among the ranks of those considered to be subversive.[58] He continued to suggest that the African American battle for equality could not be limited to a domestic audience but had consequences for the world, because the blight of racial oppression involved all peoples, whether it was articulated via the crimes of Jim Crow in the United States or through the campaigns of colonial rule worldwide.

Increasingly, Du Bois adamantly juxtaposed the superpowers: the Soviet Union was "leading and encouraging" the revolt of the colonized against colonial rule, whereas "girding itself against this is the United States of America, which arose 200 years ago as a free-thinking democracy, with limitless land and resources; but which sank into dependence on slave labor, transformed itself into a vast center of capital monopolized by closed corporations, and now seeks to replace the British empire by stopping socialism with force, and ruling the world by private capital and newly invented technique."[59]

As evidenced by his praise of the Soviet Union and denigration of U.S. policy, Du Bois did not hesitate, particularly toward the end of his life, in his ideological support for communism and for nations that embraced it. Believing that his travels made him one of the foremost experts on the subject, Du Bois could convincingly explain the benefits of communism with almost unparalleled clarity and precision, forgoing the idea of civil rights and looking more broadly at how the world worked in terms of equality, while simultaneously, as observed by Jodi Melamed, declining "to witness for America":[60] "I believe in communism. I mean by communism, a planned way of life in the production of wealth and work designed for building a state whose object is the highest welfare of its people and not merely the profit of a part. . . . After earnest observation I now believe that private ownership of capital and free enterprise are leading the world to disaster. . . . If, because of this belief and such action, I become the victim of attack and calumny, I will react in the way that seems to me best for the world in which I live and which I have tried earnestly to serve."[61] Du Bois's use of Marxist frameworks was not new in the postwar period, of course, but had a long evolution within his scholarship.[62] In *Black Reconstruction in America, 1860–1880,* for example, published in 1935, Du Bois powerfully indicted capitalism, arguing in almost unprecedented fashion that America's emergence as a global power came at the expense of black bodies.[63] His final autobiography, Melamed argues, stands not as "an American communist text, but within the intellectual tradition of Black Marxism in the United States."[64]

Du Bois wanted to make clear that in order to combat racial oppression, African American workers had to align themselves with a global black working class. However, it was not until the Cold War that Du Bois (among others) really came under fire for his increasingly leftist leanings. According to Thomas Borstelmann, the Truman administration's concentration on the Korean War proved to be the breaking point, putting civil rights agendas low on the list of national priorities and targeting civil rights activists, rather than Jim Crow policy, as the problem in its clash with the Soviet Union over the postcolonial world.[65] Increased propaganda efforts in Africa amplified the government's attempt to damage the reputation of figures such as Du Bois.

Of particular concern to the State Department was Du Bois's involvement in the Peace Information Center (PIC), formed in 1950 to advertise the Stockholm Peace Appeal, which advocated nuclear disarmament. Its first major action came on July 13, 1950, a little more than two weeks after the start of the Korean War, when it published the first *Peacegram*, which claimed that the Stockholm Peace Appeal had been endorsed by 1.5 million people. Secretary of state Dean Acheson countered that the Stockholm Appeal was merely "a propaganda trick in the spurious 'peace offensive' of the Soviet Union," to which PIC chair Du Bois responded by declaring that Acheson's stance lacked any "intimation of a desire for peace, or a realization of the horror of another world war or of sympathy with the crippled, impoverished and dead who pay for [the] fighting." A few weeks later, on August 11, William Foley, head of the Foreign Agents Registration Section of the Justice Department notified Du Bois that the PIC had to register "as an agent of a foreign principal within the United States."[66]

Du Bois failed to take Foley's request seriously, as he felt his stance on the Stockholm Peace Appeal centered on the eradication of nuclear weaponry and had little to do with any kind of pro-Soviet stance. The membership of the NAACP agreed, voting to support him against the Justice Department despite a declaration by Walter White that the PIC was about "Communist-inspired propaganda."[67] Instead of dealing with the Justice Department's demands, Du Bois chose to fly instead to Prague for a peace conference, but then returned at the request of PIC prodigy Abbott Simon, who felt that the Justice Department's demand needed to be addressed. On October 12, 1950, the PIC decided that the best way to deal with the problem was to disband the organization altogether. However, the Justice Department refused to accept this as a solution and on February 2, 1951, reissued its order that the PIC—which now did not even exist—register as a foreign power. Within a week, a Washington, D.C., grand jury indicted the PIC officers, including Du Bois, in *U.S. v. Peace Information Center*. The case was eventually dismissed and proved to be a greater victory for Du Bois, whom many campaigned around to "save," making it, according to David Levering Lewis, "a rare courtroom victory in this Red Scare era."[68]

But despite the acquittal, many still had an impression of Du Bois as one guilty of treason, and thus the Cold War continued to have ramifications for him. His work in the CAA also came under fire, as the U.S. attorney general's Subversive Activities Control Board stated in 1952 that the organization was "substantially directed, dominated or controlled by the Communist Party, USA."[69] When the CAA closed its doors, in 1954, the battle against Du Bois continued, particularly as his disillusionment with U.S. policy grew. His critiques of it ventured further to the left when the State Department revoked his passport, just as it had done with Robeson. But Du Bois continued to use his pen, which few seemed able to curb, to continue his fight for economic and social equality. His list of offenses to Cold Warriors and mainstream civil rights activists alike was long and distinguished, as Lewis explains:

> Du Bois's opposition to the Marshall Plan, NATO, the Point Four program for the developing world, and the Korean War as instruments of capitalist imperialism were heresies that most of the spokespersons for the race deemed to be evidence of unreality bordering on the certifiable, an opinion Walter White allowed to be attributed to him over the voice of America. His causes were not theirs—unrelated, dangerous civil liberties issues that brought guilt by association: endorsing We Charge Genocide, the Civil Rights Congress's 1951 petition that Robeson and William Patterson carried to the United Nations; defending the Rosenbergs . . . serving as character witness in the Smith Act trial of Ben Gold . . . [and] testifying on behalf of James Jackson and Alexander Trachtenberg, the publisher, in the second round of Smith Act trials of CPUSA functionaries.[70]

Du Bois reclaimed his right to travel in 1958, after the Supreme Court declared that a U.S. citizen could not be denied a passport because of his or her political beliefs, and he hit the road for the next year, eventually relocating to Ghana in 1961 at the invitation of president Kwame Nkrumah to work on what was to be his last (and never-finished) project, *Encyclopedia Africana*.[71] As he readied himself to relocate, the Supreme Court issued a decision that sustained the controversial 1950

McCarran Internal Security Act, which included stipulations for the required registration of "Communist-infiltrated organizations," and prevented anyone whose work exhibited communist tendencies from entering the United States.[72]

Whether impelled by the McCarran Act or other reasons, Du Bois hit a breaking point of sorts. On October 1, 1961, at ninety-three years old, he applied for official membership in the Communist Party of the USA before leaving for Ghana, essentially ensuring that he would not be able to return under the reinforced McCarran Act. In his application, he wrote, "Today, I have reached a firm conclusion. Capitalism cannot reform itself; it is doomed to self-destruction."[73] In response to Du Bois's newly official status as a Communist, the United States refused to renew his passport. On February 17, 1963, Du Bois became a citizen of Ghana, signifying that, as Von Eschen articulates, "there was no longer a home in America for his generation of anti-colonial activists."[74]

Of course, at this point in Du Bois's career and life, acquiring the official stamp of Communism was merely a symbolic act, as the emphasis on Cold War politics in the postwar period had changed the path of civil rights irrevocably. The man who had once tried the patriotic route, making his famous call for African Americans to "close ranks" during World War I, had opted for another path, one that announced in no uncertain terms that he felt the United States and its political system had failed him, and that a sense of American national belonging could not be ethically or feasibly prioritized above international conceptions of race and rights. Du Bois refused to see the Cold War as others did, as a battle between "us" and "them" or a battle between the United States and the USSR. Rather, he remained committed to writing about how neocolonial capitalism continued to shackle those who were part of the diasporas of labor that centered largely on Asia and Africa, and how belief in democracy remained an impossibility because one could not believe in something that simply did not exist.

In doing so, Du Bois ensured that his life—and with it his legacy—could not be represented by the strategies of civil rights that he had framed long before, strategies that only in his last years began to gain a visible and meaningful space in the American cultural and political landscape. Instead, because of his own intellectual and political evolutions,

Du Bois ended his life with an avowal of faith in the political system of America's enemy and a flight to the continent of (some) of his ancestors. What remained to be seen was whether or not the oeuvre of a man who lived so long and wrote so prolifically could again find a place within the history that he had contributed so much to through most of the twentieth century.

CHAPTER THREE

Her Proudest Contribution
to History

Regardless of the fact that in his later years, Dr. Du Bois chose another path, it is incontrovertible that at the dawn of the twentieth century, his was the voice calling you to gather here today in this cause.
—**Roy Wilkins, NAACP executive secretary, March on**
  Washington, 1963

D<small>U</small> B<small>OIS'S</small> <small>INCREASINGLY LEFTIST LEANINGS</small> ensured that many people in Great Barrington, despite the poetics regarding his beloved boyhood home in each of his autobiographical writings, echoed the accusations and conclusions that essentially had been foregone for the folks at the State Department. These were the ones who opposed the emergent campaign to memorialize Du Bois's years in Great Barrington shortly after his passing, and they included, particularly, members of the twelve local chapters of the American Legion, the Knights of Columbus, the Daughters of the American Revolution, the John Birch Society, and chapters of various veterans' groups in Great Barrington, West Stockbridge, Dalton, and Pittsfield.[1]

Support for celebrating Du Bois came from a wide range of residents with varying degrees of localness, including Harry Belafonte; U.S. representative Silvio O. Conte; playwright William Gibson and illustrator Norman Rockwell, both of whom lived in Stockbridge; Sidney Poitier, who owned a home just over the border, in New York State; and renowned Protestant theologian Reinhold Niebuhr, who first delivered his famous

"Serenity Prayer" in Heath, Massachusetts, located on the Berkshire County border, where he and his family spent summers.[2] John W. P. Mooney, a local cable newscaster, demonstrated ardent support for the campaign and articulated its overarching goal. "It would be ironic, indeed, if the town of his boyhood denied the legacy of freedom that he attempted to leave," Mooney said, "and denied as well a memorial to a man who is very probably her proudest contribution to history."[3]

A BERKSHIRE ENIGMA: WALTER WILSON

Most important to the local momentum of the cause was Walter Wilson. Wilson was not alone in his idea to commemorate the beginnings of Du Bois in Great Barrington, but he forcefully pushed forward the idea and created the foundations necessary to make it happen.

Piecing together Wilson's background is a difficult task, as he had no children and left no papers. He was never famous beyond the realm of the regional, but because of his vibrant and engaging personality, many local to the Berkshires have vivid memories of him. Tales of his varied legacy still circulate regularly through aging social circles in the Berkshires and in New York, including those of his lawyer of many years, William Simons; his partner in the Du Bois land deal, Edmund Gordon; and local Great Barrington activist Elaine Gunn, who played a central role in the movement to memorialize Du Bois alongside her friend the late Ruth Jones. Because of Wilson's work for social (and socialist) reform, his notable collection of Shaker furniture, and his extensive (and controversial) real estate dealings, somewhat of a paper trail ranges through a variety of publications from the papers of the American Civil Liberties Union to the local Berkshire newspapers, particularly the *Berkshire Eagle,* including a letter he wrote to the newspaper's publisher.

Gunn remembers Wilson as "a true southern gentleman, soft-spoken and delightful."[4] Born in 1903, in Tennessee, Wilson moved to Texas as a teenager. Finishing little formal education, he took a job in Houston as a longshoreman, but he wanted to be a writer. In the early 1920s, Wilson moved to New York City and enrolled in night courses while he spent his days working on the docks and working with trade unions. Influenced by both his hard labor and his thirst for learning, he took a job as southern secretary for the American Civil Liberties Union (ACLU). According to one profile written on Wilson, with this new role he became "deeply involved in civil rights work in the South long before that occupation was fashionable."[5]

According to William Simons, Wilson's personal attorney (and later a superior court judge), Wilson carried a membership card from the American Communist Party. It seemed to be general knowledge among those close to him, whereas those who were critical of Wilson and often referred to him as "that Communist" likely had no idea how close they might be to the truth.[6] Communist or not, according to ACLU records and Simons's recollection, as early as 1930 Wilson worked in the South as part of the organization's efforts to combat unjust prosecution against civil liberties, especially the right to organize. The work was "clearly dangerous," recalls Simons. "I had a great deal of respect for him and what he did in the South."[7] Indeed, it was a critical period to be working for the ACLU, because, as the group outlined in its annual report, "1930 was the worst year since the war for free speech prosecutions and for meetings broken up or prohibited. Lynchings, too, showed a sharp rise over the previous two years."[8] The ACLU was particularly concerned about the protection of three key groups—"Negroes, strikers, and Communists"—as they were considered to "bear the largest burden of repression."[9] In the South, Wilson represented the ACLU as part of its "local committees" program, designed to send aid to areas where problems were considered to be "most acute." According to the report, "In the South, where strikes and Communist agitation have aroused violent repression, Walter Wilson represented the Union in organizing committees to oppose prosecutions in Atlanta and Birmingham, and aided in the prosecution of lawless officials in North Carolina."[10]

Wilson, still an aspiring writer, put pen to paper on behalf of the ACLU, publishing pamphlets in the 1930s such as *Call Out the Militia: A Study of the Use of the National Guard in Strikes* (cowritten with Albert Deutsch) and *The Militia: Friend or Foe of Liberty?*[11] Also in this period, he published *The American Legion and Civil Liberty* (1936) and *Forced Labor in the United States* (ca. 1933), which included an introduction by Theodore Dreiser. He became something of a freelance expert on chain gangs, tenant farming, and the racial politics of labor relations, writing for publications such as *Harper's, New Republic, Crisis, Reader's Digest,* and the journal of the United Mine Workers.

Wilson married Fannie Sher, described by Simons (and everyone else!) as "a lovely woman." Wilson met her in the late 1930s in night school in New York City. She was a Russian immigrant, born on August 17, 1903, who worked as a social worker for New York State.[12] In 1939, Wilson moved with Fannie to East Chatham, New York, which abuts the Berkshires, to try his hand at business, specifically real estate, while living in a rural setting that would cultivate his writing endeavors. Running the Berkshire Farm Agency out of his home, he soon came to own approximately five thousand acres of property, mostly in southern Berkshire County, and, according to the *Eagle,* "acquired a reputation as a man who combines a liberal philosophy with hard-nosed business tactics."[13]

Simons agrees. While working as an assistant district attorney, Simons, a New York University Law School graduate and Korean War veteran, began a civil practice in Pittsfield, Massachusetts, the county seat and "metropolitan center" of the Berkshires. The district attorney position, though foundational to his career, was only part-time, so he needed to cultivate a private practice. Wilson was one of his first clients, and without question his first big client. "He was my money," Simons remembers. "As a client he was very demanding, but I liked him. He discovered the value of Berkshire land way before anyone else. He made things happen."

Wilson immersed himself in both the business and cultural life of the Berkshires, demonstrating an acute sense of important architecture and culture by buying shares in prestigious properties. In 1952, for example, he purchased the Bellefontaine Mansion for $28,500. The estate was built in 1897, and designed by architects J. M. Carrere and Thomas Hastings (who also designed the New York Public Library) to be a copy of Louis XIV's Petit Trianon. It is now the home of the Canyon Ranch Spa and Resort.[14] He also claimed to have had shares in Avaloch, an 1885 estate-turned-hotel that is best known for its days as Alice's Restaurant, enshrined by Arlo Guthrie in a song about a 1966 trash-dumping incident in nearby Stockbridge (it is now the Apple Tree Inn); Wheatleigh, an 1893 estate that now, according to the likes of *Travel and Leisure,* the *New York Times Magazine,* and Andrew Harper's prestigious *Hideaway*

Report, is one of the finest hotels in the United States; and Philip and Stephanie Barber's Music Inn, which was centered on a barn on the same property as Wheatleigh and housed one of the finest summer jazz programs in the world.[15]

Ignoring the two hundred years of history that placed Berkshire County as a rural refuge for city folk from New York and Boston, Wilson claimed to have created the real estate market for second-homers in the Berkshires. One of his breakthrough developments began in the late 1950s, when he purchased the former Hanna Farm in Stockbridge on Lake Mahkeenac, a mile-wide freshwater pond better known in the Berkshires as the Stockbridge Bowl (and not far from where Nathaniel Hawthorne wrote *House of the Seven Gables,* in 1850).[16] The Hanna Farm has played various important roles in Berkshire culture; perhaps most important, it was an early site of the Berkshire Symphonic Festival, founded by Gertrude Robinson and her friends in 1934 and now known as the Tanglewood Music Festival, summer home of the Boston Symphony Orchestra. Upon buying the seventy-acre farm, Wilson gave the main house to the Stockbridge School and then began his development plans for the remainder of the property.[17] He turned it into a summer-cottage colony and advertised the units primarily to artists who worked in television in New York City, such as Don Shirley, an Emmy Award–nominated art director for "The Perry Como Show," and to other notables who summered in the Berkshires, such as record publisher Harold Lewis, cellist Richard Kapuscinski, and famed trumpeter Armando Ghitalla.[18] "As a result," the *Berkshire Eagle* observed, "a little colony of New York City refugees has grown up in the area."[19]

With his success at selling properties as second residences, Wilson began to develop what he called "leisure-home development" in the southern parts of Berkshire county, such as West Stockbridge, Lenox, and Richmond, as well as the so-called hill towns of Becket and Peru. As the principal of Berkshire Land Ventures, which he owned with Philip Brent, an accountant from New York City, Wilson considered himself to be brokering deals that were far ahead of his time, being one of the first—if not *the* first—to commercially promote the Berkshires as a rural sanctuary that lay equidistant between New York City and Boston (approximately a 2½ hour drive either way). "No other area can make this claim," he said, "and I think it is about time we took advantage of our location."[20] Many agreed that Wilson was a path breaker, with one opinion piece in the *Eagle* declaring him an "apostle of a new industry." However, Wilson's idea about development confused many. Wilson came across as a contradiction, a businessman who was one of the largest private landholders in Berkshire County, yet a man who espoused land conservation and social justice.[21]

Following the development at Stockbridge Bowl, Berkshire Land Ventures acquired three thousand acres in the hill towns of Peru and Becket. Wilson's goal was to develop the area with houses that had been part of Victory Hill, a project in nearby Pittsfield composed of a series of Levittown-like homes manufactured for veterans, which had been shut down when the houses themselves were condemned. He purchased the condemned homes and moved them to his development, intending to sell them off individually on small plots. However, the zoning of the towns did not allow him to develop the project to what he felt was its full potential. The towns, according to Wilson, needed to create more flexibility in order for him—and therefore them—to be successful.[22] Summer homes, and the people that inhabited them, Wilson argued, would provide an increased cash flow for the Berkshires. The county needed to reassess its ideas about second-homers, he advised, discover the positive impact that they had on the local economy, and, in his words, "begin treating these people as citizens."[23]

In trying to develop such remote areas, Wilson often brought lawsuits against the towns where he wanted to build. In 1966, he brought a land-damage case to court, in which he petitioned for damages with regard to land he owned in South Berkshire County that had been taken by eminent domain. The case became somewhat controversial, because Wilson argued that his property was "interior land" and therefore worth more than he had been paid for it.[24] When these fights in Peru and Becket dragged on for months, Wilson abandoned the original plan and shifted his idea of "leisure-home developments" to what he called a "large-lot philosophy"; he would sell only large tracts of land, five acres or greater, to build individual houses, maintaining open space in the Berkshires rather than dotting the hillsides with multiple houses.[25] One of his largest endeavors was the Dean Hill area in the small town of

Richmond, which is located next to Pittsfield, Lenox, and Stockbridge. In Richmond, Wilson bought a total of 225 acres for $100,000, in 1961, but soon lost 25 acres to the town for the building of a landfill on Cone Hill Road. Wilson successfully sued for the land value as well as for the damage that he claimed had been done to the additional acreage, and was granted $17,500 by a superior-court jury after an eight-day trial, which was believed to be a record for a land-damage case in the area at the time.[26] At one point, Wilson found himself the object of a lawsuit, when one of his lawyers, attorney Joel S. Greenberg, filed a $500 attachment against Berkshire Land Ventures for legal fees and services rendered.[27]

Simons, too, would eventually sever his association with Wilson, although not until 1979. According to Simons, their relationship dissolved because Wilson never wanted to spend the money that would make his transactions completely honest. This lack of follow-through led to what Simons describes as some less-than-scrupulous business practices, and Simons did not want to write bad deeds or bad titles based on shoddy work. Wilson developed the Stockbridge Bowl properties, for example, with bad waterlines and no driveways. So although people initially loved their new summer cottages, they "turned irate," according to Simons. "The idea of making something right was not in his [Wilson's] vocabulary." After Wilson moved the Victory Hill houses to Becket, for example, he tried to sell a substandard one to a blind man. Simons finally put his foot down and refused to represent Wilson on the deal. "He couldn't understand this idea of *ethics*," he remembers.[28]

Despite the various controversies that surrounded his business dealings, Wilson maintained a successful career as a real estate developer. "I deserve to be fabulously wealthy, but I'm not," he said, though he did admit to living with "ample security." While making money in the cutthroat worlds of real estate and land development, he maintained his civic foundations. He gave, for example, an acre of land to the town of Stockbridge, which was developed into Wilson Park. "If I had been in town, I never would have let them do that," he said. "Any park bearing my name should have at least a thousand acres."[29]

Such a lack of modesty was a notable aspect of his personality. Described by one local journalist as a vain man, he was known to wear

hats in order to cover his baldness, and he refused to give his age to anyone who asked.[30] He also continued to confuse people. One local profile
described him as a "real-estate man and historian, a born Southerner
who has an unusual sensitivity to the plight of the American Negro."[31]
Indeed, while Wilson continued to acquire property and further his ideas
on leisure-home development, he also continued his social interests,
working on a history of the Ku Klux Klan, for example, and an investigation into segregation. In a letter written to *Berkshire Eagle* publisher
Lawrence K. "Pete" Miller, in 1946, which apparently followed up a
conversation between the two, Wilson indicated that he had enclosed a
portion of a "rough draft" of his "interpretation of Jim Crow," indicating
the extensive reach of his work as well as his determination to establish
himself as a social reformer and writer:

> As you know Charles A. Beard once wrote a very influential book
> using the method of economic determinism in explaining the origin of
> the U.S. Constitution. I think he made sense in showing the influence
> of the Shay Rebellion [*sic*] as the immediate reason for calling the
> Constitutional Convention and in explaining the influence of class
> interests on the Constitution itself. In my article I have tried to use
> the same method in interpreting Jim Crow. My chief hobby is reading
> social history of the South and I am very much interested in current
> social reform activities there. Besides I have at various times . . .
> made several personal investigations of social conditions there for
> various organizations and publications and for my own satisfaction,
> the last two being studies of the TVA. Before that the last was for the
> NATION magazine and READER'S DIGEST. During the great textile
> worker revolt in 1929–30 (Marion, Elizabethton, Gastonia, Danville
> etc.) and during other disturbances I was the Southern Secretary of
> the American Civil Liberties Union. I wrote an article for HARPERS
> magazine entitled CHAIN GANG AND PROFIT. I did a piece of
> original research on the famous but then little known Coal Creek
> Rebellion in Tennessee which was published in the United Mine
> Workers Journal. I did an article on the tenant-peonage system for
> THE NEW REPUBLIC. Also a series called JIM CROW IN
> UNIFORM for the CRISIS, the official organ of the NAACP. Among
> the recent students of conditions in the South I am most impressed
> with Prof. C. Vann Woodward, Dept. History at Johns Hopkins

University. From my reading, my experience as a southerner and from my own work in the field of civil liberties I have reached the conclusions expressed in this article. It is a black and white; right and wrong treatment. But it would take a book to put in the many shadings and point out the exceptions.[32]

Wilson likely was trying to get his piece published by Miller in one of his three family-owned newspapers, yet it seems he also wanted to be acknowledged as a newly arrived asset to the Berkshire community, one who brought an extensive knowledge of increasingly relevant events regarding race and labor. Miller was one of the power brokers of Berkshire cultural life, helming one of the most highly praised small newspapers in the world—the *Berkshire Eagle*—and connected to seemingly everyone who was anyone in Berkshire society. His wife, Amy Bess, was heavily involved in many Berkshire social circles and known especially for her antique and Shaker furniture collection. She played the key role in safeguarding Hancock Shaker Village, now a museum dedicated to the preservation of Shaker artifacts and the teaching of Shaker culture. In the late 1950s, Amy Bess led the campaign to save the village from a developer, taking over its presidency in 1959 and remaining in the position until 1990.[33]

Wilson's own interest in the Shaker communities that dotted the Berkshires undoubtedly gave him something to talk about with a couple like the Millers, from whom he learned that Shaker collections were becoming an excellent investment. He continued to avidly collect Shaker furniture and to broaden his interests in Shaker culture, working with local Shaker groups in New York State and the Berkshires. Of his interest in Shakers, he once said, "They were Communist, too."[34]

Wilson's interests, then, were seemingly antagonistic: he was developer and intellectual, businessman and socialist. He was a raging capitalist but had a tremendous sense of social justice, so although he did not always want to make things right in business, he wanted to make things right in the world. "He was able to compartmentalize," explains Simons. "He was a very complicated guy—a country persona but also a sharp, rather unethical businessman. He was quite a salesman, and stirred very polarized feelings—people either loved him or hated him." One local journalist agreed, deeming him "a Berkshire enigma" who was "applauded by some, maligned and mistrusted by others . . . informal in dress and talk; yet . . . very much a part of the Chatham area's intellectual society."[35]

Wilson eventually decided that he did not want to limit himself to real estate, and he founded Walter Wilson Publishing Associates, based in Lenox. The first project of the press was a reprint of a rare Shaker pamphlet, entitled *Their Reasons for Refusing to Aid or Abet the Cause of War and Bloodshed*. The document, written in 1815 in the New Lebanon Shaker community, was followed by a second one, *The Shakers and Race Hate*. Wilson's intention was to refocus public interest in Shaker culture in terms of social reform rather than craftsmanship, farming, and furniture.[36] He also continued his interest in African American history, and his research in this area, as well as his unparalleled knowledge regarding South Berkshire real estate, led him to discover not only that W. E. B. Du Bois had been born in Great Barrington but also that the Burghardt plot was for sale. Du Bois himself had owned the property, from 1928 to 1954, with hopes of someday retiring in the Berkshires, but he sold it to James and Elsie Bowen, who had now put it on the market.[37] For Walter Wilson, the Bowens had created an opportunity that he had been looking for.

"A PATRIOTIC ENDEAVOR"

In 1967, Wilson purchased the Burghardt plot from James G. and Elsie Bowen. The Bowens had bought the land from Du Bois himself, who had last visited Great Barrington in the fall of 1956.[38] Wilson made the purchase in partnership with eminent scholar and civil rights activist Edmund W. Gordon, who had known Du Bois in Brooklyn in the 1950s.[39] As Gordon recalls, he met Wilson when he was looking for a realtor to help him find a second home in or near the Berkshires, in the late 1950s or early 1960s. Gordon was a fan of the Boston Symphony Orchestra and thought that residing near Tanglewood, the symphony's summer home, would be ideal. While combing the *New York Times* real estate section, he came across an advertisement for Wilson's agency, Berkshire Farm, and noticed it was one of the few ads—indeed, perhaps the only one— that included an equal opportunity declaration. "Walter was making it known he was accepting of all people," Gordon remembers. He called Wilson, who found him a property named Fog Hill, off Route 22 in Austerlitz, New York, just over the border from the Berkshires and near Wilson's own home, in East Chatham. The two made a second business transaction when Wilson called Gordon about some land that he had found in Belize for a mere $25 per acre; Gordon agreed it was a bargain and bought it.[40]

Through the course of their real estate dealings, Gordon and Wilson became friends. They found they shared a love for Shaker furniture—Gordon remembers that Wilson and his wife had a large collection—and they had similar ideas about social justice. Gordon knew that Wilson's background included a stint as secretary for the ACLU, but he disagrees with Simons that Wilson ever officially joined the American Communist Party. "Walter never really closely allied to the Radical Left," Gordon says. In relation to Communist membership, he continues, "That had more to do with what people thought of him rather than his personal idea of himself." Gordon claims a distinction between being progressive and being liberal, and says, "Walter was clearly a liberal who tended to the progressive side."

During one of their many conversations, Gordon and Wilson discussed Du Bois's background in the Berkshires, after which Wilson set out to find the homestead, successfully. "He was very good at finding things," says Simons. "Walter discovered it," Gordon remembers, "and said it was for sale. . . . [I said,] 'Let's buy it.'" Ever the real estate entrepreneur, Wilson quickly moved forward into a partnership with Gordon and purchased the five acres on which Du Bois's boyhood home had stood, on Route 23, which, in addition to a pine grove and a healthy representation of Berkshire trees, included an oak that measured some sixteen feet around. Wilson and others dubbed the tree "the Du Bois oak."[41]

The two sought to incorporate the purchase as a foundation and created, toward that effort, the W. E. B. Du Bois Memorial Committee. In the days when their working relationship was still good, Wilson turned to Simons, an increasingly prominent attorney, for help, asked if he could put Simons's name on the committee letterhead, and asked if Simons would deal with the title and the deed transaction. Simons said yes to all, pro bono: "Walter had a whole slew of people doing things.

I saw it as a contribution," he says. "I was glad to help." According to Simons, Wilson also sought Brent's help for the project. "Phil got the tax-exempt status," remembers Simons, "no easy task."

With the deed secured and the tax-exempt status successfully obtained, everything was in place for people to begin to donate money to the memorial committee. However, with the purchase of the land and the creation of the committee, the first groundswell against Du Bois emerged, and as the plans of Wilson and Gordon solidified, Gordon remembers, so did the opposition.

Some folks in Berkshire County instantly dismissed the project to memorialize Du Bois because of Wilson's involvement. Because of his extensive network of real estate projects and the controversy that often surrounded them, many felt that Wilson was trying to use the Du Bois land only to make money. Simons counters: "Walter's interest in Du Bois was totally unselfish—he truly admired him. After he spoke to me a couple of times to get me to work on the project, I went to the library and took out a few books—[*Dusk of Dawn*] and so on—and became really interested. I found how Du Bois was so fond of Great Barrington." Wilson, too, denied any kind of commercial interest in the land and responded to his critics by pointing out that he had rejected all monetary offers for the plot, including one from a man who wanted to build a motel on the site.[42]

Opposition came as well from those who regarded Gordon's New York circle with trepidation. Gordon and his friends were part of what could be called a summer black intelligentsia, located largely on the border between Berkshire County and New York State's Columbia County. Locals resented such outsiders' entering into the small-town politics of the Berkshires during a time of tremendous national turbulence, especially in terms of national race relations and politics. Moreover, Gordon's partnership with Wilson caused concern within Gordon's New York circle. There was dissension among his friends because they opposed the major role that Wilson played in establishing the memorial committee. "I knew his personal history—his interest in Du Bois was the next step of an expression of his interest in social justice," Gordon says. "But some of my friends were troubled that I was involved with a Caucasian man in resurrecting Du Bois." To Gordon's friends, Wilson "was an outsider—

a Johnny-come-lately who didn't understand." However, Gordon's appreciation of Wilson's social sensibilities, and his awareness of how important maintaining a local leader on the Memorial Committee was to its success, ensured that Wilson's role remained at the forefront. And Gordon disagreed to a large degree with his friends: Wilson did have an understanding. "There are some European Americans who are more sympathetic to black causes than black folks themselves," he says. There are multiple levels of knowledge and understanding, he argues, asserting that although many in black circles divide people into categories of politics—"colored, Negro, black folks"—"I have tried to avoid making that distinction." Yet Gordon maintained, when pressed to label Wilson, that he was "black."

According to Elaine Gunn, the local black activists differed from their New York counterparts when it came to Wilson's involvement. Gunn had grown up in Hagerstown, Maryland, and moved to the Berkshires with her family while she was still in high school. After she moved to Manhattan to attend New York University, she returned to Great Barrington, where she married, raised her family, and taught at a local school, Bryant Elementary. Gunn became involved in the Du Bois movement because of her friend Ruth Jones, who worked closely with Wilson.[43] From Gunn's perspective, no one ever really thought about the fact that Wilson was white; people simply admired him for his devotion to the memory of Du Bois. "There weren't that many folks—black or white—in this area who knew about Du Bois, so I don't remember anyone voicing opposition to Walter," she says. "Those of us in his corner were there because we thought it was a good thing to do. I don't remember any black folks saying he shouldn't be involved in this. He was doing the work, he wasn't asking anyone else to do what he wouldn't." As for Wilson's political leanings, Gunn remembers that no one ever really talked about them. She herself had first encountered communism when she was at NYU. "They [Communists] were lovely people," she remembers. "I was from Stockbridge, what did I know about Communism? So I went to a few meetings, I listened, but I was always careful not to sign anything." When it came to understanding Wilson's ideologies, she, like others, simply labeled him "progressive," but she admits that the term was a mask for something else. "He was 'progressive,' that's what we always said," Gunn remembers. "It was almost a code word." Gordon agrees. Although he saw himself as a Marxist, the idea of whether or not someone was "officially" a communist was simply not a topic for conversation. "The McCarthy era taught us not to talk about it," he says. "If someone had a card, that was their business."

Whereas Gordon's friends somewhat grudgingly accepted Wilson because of the need to have a local on the memorial committee, and the local black community had no problem working with him, the association of Wilson and the committee simply did not make it local enough for many in Great Barrington. Historically, there had been resistance that stemmed from the antagonistic relationship between Berkshire County residents and their summer citizens. As a real estate developer, Wilson knew well and had become frustrated with the bitterness between the two camps: those who "belonged," worked, and raised their families in the Berkshires, and those who came for the esteemed cultural program every summer, or to gaze at the foliage in the fall, or to hit the ski slopes when the snow came. From his point of view, it was not productive to resent this "outsider" group, as they contributed an increasingly large percentage of the local economy, even though this solidified their stereotype as arty, intellectual, snobbish types with money to burn.

Gordon also understood that the hostility toward the memorial committee stemmed partially from the tense relationship between Berkshire locals and summer visitors, and he worked to ensure that the organization was not considered merely to be the work of New Yorkers. "That very factor was one that we worried about—that's why our efforts through Walter focused on local people, although most were somehow connected to the NAACP," Gordon says. "Even Du Bois was thought to have deserted the area for New York."

Gordon's observation is a critical one. Year-round residents both disputed the localness of the committee because of its members and asked, according to Gordon, just how "local" Du Bois was—in part because he had left the Berkshires so long ago and in part because he had renounced his country and its political system, moved to Ghana, and joined the Communist Party. In other words, his political leanings had exiled him as much as, if not more than, his geographical location.

Thus, for many, Du Bois could not be considered native in any way, particularly when compared to the likes of Herman Melville, who wrote some of his most important works while at Arrowhead; Norman Rockwell, who painted Berkshire locals for the last few decades of his career; or Daniel Chester French, whose most important work took place in his Stockbridge studio. Quickly it became apparent that the Du Bois Memorial Committee had its work cut out for it.

This is not to say that all of the Berkshires had remained ignorant about one of the area's native sons before the memorial committee formed. The *Berkshire Eagle* had kept track of Du Bois throughout his career. In the last years before his death, for example, the *Eagle* had noted his ninety-second birthday in 1960, his official joining of the Communist Party in 1961, and his move to Ghana in 1963, and ran a lengthy obituary that same year. It also noted in 1965 that emerging "Du Bois Clubs" springing up throughout the country were named for a "Berkshirite."[44]

However, with the announcement of the memorial committee, on February 12, 1968, and despite an endorsement from the Berkshire County Historical Society, criticism came quickly regarding Du Bois, largely supported by a small weekly newspaper based in Great Barrington, the *Berkshire Courier*. Like the *Eagle*, the *Courier* had often included items about Du Bois in its pages, proudly hailing its "illustrious son" on his eighty-second birthday as "one of the outstanding literary men in the country."[45] However, as a few Great Barrington residents and members of the Daughters of the American Revolution (DAR) spoke up against the creation of the memorial committee, an editorial in the *Courier* stated that "only in America could such a proposal be made. In other countries, the proponents of such an idea would be tried for treason." Accompanying the editorial, the *Courier* printed a letter to the editor railing against the plans of the memorial committee: "The first resistance to the British that resulted in the Revolutionary War started in Great Barrington. The Communists have vowed to take away the freedom we won then. I honor Du Bois for his ability to rise to such heights of 'non-affluence,' but I do not believe that it is fitting or proper to honor with a memorial in Great Barrington, or anywhere else in the United States, a member of any party that is now trying so hard to overthrow our government."[46]

The committee continued its efforts despite this early dissent. Within a few weeks of the announcement of its creation, Wilson and Gordon went to the centennial celebration of Du Bois's birth at Carnegie Hall in New York to present the Great Barrington memorial proposal. The celebration was one of Martin Luther King's last public speaking engagements, coming just five weeks before his assassination. At Carnegie Hall on February 23, King hailed Du Bois "as a model of militant manhood and integrity. He defied them, and though they heaped venom and scorn on him, his powerful voice was never still."[47] At the event, Gordon made a presentation about the Du Bois Memorial Committee, and both Wilson and Gordon had a chance to speak with King, who agreed to join the committee.[48] He would not have a chance to make much of an impact on it.

Upon Wilson and Gordon's return to the Berkshires, John Volpe, the governor of Massachusetts, announced that he would arrange a meeting between state officials and the memorial committee to see what role the state might have in creating a tribute to Du Bois.[49] Volpe's announcement undoubtedly occurred because just a few weeks earlier, before the Du Bois centennial celebration in New York, a group of luminaries, including Sidney Poitier, A. Philip Randolph, Aaron Copland, John Hope Franklin, C. Vann Woodward, Floyd McKissick, and Roy Wilkins, had written to him asking for his support in creating a state memorial to Du Bois.[50]

Although having allies such as King and Volpe seemed to add a needed legitimacy to the committee's efforts, in a short period of time, opponents continued to organize against the group. After initial negative reaction from a variety of residents and a few vocal members of the DAR, members of the Great Barrington chapter of the Veterans of Foreign Wars, VFW Post 8348, unanimously voted that its membership, ninety-seven men strong, would "strongly oppose" a memorial to Du Bois. Great Barrington selectman Cecil E. Brooks supported the VFW's action and predicted that if the campaign for such a memorial continued, there was "going to be a conflict."[51] Such a stance was to be expected, as veterans' groups have played a dominant role in voicing what historian Michael Sherry has called "patriotic orthodoxy," a practice that eliminates multiple interpretations of the past with a firm viewpoint of what history should be. According to Sherry, patriotic culture changed in the Vietnam era as people lost faith in the United States and its policies. As antiwar counterculture activists "opted out of it," patriotism became synonymous with conformist politics: "Many conservatives began a quarter-century-long campaign to use patriotism to regain power and defeat their real and imagined enemies at home," producing a "singular version of the American past."[52] Along these lines, the figure of Du Bois could be defined only by what the veterans considered to be his worst trait, support for communism, regardless of the breadth of his historical importance.

The *Berkshire Courier* also supported the VFW's stance against the memorial, calling the proposal "traitorous" in an editorial entitled "No Memorial, No Thank You." "We do not feel a monument should be erected in our town to a man who did not serve his country in a responsible manner," the *Courier* argued, speculating that Du Bois belonged to some ten different communist groups.[53] A letter to the editor of the *Berkshire Eagle* supported these claims, citing copies of a report by the House of Representatives that documented findings of a special committee investigation into tax-exempt organizations. The report cited eight pages that listed "some of the aid and support to Communist causes, Communist fronts, Communist individuals and Communist publications that Dr. W.E.B. Du Bois provided from 1940 to 1952." For example, the report mentioned that the Workers' Bookshops advertised Du Bois's writings; that he contributed to publications such as *Soviet Russia Today, New Masses* magazine, and *Mainstream* magazine; that his pamphlet *I Take My Stand for Peace* was published by the New Century Publishers, which published many Communist Party pieces; that he played a role in the World Peace Congress in 1949, in Paris; and that communists used his name for the various W. E. B. Du Bois Clubs, created, according to the writer of the letter, "for the purpose of ensnaring gullible young people into serving Communist purposes." The report, the writer continued, "logically justifies my opinion that by 1940 Du Bois was firmly committed to support of the Communist conspiracy. 'Senility' apologists for Du Bois please note!" Erecting a memorial to Du Bois in Great Barrington, the writer concluded, "will make easier such [Communist] trickery."[54]

Although the *Courier* increased its negative campaign against the project of the Du Bois Memorial Committee as a battle against communism, and some readers of the *Berkshire Eagle* seemed to largely align themselves with those views, the *Eagle* itself entered the fray by publishing a full-page "special report" on Du Bois, entitled "Prophet Not without Honor," written by *Eagle* reporter William Bell. The story documented Du Bois's life and included photos of him in various stages of his life as well as a drawing of the original house that once stood on the Great Barrington site now owned by Wilson and Gordon. The article argued that although Du Bois had ended his life outside of the United States, both physically and politically, that fact "does not wipe out his record of fighting for human rights." Rather than stir hysteria over the issue of the memorial, the story sought to "review the facts" in order to create a balanced history. Bell asked that, instead of responding to the proposal with knee-jerk reactions, people think about how the emerging controversy raised interesting questions about history, especially in terms of what happens when figures of historical importance reach old age. He urged people to avoid judging another person only on "a portion of his life," deeming such a response "absurd." Bell thoughtfully concluded thus: "Berkshire County had a great man in its midst in the person of Du Bois. The question before us now is this: are we big enough in heart and mind, and broad enough in sympathy to pay Du Bois the tribute he deserves; or shall we let the view through the wrong end of the telescope divide the issue for us?"[55]

The piece generated some mail from readers, who in general found it to be thoughtful and well researched. One letter to the editor, from a woman in South Egremont, asked that the various DAR and VFW organizations that had come out against the memorial "become as well informed as Mr. Bell before they pronounce judgment";[56] another took issue with Bell's deeming Du Bois "Great Barrington's most famous native son." The writer continued,

> They had better smile when they say it if the views of some of the
> descendants of the provincials who sent him to college count. While
> it would seem that *notorious* rather than *prominent* would be more
> applicable to many of the national groups that support the erection
> of this monument, they may have done the community a service in

making Du Bois's views public. In the spirit of objectivity displayed in *The Eagle's* article, may I suggest that the monument be three-faced. Then proper honor could be given to two other famous men who have not been properly appreciated in their own countries: Benedict Arnold and Vidkun Quisling.[57]

Although the writer's comparison of Du Bois to Arnold and Quisling may appear extreme, the letter articulated several of the themes underlying the movement against the memorial, particularly that the memorial committee was not a local group but a national one, and that those who had local clout—"the provincials"—as well as those who could claim to have blood ties to ancestors who had actually done something for Du Bois, were not being listened to. For this writer, the argument went beyond Du Bois himself and back to the familiar pitting of the local citizenry of Berkshire County against those who visited for the summer season. And he was not alone. In a letter to the editor that cited the House report regarding Du Bois's communist activities, the writer went one step further, concluding not only that Du Bois's membership in the Communist Party made him ungrateful to the community that had "allowed" him to succeed but also that joining the party was an act of sedition in which Du Bois had "ill repaid those fellow Americans of his community who donated to finance his education, thereby increasing his capacity for treasonous activity against his country."[58]

Another response to the *Eagle* feature came in an editorial in the *Berkshire Courier,* which attacked both the piece and Du Bois, using the piece to fuel its own campaign against the memorial committee: "The Berkshire Eagle lauds the many achievements of Du Bois. . . . However, . . . [it] brushes aside . . . the fact that Du Bois was affiliated for many years with the Communists. . . . There are still a few misguided souls who refuse to recognize that Du Bois was an out-and-out Communist—a man who worked for many years to downgrade and weaken the United States."[59] From the *Courier's* point of view, supporters of the memorial committee were confused.

As a range of organizations and public figures continued to come out with their stances on the memorial project, it became clear that the debate increasingly posed those against the Du Bois memorial as patriotic, and those who either joined or supported the committee to be treasonous, making the various war veterans' groups, among others, the "good guys" and civil rights and peace organizations, at best, disloyal, and, from the perspective of many, subversive "bad guys." In the midst of the mounting opposition, the Berkshire County chapter of the NAACP, for example, announced that it had voted, according to president Willard H. Durant, to support the memorial committee's efforts.[60] Within a month of the local chapter's decision, the national body of the NAACP also endorsed the memorialization efforts.[61] In 1968, with civil rights groups such as SNCC and the Black Panthers taking center stage away from antecedent and seemingly more traditional and conservative groups such as CORE and the SCLC, it seemed somewhat unbelievable that the group Du Bois had helped found in 1909 would, at that point, be construed as subversive.

One letter to the editor of the *Eagle* warned "patriotic organizations" to put the Du Bois case to rest; not because she wanted a memorial but because she feared what might happen if the debate continued. Making apparent reference to the very public spectacles staged by civil rights activists in the South, she warned:

> We are inviting outside interference at a time when there are many willing to interfere. We are preparing a marvelous bed for radicals, kooks, agitators and other undesirables from outside. What better chance to make themselves heard, to gain publicity, glory or make first coup than to come up here and help stir up a little mayhem this summer? The longer we keep this ridiculous tempest in a teapot going, each contributor adding more fuel on one side or the other, the more probable the chances that someone will avail himself of this perfect opportunity. . . . Let's not forget, we have taverns and burlesque house and worse, but we need not frequent them or patronize them. Nor need we necessarily frequent this memorial.[62]

The battle escalated. Whereas the NAACP put the Du Bois memorial to a positive vote, in nearby Dalton, American Legion Post 155 voted against it, as did (unanimously) the Dalton chapter of the VFW, to show support of its Great Barrington counterpart. American Legion Post 254 in West Stockbridge wrote a letter to Volpe asking him to change his stance. That post joined the Great Barrington American Legion, the Pittsfield American Legion, and the Great Barrington Knights of Columbus, all of which stated that they intended to begin letter-writing campaigns against the memorial, according to William Drambour of Post 127 in Great Barrington, "because of Du Bois' membership in the Communist Party."[63]

Undoubtedly under pressure from its twelve member chapters, the Berkshire County Council of the American Legion placed on its agenda a resolution, drawn up by Southern Berkshire Post 127, asking for "a very firm stand" against a Du Bois memorial: it passed. With this resolution, all legion posts and three VFW posts had publicly stated opposition to the Du Bois memorial project. However, the DAR, which had been considered one of the first groups to oppose the proposal, recanted somewhat. "The reported opposition," said member Lila S. Parrish, "has been only the opinion of a few." The DAR's official stance, she continued, was that it had no official stance.[64]

Even though the governor of Massachusetts had promised to help the Du Bois Memorial Committee in arranging meetings with state officials, a handful of state politicians came out in the opposite camp, indicating that the controversy materializing in the Berkshires was beginning to get noticed in Boston. State senator George D. Hammond became the first politician outside the local Great Barrington government to join the resistance, stating, "I oppose whole-heartedly a memorial to a Communist," and state representative Sidney Q. Curtiss said that he would vote against the use of any state funds for the memorial project, citing as reasons Du Bois's membership in the Communist Party and his renouncement of his U.S. citizenship before he died.[65]

Not all elected officials agreed, however—although for complex reasons. Senator Edward W. Brooke, who in 1966 was the first African American elected to the U.S. Senate in eighty-five years, became an ardent supporter of the project and member of the memorial committee, arguing that the "erratic radicalism" of Du Bois in old age should not be allowed to overshadow "the essential greatness and goodness of the man." Brooke argued that Du Bois's reasons for making the choices that he did late in life were useful, and that a memorial to him might enlighten those who did not understand the ramifications of racism on the individual. Thus, although Brooke provided support, he did so by pathologizing Du Bois, painting him as an old man who had been so irreparably scarred by racism that he had made the irrational decision—rather than the studied and thoughtful conclusion—to choose communism over democracy:

Many well-intentioned and sincere people have written questioning
my decision to join a group . . . whose purpose it is to raise funds for
a memorial to Dr. Du Bois. Some are understandably troubled by his
espousal of communism in the twilight years of his life and question
the propriety of having any kind of memorial to "an avowed
Communist." [But the memorial could] serve as a living reminder to
all of us what can happen when the forces of intolerance, racism and
injustice make despairing men believe that causes like communism
provide the only alternative to a decent life in their homeland.[66]

Brooke was not the only figure of note to join the memorial committee's
efforts. As the opposition grew, so did the spotlight on what the group
was trying to do, and the local newspapers began keeping track of which
"Negro celebrities" were joining the cause: CORE founder James
Farmer; Stephen Gill Spottswood of the NAACP; Stephen J. Wright,
president of the United Negro College Fund and president of Fisk College; Morgan College president Martin Jenkins; and actors Roscoe Lee
Brown, Godfrey Cambridge, and Ruby Dee.[67]

However, the assault against the memorial continued. Pittsfield's Veterans of World War I came out against the plan, as well as a new organization in Great Barrington, the Affiliation of Anti-Communists, formed
with the explicit mission of defeating any kind of effort to memorialize
Du Bois. The group's leader was Raymond Bonneville, a thirty-six-year-
old part-time household-supplies salesman who had a reputation for engaging intensely in local politics by forming small organizations to fight
a variety of causes. He had previously formed a coalition to oppose the
reevaluation of Great Barrington, although he lost control of the group
to another member; and he had also formed a coalition to take down an
apartment building in the center of the town. Speaking of his new organization, which he defined as "militantly anti-Communist and militantly
anti-Socialist," Bonneville made no bones that the Du Bois memorial
was his number one target. Twenty people assembled at the group's first
meeting. "We're going to start a six-month program of self-education so
we can learn about the harm communism has caused," Bonneville told
the press. "Then we'll be ready to fight it."[68]

As Bonneville's group exemplifies, the associations made between
Du Bois and communism together with his renunciation of American

citizenship were the most common reasons cited in objections to the memorial committee's proposal. Bonneville's admission that his group needed to study communism for a lengthy period of time before jumping into full combat against the memorial project demonstrated how communism served as an easy way to oppose the memorial committee. For members of the committee, the degree of this kind of ignorance was infuriating. "People forget the reason why Du Bois joined [the Communist Party]—he had been trying to make it better for black people in this country, and it didn't happen, so he tried something else," says Elaine Gunn. "You feel sorry that he had to leave the country, but he never gave up his citizenship. That's the thing that people are still harping on; they say, why should we honor a man who gave it up?—but he didn't."

Aside from Du Bois's self-expatriation to Ghana and his membership in the American Communist Party, opposition to the memorial likely was also fueled by the makeup of the Du Bois Memorial Committee itself, which was populated increasingly with the "outsider" intelligentsia so many locals scorned, and with many who did not reside in the Berkshires at all. By the first week of April 1968, the *Berkshire Eagle* counted seventy-eight members on the committee, including famed journalist-historian William L. Shirer (*The Fall of the Third Reich*), who lived in Lenox; science journalist Gerard Piel (*Scientific American*); sociologist Robert Coles; Patrick E. Goman, of the Amalgamated Meat Cutters and Butcher Workers union; Jewish businessman Kivie Kaplan, who had taken the reins of the NAACP as president in 1966; sociologist Charles R. Lawrence of Brooklyn College; the president of Barnard College, Millicent McIntosh, who had a home in South Berkshire; and civil rights leader and Morehouse College president Benjamin Mays.

Even the *Berkshire Eagle,* an early supporter of the committee's efforts, had to acknowledge that the future of the memorial seemed grim; columnist John W. Tynan Jr., of the South Berkshire bureau, admitted, amid his own publication's swelling support for the memorial campaign, that it was the "wrong town, wrong time" for a tribute to Du Bois. Tynan allowed that Du Bois was "a noted civil rights crusader and historian," but he also acknowledged the bases for the opposition, including Du Bois's membership in the Communist Party and his association with a variety of communist bodies since 1942; and many people's sense that

Du Bois "did more harm than good to the civil rights movement," serving as the "inspiration for extremists such as H. Rap Brown and Stokely Carmichael." Tynan felt that the bottom line was one simple fact that few people recognized: "Great Barrington wants nothing to do with a memorial to Du Bois. Every organized veterans' group in town has opposed the memorial. Even the Knights of Columbus have gone on record against it. Only a few individuals here have spoken in favor of it."[69]

Tynan, for the most part, summarized the battle over Du Bois as it stood to date, yet he introduced a new camp in the controversy—those who disagreed with Du Bois's approach to civil rights. An early letter to the editor of the *Berkshire Eagle* charged that if those on the Du Bois Memorial Committee had "ever taken the trouble to read his books and to find out what the man stood for," they would have found why Du Bois was "the hero of all the black racists down to Stocklely [*sic*] Carmichael and Rap Brown." According to the letter, "Du Bois is the enemy of all satisfactory race relations and should not be glorified to by an ill conceived memorial." The writer, from Lenox, found the fact that Du Bois once claimed that Karl Marx was the "greatest of modern philosophers" to be "beside the point." For him, Du Bois's connection to communism was not as important as his finding that Du Bois and his followers had "set back the natural trend of friendship between the races about 100 years or more." "The general idea of all this," argued the writer," is to vote the whites out of large areas of the U.S., take over in the name of black leadership and then set up some vague sort of communal living."[70] One reader, from Pennsylvania, agreed wholeheartedly, writing a letter to the editor in support of the earlier writer's letter: "I add my voice to his and to that of the various patriotic organizations opposed to creation of the memorial. Were he alive today, Mr. Du Bois's words and actions might well be a distinct detriment rather than an advantage in helping to solve our racial problems."[71]

BENEDICT ARNOLD'S LEG AND THE MODERN KNOW-NOTHINGS

As the debate over Du Bois escalated, Walter Wilson himself issued a public statement on March 7, 1968, in the form of a letter to the editor of the *Eagle,* to clarify his position regarding what he cleverly dubbed the "fascinating, fast-growing Berkshire monument industry."[72] With it, he firmly entrenched the idea to commemorate Du Bois within the long-standing American tradition of public commemoration, understanding that negotiations would have to take place among a memorial, its local audience, and its broader historical context. Wilson's understanding of the situation works well within historian Kirk Savage's historical perspective of the creation of monuments in America in a broader sense:

> Monuments emerged within a public sphere that communicated between actual communities of people and the abstract machinery of the nation-state. Monuments were one space in which local communities based on geography or interest or both could define themselves and speak to or for the larger collective. The relationship between the local community and the more abstract collective was complex and . . . quite strained. Monuments did not simply serve the official demands of the state. Nor did they simply channel spontaneous popular sentiments. . . . The process of commemoration was in fact reciprocal: the monument manufactured its own public, but that public in turn had opinions about what constituted proper commemoration.[73]

In his letter, Wilson claimed that he first got the idea for a memorial to Du Bois after visiting the national historical park in nearby Saratoga, New York, that commemorates the critical American victory over the British in 1777. Wilson was particularly struck by the monument to Benedict Arnold's leg. The monument sits on the site where Arnold was wounded during the battle of Freeman's Farm, during which he skillfully led his men in a charge against the British but was severely wounded in the process. He lived, of course, to turn his reputation from that of war hero to traitor, attempting to give the keys of West Point to the British and becoming the ultimate symbol of treason.[74]

Wilson was struck by the memorial because he felt that it recognized Arnold's service *before* he became a traitor: "Maybe here we have found a sensible formula to use when erecting monuments. How much of a body would I give to this or that great one? Arnold got a leg. Who should have a whole body? I couldn't think of a single example. None of my heroes rated a full perfect body from head to toenail—not even F.D.R. and J.F.K. The country is full of complete statues—to many leaders of

the original Ku Klux Klan, for example, in public places all over the
South and in Washington, D.C.—but do the favored ones really rate per-
fection?"[75] Wilson wrote that he decided to focus on civil rights figures
using what he called the "Benedict Arnold Leg Formula," thinking about
notables such as the always mentioned "Mum Bett" Freeman; Crispus
Attucks, a man of African heritage shot and killed in 1770, making him
the first casualty of the Boston Massacre; abolitionist Charles Sumner;
Thaddeus Stevens, the antislavery congressman; and Robert Gould
Shaw, the white leader of the entirely black Massachusetts 54th Regi-
ment during the Civil War, made famous by Robert Lowell's 1960 poem
"For the Union Dead."

Wilson then wrote that his thoughts rested on "the two great modern names." "How much of a whole body on a statue should Booker T.
Washington have?" Wilson asked, wondering whether Washington deserved his many honors. Wilson was concerned about who had embraced
Washington's legacy, noting that "the lily-white Virginia Legislature purchased his birthplace and erected a replica of the Washington cabin-
home on it" and that the U.S. government had spent a great deal of
money on turning the homestead into a national historic site "in order
to perpetuate the 'ideals' of this influential man." The campaign to
turn Washington's birthplace into a place of national importance had,
according to Wilson, the full support of "the Southern racist members
of Congress," who were "using the white-exploiter prerogative of pick-
ing and honoring Negro leaders."[76]

The other name, according to Wilson, was that of "the man who almost
single-handedly destroyed the B.T.W. influence," W. E. B. Du Bois, a
"great modern Negro and American leader." Wilson called Du Bois one
of the "few renaissance men" in the United States—a poet, playwright,
educator, historian, editor, novelist, and activist. Washington's ideals,
argued Wilson, were dead before Washington himself was, yet the influence of Du Bois "is probably just beginning." And yet, pointed out
Wilson, there was no monument to the great man. He asked the residents of Berkshire County that if they were to apply the Benedict Arnold
Leg Formula, would they give Du Bois merely a little toe? "Would you
leave off one leg? Or two? Or both arms?" Wilson asked. "If so, take
care to greatly enlarge his heart and his brain."[77]

Georgia legislator Julian Bond, center, was a favorite target of interviewers

Footnote to History

LAST SATURDAY, eight hundred people came to Egremont Plain in Great Barrington where a century earlier a little boy had lived and played in the house of the black Burghardts. They came to honor that boy, who grew into a powerful spokesman for his people, who saw his country reject and persecute him, who in turn rejected his country with a cry of bitterness—and yet, with the engaging inconsistency of humankind, continued to love it.

W.E.B. Du Bois never forgot, up to his death at a great age on an African shore, "the wide and lonely plain beneath the benediction of grey-blue mountains and the low music of rivers." And so, as his widow had predicted, while people spoke and sang and dedicated a park to Du Bois, his spirit seemed to hover over the Berkshire Hills, rejoiced still by some of his countrymen but keeping the dignity of one who learned to love freedom in the town where the first American resistance to tyranny was born 195 years ago.

Audience seating was somewhat catch-as-catch-can

Photographs by
Walter Scott

Cofounder Walter Wilson

Great Barrington police were out in force, but unobtrusively

The black news media were well represented

Dr. Edmund S. Gordon, cofounder of the DuBois Memorial Foundation

The Rev. Frederick Kirkpatrick of the New Stage Youth Theatre

Actor Ossie Davis

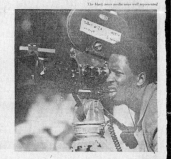

The *Berkshire Eagle*, October 23, 1968.

Georgia legislator Julian Bond, center, was a favorite target of interviewers

L̲AST SATURDAY, eight hundred people came to Egremont Plain in Great Barrington where a century earlier a little boy had lived and played in the house of the black Burghardts. They came to honor that boy, who grew into a powerful spokesman for his people, who saw his country reject and persecute him, who in turn rejected his country with a cry of bitterness—and yet, with the engaging inconsistency of humankind, continued to love it.

W.E.B. Du Bois never forgot, up to his death at a great age on an African shore, "the wide and lovely plain beneath the benediction of grey-blue mountains and the low music of rivers." And so, as his widow had predicted, while people spoke and sang and dedicated a park to Du Bois, his spirit seemed to hover over the Berkshire Hills, rejected still by some of his countrymen but keeping the dignity of one who learned to love freedom in the town where the first American resistance to tyranny was born 195 years ago.

Audience seating was somewhat catch-as-catch-can

Great Barrington police were out in force, but unobtrusively

The black news media were well represented

Walter Wilson, July 1973.

From left: White House staffer Gerald Wallette stands with Edmund W. Gordon, Walter Wilson, and Ruth D. Jones at the Tanglewood ceremony celebrating the designation of National Historic Landmark to the site of the boyhood home of W. E. B. Du Bois, Lenox, Massachusetts, October 22, 1979.

Shirley Graham Du Bois stands with Edmund Gordon and Howard Melish in Great
Barrington, Massachusetts, October 17, 1970.

The site of Du Bois's boyhood home, on Route 23 in Great Barrington, Massachusetts, just a few days after being designated a National Historic Landmark, October 20, 1979.

Mahaiwe Cemetery, in Great Barrington, Massachusetts, the burial site of Du Bois's wife Nina and son Burghardt.

In 1994, the Great Barrington Historical Society erected a plaque next to the graves of Burghardt and Nina.

The only roadside marker for the Du Bois home site, the National Historic Landmark plaque at the side of Route 23, Great Barrington, Massachusetts.

One of several markers along a refurbished trail to the site of Du Bois's boyhood home, now well hidden by trees.

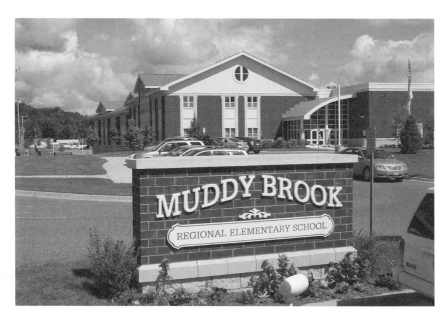

Muddy Brook Regional Elementary School.

Wilson maintained that it was Du Bois he thought of while looking at the monument in Saratoga to Arnold's leg, thinking of the lack of
presence in Berkshire County that its greatest resident had, and finding
the reason to be of the most disturbing nature:

> None of the beautiful books about our purple hills ever mentioned
> him and he was not found worthy of mention among the names of men
> and women praised beyond measure in chamber of commerce and
> tourist bureau publications. Since this goes way back to the time
> when he became a nominal Communist—even takes in the 1920s and
> 1930s when he was a leading anti-Communist—what was the reason
> for the insulting ignoring? It was because he was black, of course. . . .
> I left the Saratoga park resolved to help make amends to Du Bois and
> the Negro people if ever opportunity offered. I'd confound the John
> Birchers, the DAR, and the racist individuals who hate and should
> hate W.E.B. Du Bois. Unlike Washington, he made the proper
> friends and more important, perhaps, the proper unforgiving enemies.
> Why not? He fought 'em alive and he fights 'em dead. So last spring,
> when I saw a "For Sale" sign on the old Du Bois childhood home site,
> I put down a heavy deposit, signed a contract and bought five acres
> for $5,000. Then I went to see my friend and summer neighbor,
> Dr. Edmund W. Gordon, and told him what I had so rashly done. In
> his quiet way he said, "Put me down for half of cost and expenses."
> I put in the rest and the deed was done. We decided to put together
> a national committee of sponsors and offer the site to the
> commonwealth. This is the extent of our subversive intent. If it be
> treason I confess publicly and unrepentantly.[78]

In the conclusion of his letter, then, a letter that began rather lightly
with a story of a visit to a national historic site, Wilson praised Du Bois
for having the right kind of enemies—enemies that no one with a progressive worldview would want as friends. He also directly addressed
those who opposed a memorial to Du Bois—not as patriots fighting
against communism but as racists fighting a tribute to a black man.

Some agreed with Wilson's reasoning. "Does a memorial necessar-
ily connote approval of all phases of the life of the memorialized?"
asked a minister from the small village of Housatonic, wondering which
action truly defined patriotism: that of "the non-Communist who commits

acts harmful to his country or a nominal 'Communist' who does nothing of this nature?" He concluded that the opposition to the Du Bois memorial fell into a "'fear of communism' pattern'" rather than a pattern of freedom.[79]

Others, not surprisingly, dismissed Wilson's points across the board. No readers, of course, admitted that their reasons for waging war against the Du Bois memorial were racist in nature; they chose to couch their beliefs in a more codified manner. One *Eagle* reader responded that the Benedict Arnold Leg Formula could not be applied in this situation, because "Du Bois was so mad when he took off he didn't even leave us a leg to remember him by."[80] Some, rather than use the communist angle, took apart Du Bois's framing of civil rights. One *Eagle* reader, for example, from West Lebanon, New York, in what was undoubtedly considered to be a "liberal" opinion, wrote a letter that brought together Du Bois's identity, his political affiliations, and civil rights, bringing to the forefront the idea that Du Bois, for many reasons, did not belong, despite the opportunities that allowed so many outsiders to gain a place within the border of the United States:

> Are our memories so short that we can forget the many atrocities
> Russia has inflicted on us; that now we are thinking of putting up a
> memorial to a man, once a U.S. citizen, but who gave up his
> citizenship and became an acknowledged Communist? That Du Bois
> was a Negro is beside the point, but at present to civil righters it is
> apropos. We, as a country, have been slow in rectifying the wrongs
> done to the Negro people, but wrongs cannot be rectified overnight or
> by laws made by politicians. . . . Everyone must earn the right to take
> his proper place in society. This the Irish, the Jews, the Germans,
> the Italians and many respected Negroes have done. Dr. Du Bois
> relinquished that right when he turned his back on America.[81]

Yet another reader made a similar, albeit shorter, point, declaring herself a "proud American" who supported civil rights but opposed the memorial on the basis that Du Bois "chose communism and disowned his country." She concluded her letter by assuring others that she was "not against equality for Negroes. I'm sure our proud American Negroes will not let their cause be used as a decoy for the glory of communism."[82] Still another reader criticized Du Bois even more clearly, for relinquishing "all claim to recognition in the United States, the country which brought him financial independence and fame."[83]

Beyond those who saw Du Bois as ungrateful to the democratic ideals that "allowed" him success, and those who disagreed with Du Bois's approach to race relations and civil rights, were those who barely masked their obvious and deeply embedded racism with anticommunist rhetoric. For some, it was a self-conscious strategy. The newly formed Affiliation of Anti-Communists, for example, attempted to launch a preemptive strike against those who deemed their actions racist. According to Bonneville, each member would be screened for racial bias before being allowed to officially join.[84]

It seems that many residents of the Berkshires were able to easily locate within their historical trajectories Mum Bett, a more comfortable black figure in her role as servant, or Crispus Attucks, famous because of death, but Du Bois made for a more complicated subject. Wilson continually dismissed the opposition in the local press, claiming that if groups such as the American Legion and the VFW prevented the creation of a public monument, he would simply work to create a private one. Further, he astutely continued to speculate that the opposition was not merely about Du Bois joining the Communist Party or renouncing the United States. "I suspect there's a racist pattern in all this opposition," he said. "It's not all anti-Communist."[85] Wilson had no patience for such posturing. "I'm convinced that this Communist business is a mask for racial bigotry," he observed. "Dr. Du Bois was the greatest humanitarian to ever come from this part of the country and we should honor him."[86] The *New York Times* concurred that racial prejudice was likely the root of the conflict: "Although no one talks about it openly, some residents are said to fear an influx of Negro visitors to the [proposed memorial] park."[87]

Wilson also had no patience for those whom he felt masked their racist arguments with "patriotic" claims that Du Bois could not be memorialized because he did not die an American citizen. In a second letter to the editor of the *Eagle,* he argued that dying in Ghana was not synonymous with "treason and crime." "If so," he continued, "what becomes of our much-extolled 'melting pot'?" Many great Americans, he reasoned, came from elsewhere, and Du Bois's choice of citizenship was a "false" reason for dismissing his worthiness of a monument. "The fact that Dr. Du Bois became a citizen of Ghana in 1963, a brief half-dozen months before his death, isn't the real reason the modern 'Know Nothings' oppose the memorial," Wilson continued. Rather than consider Du Bois not eligible for remembering, perhaps those opposed to the monument should think about why he changed his citizenship: "Rightly or wrongly, he felt that his country had repudiated him and his work and had dishonored him by imprisoning him for circulating the Stockholm Peace Petition." He moved to Ghana with a promise of support and funds for his lifelong project of creating an African encyclopedia, Wilson pointed out. Should he really be punished for taking the opportunity to live free of "persecution and dishonor" and "do the work nearest to [his] dreams"?[88]

That April, an editorial in the *Nation*, anonymous but possibly written by Wilson, gave the memorial campaign further national attention, offering readers a summary of what had been happening in the Berkshires and locating the opposition to the memorial movement as part of the "'Communist phobia' that plagued the United States": "In the eyes of such opponents, the taint of communism is enough to make all of a man's achievements count for naught. . . . The enlightened patriotic citizens of the Housatonic Valley should be proud of their distinguished son, and they should proclaim their pride to the world."[89]

However, the debate over Du Bois retreated to the back burner on April 4, 1968, as news of Martin Luther King Jr.'s assassination took hold, yet it also galvanized the movement, bringing together the politics of the local and the national into even clearer focus. The aftermath of riots and violence that King's death provoked seemed to sharpen the fears of many opposed to the Du Bois memorial, but it also motivated those in favor of a memorial. According to Elaine Gunn, King's death was a turning point, particularly when a group of area residents gathered together in Park Square, in the center of Pittsfield, for a King memorial. She remembers being there with Wilson; her uncle, David Gunn, who was an officer of the local NAACP chapter; and Ruth Jones, among others. Wilson kept telling people at the memorial that there should be something similar in Great Barrington for Du Bois. "So we all started talking about how we could do that," Gunn says. "Walter had a list of names from around the country, and had a list of important people from around the area—the Cranes, Bill Gibson, Norman Rockwell. What I remember then is that Walter began to talk about people who should be involved, including the NAACP—that's where Uncle David came in, because he was key to keeping the organization together in the county." According to Gunn, Wilson then turned to Jones, who was working at the relatively new Simon's Rock College in Great Barrington, for organizational help. Jones asked the college's founder and president, Elizabeth Blodgett Hall, if they could use the campus to meet, and Hall readily agreed. Thus, Jones was able to do organizational work for the Du Bois Memorial Committee using the college's resources, including its mailing lists, and the group took another step toward turning the property Wilson and Gordon had purchased into something significant.[90]

But in Great Barrington, connections made between King's death and the burgeoning Du Bois movement created venomous conversation among locals, exemplified at a panel discussion that took place to honor King's legacy. During the session, the Reverend Lawrence Larson of the town's St. James Episcopal Church raised the issue of the opponents of the Du Bois memorial and made a correlation between the local controversy and King's death, once again making clear that anticommunist rhetoric was likely covering racist perspectives. "If they are not ashamed now . . . ," he said, leaving the sentence hanging, indicating that those who contested the memorial committee—or at least its cause— had something in common with those who had brought down the nation's leading civil rights leader. Larson's statements infuriated the *Berkshire Courier,* which railed against the pastor in an editorial:

> Ashamed! Ashamed of what, we ask? It was not a group of bigots
> who expressed their opposition to the Du Bois memorial. Instead,
> it was a group of Americans, concerned with the costly war against
> communism, who spoke out against what would, in effect, be a
> monument in our backyard to a Communist. . . . Insinuations by a
> clergyman who attempts to turn a patriotic endeavor into a race issue
> are not called for. The minister . . . is the one who should be
> ashamed—ashamed for apparently attempting to turn an issue
> involving communism v. democracy into one which would be racist
> in nature.[91]

Perhaps more important was the reaction of those who made connections between the legacies of King and Du Bois to create something other than rage. As Gunn indicated, King's death reinforced Walter Wilson's desire and also intensified her own understanding of the movement. Gunn admits that she first got involved in the Du Bois memorial movement because of her friendship with Ruth Jones, and because she enjoyed the social aspect of it. "I attended the meetings with her—we were young married folks raising our children, and it was something to do in Great Barrington," she says. "What was happening in the South— we were here and couldn't get involved physically, but we could watch it and sympathize. We were watching, on television, but we couldn't get there." According to Gunn, King's assassination electrified local action: "It wasn't until after King's assassination that the Du Bois thing really got going. We had been in the local NAACP, and [in] a community movement to send things like clothing to the South, but that was it. King's death made Walter raise the bar—there needed to be something on par for Du Bois, not just honor [for] King."

Some who climbed on board in the wake of King's death were motivated to propose alternative ideas to the Du Bois memorial. One example was the self-proclaimed "fence-sitter," a veteran of the Korean War who did not want to honor anyone "who had leanings toward the very thing we fought against" but still wanted to "honor an American who has done much for his country and race." This man suggested that rather than build a monument to Du Bois, which some might "desecrate . . . so as to cast an unfavorable light on their fellow Berkshirites," the two sides of the Du Bois debate should come together to "do something in Dr. King's memory," perhaps by donating money to the building of the new Second Congregational Church in Pittsfield, in order to demonstrate "racial harmony and Christian spirit . . . and a suitable memorial to a great American Negro . . . in the Berkshires."[92]

Others disputed that King and Du Bois could be compared at all, choosing instead to take the criticism of Du Bois in a new direction, regarding him as the wrong kind of black figure to herald. A letter to the editor of the *Eagle* by a man from nearby North Egremont, for example, indicated that the movement to memorialize Du Bois, which he described as an illustration of "minority disregard of majority preference," encompassed both the greater problem of the political moment—the relationship of religion to the Cold War—and the problem, in his eyes, of casting a figure like Du Bois as a black leader in the wake of the King assassination, because King "resembled Dr. Du Bois in color only":

> Those in favor [of a memorial] have simply rested their case on Dr. Du Bois's progress to a "Who's Who" status before he renounced his country and the system under which he realized the ultimate in his field. Those opposed have neither belittled nor denied his achievements, but they disapprove any commemoration anywhere, any time, of any one under these circumstances. There has been no denial by the proponents of the many W.E.B. Du Bois clubs . . . of the other ways in which he strove to advance the Communist line during the second half of his life. Some clergymen have advocated the project; others have opposed it. How anyone ordained for religious service can mindfully enshrine an individual whose adopted code includes only such religion and thought as the ruling body decrees is incomprehensible. . . . Since Dr. King tried quietly but firmly to work within our legal structure and economic system and to purge the Communistic elements from his followers, it is only logical that his tragic death should increase, not diminish, the objections to any dedication to one diametrically opposed to his way of effort. It can be said that the attention drawn by the scholarly dissensions during the past several months constitutes a service considerably beyond this immediate area. Even if a battle is lost the constructive opposition to any ramification of communism will never cease.[93]

Indeed, the debate seemed to have no end, although without question those who opposed the memorial committee were able to carve more public space for themselves than the committee could, using Du Bois's political affiliations and residency in Ghana to prevent the debate from becoming what it truly was: a battle over the memory of a black man. For some, it bordered on the absurd; one Pittsfield resident felt that, rather than memorialize Du Bois, people should focus their energies on granting a medal to Walter Wilson, for having "turned up a genuine, Berkshire-born, over-educated, confessed, card-carrying Communist. . . . And praise be to God, not only is he black but has a beard to boot!" The writer commended Wilson for having given "the vigilantes . . . their devil," noting that because Du Bois was dead, he did not have to deal with "the obscene telephone calls of the supercharged" or even "a burning cross on his lawn." Rather, those who opposed Du Bois would simply "write their letters, pass resolutions and let off steam." Dubbing himself one of the "middle-of-the-roaders," the writer thanked Wilson for focusing the ire of these people against someone who could not respond. "What a comfort to tortured doubts Walter Wilson hath wrought," he concluded.[94]

For John O. LaFontana, a local journalist from Great Barrington, the debate created worry that the Berkshires, where "the first blow for freedom from which the British yoke was struck," would fail to fulfill its historic legacy, one that was already marked by a monument to Shays's Rebellion and for which the local DAR chapter chose "First Resistance" as its chapter name. But rather than see a memorial to Du Bois as continuing the democratic vocation of the region, this Great Barrington resident finds that "patriotism has been outraged because the memorial honors a man who died a Communist." Rather than see Du Bois's Communist affiliation as a question of patriotism, LaFontana urged his fellow residents to see it as a moral problem demonstrating why Du Bois chose Ghana over the United States and communism over democracy, and delving into the ramifications of a society that proclaimed itself "the land of the free and home of the brave" but practiced segregation, discrimination, and racial violence. "We say communism denies freedom to society," he wrote. "That is why we fear and despise it. It robs us of our dignity, our soul, our freedom. Yet the Negro is denied these same things."[95]

Further, LaFontana understood, as did Wilson and others, that the debate over Du Bois could not be merely about treason and communism: it had to be about race, because for Du Bois, American political ideology could be understood—and refuted—through no other lens:

> There are those who oppose the memorial saying it is a question of
> patriotism and principle, not the color of one's skin. But in this case it
> regrettably becomes a racial question because the focal point of all
> the controversy is Dr. Du Bois, a Negro. This furor might never have
> come about had he been white. Had he been a white man, he
> undoubtedly would have been known to all and recognized as an

outstanding author, historian, teacher, and possibly a great
humanitarian. And it would be safe to assume he would not have
turned to communism. But he was born of dark skin, not of his own
choosing, and with a keen intellect. Yet all through life his intellect
could not cope with the indignities heaped upon him and his people
because of his pigmentation. To Dr. Du Bois and his fellow Negroes
the American way of life isn't all that it is supposed to be, sad as it is.
So after trying for many discouraging years for a better and more
rewarding life, not only for himself but his people, which we denied
him, he decided to try the Communist Brand. . . . We blame others,
when in reality we are at fault, for was it not our treatment of Dr.
Du Bois that caused him to turn to communism . . . ?[96]

LaFontana tried to express what others seemed to deny about understanding the full arc of Du Bois's life and politics—that for decade upon
decade he worked, as an American, to change the world, and when he
finally could work no longer, he left. LaFontana concluded that a memorial should be erected, not to Du Bois "but to ourselves, because of him,
listing our human frailties with which we are endowed. . . . Let's not
blame Dr. Du Bois for his action; rather let us put the blame where it
belongs, on ourselves."[97]

Few outside of the Du Bois Memorial Committee agreed, publicly,
with the viewpoints of LaFontana. But the campaign to celebrate Du Bois
pushed forward in the spring of 1968. While the civil rights movement
foundered in the violence that followed the fall of its central figure, King,
and more militant branches of civil rights, such as the Black Panthers,
carved more dramatic spaces for themselves in the national landscape,
the committee moved toward getting the plot of land Wilson and Gordon
had purchased into respectable shape, hoping to dedicate the site as a
formal memorial that summer. Likely, few knew just how difficult such
a goal would be to reach.

CHAPTER FOUR

Where Willie Lived and Played

I would have been hailed with approval had I died at fifty. At seventy-five my death was practically requested.
—**W. E. B. Du Bois**

T HE DU BOIS MEMORIAL COMMITTEE forged on with its mission. With the land in hand, the committee flourished, if not in local popularity then with a membership that topped one hundred by the spring of 1968, and things began to swing into motion. The committee began its campaign by creating a program to donate books to the Mason Public Library in Great Barrington. The initiative was greeted with skepticism by the *Berkshire Courier,* which railed against the committee for taking donations intended for its "Communist memorial" and putting them toward filling local libraries with books on "Negro history and culture—and even on Communism."[1]

The idea to use some of the Du Bois money in this way actually began with the *Courier.* In an editorial the week before the memorial committee announced its book-buying project, the *Courier* suggested that rather than build a monument to a communist that could "rival the statue of liberty," the committee buy "Negro books" for local libraries, as well as books that would allow children "to glean enough information . . . so they won't become Communists."[2]

A DEDICATION DELAYED

Book project aside, the focus of the committee remained on the park. In terms of the park's design, Walter Wilson's hopes fluttered between modest and grand. At the very minimum, Wilson felt the park should feature a raised platform, upon which would sit a ten-ton granite boulder with a plaque, amid a planting of some fifty trees. The plaque would be designed like an open book. The left-hand page was to feature Du Bois's biographical details: his birthday, date of death, and a brief description of his many achievements. The right-hand page was to feature an engraved bust of him, accompanied by his famous quotation—"The problem of the twentieth century is the problem of the color-line"—from *The Souls of Black Folk*.[3] However, before any of this could take place, the site needed to be cleaned up, so a "work bee" was planned by the memorial committee for May 18 to get the job done. Despite day-long rain, the work bee was a relative success; twelve of the trees had been planted, and much of the brush had been cleared away from the overgrown plot with much raking and weeding.[4] According to Elaine Gunn, this was as social as the work on Du Bois got. Although a large reason for people to get involved in the local NAACP was to meet others (a somewhat difficult undertaking for African Americans in such a small community), with the Du Bois project, says Gunn, membership generally centered on a lot of hard work. "There were a number of NAACP social things, but there was nothing social involved with Du Bois," she recalls. "We just wanted people to recognize the fact of how important he was and who he was—it wasn't going to be a party. Later, Walter would get a case of soda and we would go and pull weeds . . . [in] the lot cleaning."

Wilson originally wanted to hold the dedication of the park before the end of the Tanglewood season, likely because that would give it a higher profile and it would better ensure that the "second-homers" on the memorial committee could attend. However, before the dedication could take place, Wilson and Gordon wanted the property to be incorporated into the possession of the committee rather than remain in their private hands. So the two of them, along with Stephen Wright and William Simons, began the difficult process of incorporating the land.[5]

Wilson asked his sometime accountant and partner in Berkshire Land Ventures, Philip Brent, to help with the incorporation process. However, as Brent went to work, attorney Arthur Stavisky, on behalf of thirty residents, made a presentation to town officials questioning the legality of using the site, which was residentially zoned, for creating an "incorporated" park. Of particular concern was the issue of parking, first raised after the work bee, during which the volunteers had parked their cars alongside Route 22. Stavisky argued that this practice of parking, which would continue if the park was to have visitors, was dangerous. Yet a town selectman refused to answer Stavisky's points, stating that no bylaws had yet been violated and that the selectmen could not take action based merely on "speculation and conjecture." Town counsel William P. Murtagh concluded the proceedings by advising the group to seek a court injunction against the proposed park on its own.[6]

With the incorporation process not yet complete, among other troubles, the memorial committee failed to get the dedication together for the summer and announced that it would take place in the fall instead, during the Berkshires' foliage season. Set for October 12, 1968, the dedication would celebrate the transfer of the property from a private holding of Wilson and Gordon to the public holding of the Du Bois Memorial Foundation, put together by Brent and Wilson. The foundation would have nine incorporators, including Gordon, Wilson, Simons, Wright, and sociologist Charles Lawrence of the City University of New York.

The announcement of an actual date for the dedication ceremony brought with it another wave of opposition to Du Bois and the memorial. A local radio station, WSBS, took a telephone straw poll about the issue; 114 people responded, 78 percent of whom stated they were opposed to creating the park.[7] Raymond Bonneville's group, the Affiliation of Anti-Communists, rose again, renaming themselves the Conservative Committee. Bonneville said that the new group would absorb the old, and it would serve as representative of people in Western Massachusetts. He claimed that the group comprised more than seventy-five members (more were expected from both the John Birch Society and supporters of "Wallace for President") but that only three members would be willing to have their names released. The group's strategy, Bonneville stated, would be to continue the campaign of writing letters to the editors of local newspapers, and to begin contacting state officials to try to stop the creation of the Du Bois park.[8] Bonneville's reluctance to release any but a few of the names of members of the anti–Du Bois group demonstrates just how delicate the situation was, and how closely it reflected the protections often offered to those who opposed civil rights; members of the Ku Klux Klan, for example, regularly enjoyed anonymity in the South because of both their costuming and the safeguards their neighbors offered.

Given this opposition, the new problems concerning zoning, and the short timeline that Wilson charted to put together a full program for the dedication and to complete the intricate incorporation process, the memorial committee announced on October 1, less than two weeks away from the scheduled ceremony, that the event would be put off "indefinitely." Those opposed to the park likely found this to be a victory, many doubted whether anything would actually ever come of the park, and still others held out hope. The state attorney general, Elliot L. Richardson, summarized just how unstable the park's future was. Although he said that he felt a Du Bois memorial was "appropriate," he also felt it was out of his—and any other state official's—realm of control. "This is a matter of local concern," he stated, "which ought to be decided by local people."[9]

A DEDICATION RESCHEDULED

For Wilson, however, "delayed" did not mean vanquished, and the following year, as promised, he tried again. The memorial committee announced in February 1969 that it wanted to begin raising funds for a scholarship program, as well as to continue to develop the Du Bois property purchased by Gordon and Wilson. In terms of the dedication itself, Wilson declared that July would be the best month, because it would guarantee the largest audience, which would not be restricted to the local. "A national audience will participate," Wilson announced, stating that the reason for the delay from the previous summer was that there had been problems scheduling the prominent figures who wanted to attend.[10]

Wilson continued to work to keep Du Bois in the public eye. With the New American Library, he published an edited anthology of Du Bois's writings, and planned to publish an accompanying syllabus for the study of Du Bois.[11] He also continued to work on the physical upkeep and improvement of the Du Bois site, bringing in heavy machinery to truck in the boulder for the plaque, and creating an access road.[12]

As the park continued to take shape, the memorial committee then set about creating a program for the dedication, and decided to ask Julian Bond to be the keynote speaker. It was here that the dual personality of the memorial committee—the mixture of locals and summer residents—worked to its advantage. "I had the connection with the Du Bois community down in New York City, and the national people, like Julian Bond," recalls Gordon. "Walter was responsible for the local sponsoring group." However, despite Gordon's connection, Wilson remained the center of the movement's leadership, according to Elaine Gunn. "He was the force," she argues. "Dr. Gordon was in the New York area, but Walter was here."

Bond's invitation, which he accepted in July, was largely due to the fact that his father, Horace Mann Bond, was a key sponsor of the movement to create the Du Bois park and had been a friend of Du Bois's.[13] However, the choice of Bond as keynote speaker also spoke to the politics that the memorial committee wanted to infuse the dedication with. Bond began his impressive career of civil rights activism in 1960 while still a student at Morehouse College, leading a series of student sit-ins, and grew to prominence as the communications director for the Student Non-violent Coordinating Committee. However, at the time of Wilson's invitation, Bond was best known for the controversy that surrounded his political career. Elected to the Georgia House of Representatives in 1965, Bond was not able to take his seat, because his colleagues objected to his staunch opposition to the Vietnam War. He was then reelected to his own vacant seat, removed again, and seated only after a third election returned him to the House, backed by a unanimous U.S. Supreme Court decision that assured all of Georgia he was supposed to be there.

Increasingly, it seemed as though the dedication ceremony was going to happen. Weather, for example, became a nonissue when the Boston Symphony Orchestra offered Tanglewood as an alternate "rain" venue, a stunning show of support for the committee.[14] But the issue of zoning again came into play. A claim brought by Theodore C. Hitchcock of South Egremont Road and represented by attorney Harris N. Aaronson argued that the site could not be a park because the property was zoned "R-2," meaning it was a "low-density" area. Hitchcock, whose property circled the Du Bois site in a horseshoe, asserted that he worried for his family's safety. He maintained that during a recent cleanup event at the site, a "bare-chested Negro" used four-letter words and trespassed on his land. As well, he claimed he had heard about bomb threats on the site, and worried about his own home. Great Barrington resident Robert Parrish supported Hitchcock, warning the Board of Selectmen that "this could turn into another Woodstock."[15]

If the park had remained the property of Wilson and Gordon, private citizens, the case would have had little basis. However, in September, after much effort, the ownership of the park transferred to the newly created nonprofit Du Bois Memorial Foundation; Wilson and Gordon served as chairs, rather than private owners, and Du Bois's widow, Shirley Graham Du Bois, served as honorary chair.[16] This paved the way for Hitchcock to file his claim. Thirty residents attended a meeting on September 29 to vocalize their opposition and support Hitchcock. Walter Wilson responded that to postpone the park's dedication because of Hitchcock's claim was "moral evasion" and "discriminatory," and that regardless of any decisions rendered by the town, plans for the dedication would continue. However, the case went to the Board of Selectmen for a decision: in early October, it ruled that the park plans did, indeed, violate zoning laws, and that the dedication therefore could not take place.[17]

However, a few days after the board's ruling, town attorney Murtagh advised that the dedication be allowed, so as not to risk violating anyone's constitutional right of assembly. The Board concurred, announcing that it would consider the validity and legality of the park another time, when it could pursue action against any further use of the property for public use and assess any necessary fines (which they speculated would be approximately twenty dollars per day for any violation). Aaronson advised Hitchcock not to pursue the claim any further at that moment. "It is not our intention, because of the lateness of the hour," Murtagh concluded in a written statement, "to interfere with the dedication."[18] Murtagh's instincts proved shrewd: upon notification of the zoning issue, the Massachusetts Commission against Discrimination announced that it would send its chair, Glendora Putnam, from Boston to investigate whether or not racial bias had a role in the selectmen's decision regarding the Du Bois park.[19]

A few days before the dedication ceremony, the *Eagle* excitedly announced that the event would be hosted by actor Ossie Davis, who had emceed the Carnegie Hall centennial celebration of Du Bois's birth, the previous year, with his wife, Ruby Dee. According to Wilson, Davis had contacted him and asked to be put on the program as master of ceremonies, saying that he would cancel a conflicting engagement in order to be in Great Barrington that day.[20] Not everyone, however, was pleased with the scheduled program. Allen H. Nolan, president of the Afro-American Society of Pittsfield, publicly criticized Wilson for what he believed to be a lack of black participation in the Du Bois movement. Nolan also believed that Wilson had prevented anyone from his organization from speaking at the dedication (despite the fact that many members helped with cleaning up the site). "We feel black organizations in the county have just been ignored," Nolan said. "We don't want anything to do with it." Wilson responded that the memorial committee had "deliberately avoided" having any specific organization represented on both the committee and the dedication ceremony program, in order to ensure that all of it remained nonpartisan. He also refuted Nolan's claim about black representation, pointing out that seven of the nine incorporators of the property were "solidly black." Moreover, he argued, the speakers for the ceremony were chosen to "honor Du Bois and to rescue his name from slanders," and in order to do that, the program for the ceremony needed to focus on nationally prominent figures.[21]

For Gunn, the accusations launched at Wilson and at the dedication's agenda simply were not fair, likely coming from a lack of knowledge about Du Bois:

> Walter would say that he was disappointed that the black community had not gotten itself involved in this project, he didn't understand it. And I don't know why [few area blacks participated]. It was out there, but it was like what was happening down South—we knew about it but what could we do? Might've seemed like such a long shot. . . . People did not know about Du Bois, I didn't, Ruth Jones didn't—people had to choose to do this, so there were a lot of Great Barrington and Pittsfield people, not a lot of black people who were educated beyond high school, very few black professionals, and people—a lot of black people—seemed very satisfied with their lives; it was easy to be.

The program, despite its controversies, finally took place, on October 18, 1969, at two o'clock in the afternoon—more than a year after it had been originally scheduled. Hundreds of people—approximately eight hundred in all—watched as a park committed to the remembrance of W. E. B. Du Bois came into being. The two-hour ceremony, according to the *Berkshire Eagle*, "went off without a hitch" despite security concerns.[22] For those who had worked so hard to make the ceremony happen, including Elaine Gunn, the fact that it went so smoothly seemed somewhat amazing:

> As the date moved closer to having the dedication ceremony, yes—
> no one knew what was going to happen. Those letters to the editor
> came out once Walter formally announced it was going to happen—
> when we went public, that's when things really began to pop up and
> happen. All the veterans organizations were opposed, the merchants
> in town were opposed, the *Berkshire Courier*. The dedication kept
> getting delayed because of Bond's schedule, and the press really had
> a field day. [Attorney] Fritz [Lord] really stuck his neck out. And we
> really thought it could be dangerous—we heard that the Panthers
> were coming from Hartford, but this could've been planted by the
> FBI, we didn't know. The day of the dedication, we had been a little
> bit concerned, we weren't sure we could have it [because of the
> selectmen]. But Murtagh knew that this was private property—he
> knew we couldn't be prevented from gathering on private property.
> He played both sides. At the last selectmen meeting, he told them
> that the dedication couldn't be stopped, and he encouraged the
> selectmen to focus on getting any kind of building on the property
> blocked. So he was opposed to it personally, but he was following the
> letter of the law—we could gather there.

William Simons thinks that the idea of Black Power in the Berkshires contributed largely to the semihysteria that took place in the days leading up to the ceremony, particularly the idea that members of the Black Panther Party might come. Just the fact that a few members of the memorial committee "dressed like the Panthers—Afros, sunglasses, etc.—made people think this was a dangerous movement with all that was going on in the period." But for Edmund Gordon, fears regarding the ceremony were somewhat tempered by experience. He remembers that the concern regarding the safety of those who attended the ceremony fluctuated between "media anxiety" and "public hostility," but in any case, none of it was new to him. "We were concerned about the hostile reception," he recalls, "but we were used to it."

PEEKSKILL REDUX

Indeed, security was a worry for all sides involved. Many members of the memorial committee remembered all too well the riot that had erupted in Peekskill, New York, which sits on the Taconic Parkway between New York City and Great Barrington, at a 1949 Paul Robeson concert. "Many of us were concerned that what happened at the Robeson event would be repeated," Gordon says. "Most of us were longtime progressives and used to official hostility. I remember slight annoyance that anyone would be so upset about it."

The Peekskill incident had an eerily similar background as the movement to memorialize Du Bois in Great Barrington, not merely because Du Bois and Robeson followed somewhat similar trajectories as black intellectuals in the postwar period but also because of the similar battle lines. As Martin Duberman outlines in his epic biography of Robeson, it began when the left-leaning group People's Artists Inc. decided to hold a Robeson concert at Lakeland Acres, just outside Peekskill, on August 27, 1949, to raise funds for the Civil Rights Congress. Robeson was no stranger to performing in Peekskill; this was to be his fourth concert in the area, and the previous three had been successful and, more important, peaceful. This concert, however, came on the heels of a series of very public events that had made life more than difficult for Paul Robeson, including his famous Paris speech; the HUAC hearings, during which Jackie Robinson testified against him; and his censure of President Truman's Supreme Court appointment of attorney general Tom Clark. Upon announcement of the concert, the *Peekskill Evening Star* warned on its front page, "Robeson Concert Here Aids 'Subversive Unit'—Is Sponsored by 'People's Artists' Called Red Front in California." A letter to the paper from a member of the local American Legion cautioned that "some of the weaker minded are susceptible to their [Communists'] fallacious teachings unless something is done by the loyal Americans of this area." The writer emphasized that he was not "intimating violence," but he concluded that he believed "we should give this matter serious consideration."[23] In the backlash that followed, the Peekskill Chamber of Commerce issued a statement against the concert; the Junior Chamber of Commerce deemed the event "un-American" and urged "group action" to take place in order to "discourage" the concert from happening; and the Joint Veterans' Council asked its members to take part in anti-Robeson activities.

Further similarities between Peekskill and Great Barrington are undeniable. Like the Berkshires, Peekskill had played a critical role in the American Revolution: George Washington established his headquarters there for a time, because he considered it to be a strategic location on the Hudson River, and there he confirmed Benedict Arnold as commander of West Point. Further, in the early postwar period, while remaining a largely working-class community, Peekskill became a destination for New York City folks in the summer, most of whom were Jewish and leaned left politically. Like residents of the Berkshires, those who lived in Peekskill year-round developed a difficult relationship with the outsiders, whom they commonly cast as wealthy and radical.

Two of these so-called outsiders, Manhattanites Sam and Helen Rosen, were to be Robeson's hosts for the concert. Robeson arrived without incident by train and was picked up by Helen at the station. However, news emerged that groups such as the VFW and the American Legion were organizing to create some kind of action at the concert. When Robeson arrived at Lakeland Acres, unrest greeted him. Traffic became blocked as groups of men examined each car as it arrived. The men pulled some passengers out of their cars, to the delight of the watching crowd, who yelled epithets such as "Dirty kike" and "Dirty Commie." The police simply stood by. Helen Rosen later remembered seeing a burning cross, after which the cars escorting Robeson turned and left the site. Robeson left for New York City the next day, where he gave a press conference outlining what had occurred: he called it "an attack on the whole Negro people" and issued a call for an investigation of the incident by the Justice Department.

The Rosens called a protest meeting at their country house and asked the state police for protection (unsuccessfully) because of the barrage of telephone threats they had received. Some fifteen hundred people who attended the meeting formed the Westchester Committee for Law and Order, which decided that Robeson should return to Peekskill to perform. A variety of unions, including the United Electrical Workers and the Longshoremen, promised that their members would protect the event, and each group also left men to stand guard on the Rosens' porch.

While these plans were put into place, however, different versions of what had happened on August 27 began to emerge. A headline in the *London Daily Mirror* claimed that Robeson had "asked for it," whereas the *New York Daily Worker,* not unexpectedly, determined that a "lynch mob" had "run amuck" in Peekskill. An FBI agent who had been in Peekskill admitted that the affair had been "started by vets," but J. Edgar Hoover—certainly no friend to figures like Robeson and Du Bois—concluded that the Justice Department would "conduct no investigation unless requested." For their part, the local veterans' groups denied that their members were responsible for the violence, and the state police denied being asked by anyone in Peekskill for protection. Conversely, the American Legion proudly admitted its involvement: "Our objective was to prevent the Paul Robeson concert and I think our objective was reached."

On the opposite end of the spectrum, the American Civil Liberties Union felt there was much for authorities to apologize for, concluding that throughout "the three hours of rioting . . . a sufficient number of law enforcement officials . . . did not appear on the scene." Others who came out on Robeson's behalf included novelist Howard Fast, the Jewish War Veterans, Henry A. Wallace, the New York NAACP, and Rabbi Irving Miller, chair of the American Jewish Congress. The FBI kept track of this last group.

Under pressure, New York governor Thomas E. Dewey, who had initially refused comment on the riot, instructed the Westchester County district attorney, George M. Fanelli, to investigate. Fanelli responded that he had been investigating pictures taken at the riot, especially a "particularly revealing" photograph of a black man brandishing a knife, and had also noticed that among the garbage left at Lakeland Acres were Communist pamphlets. As Fanelli dove into the case, on August 30 approximately three thousand people, including Robeson, met at the

Golden Gate Ballroom in Harlem as part of efforts begun by the Emergency Committee to Protest the Peekskill Riot. At the gathering, Robeson gave a powerful speech in which he predicted, with what Duberman describes as "calculated optimism," that the riot marked "a real turn in the anti-Fascist struggle in America." "We are part of a very historic departure," he told the crowd. "This means that from now on out we take the offensive. *We* take it! We'll have our meetings and our concerts all over these United States. . . . I'll be back with my friends in Peekskill."

After much discussion, particularly within the Communist Party, Robeson scheduled a second attempt at a Peekskill concert for the afternoon of September 4, at the Hollow Brook Golf Course, approximately three miles from the town center. The reaction in Peekskill was immediate: veterans' groups planned protest parades, American flags proliferated throughout town, and bumper stickers stating "Wake Up America—Peekskill Did!" adorned the backs of cars. Many summer residents, feeling the heat, secured their homes and returned to Manhattan. The newly formed Westchester Committee for Law and Order campaigned state and local officials to make certain the concert could take place peacefully. However, given that Robeson was hanged in effigy twice the night before the concert, there could be little guarantee.

On September 4, union members went to the concert site early in order to set up defense lines, while the state police set up their own configuration, including a helicopter overhead, and ambulances stood on call. By the middle of the day, around 20,000 people—some who wanted to hear Robeson sing, others who wanted to make a political point—began to enter the concert venue. They were greeted by some 8,000 veterans, many of whom screamed anti-Semitic and racist slurs and threatened, "We'll kill you!" and "You'll get in, but you won't get out!"

Robeson arrived unscathed, staying in his car at the advice of his security detachment, and the concert began on time, with union guards encircling the stage as Pete Seeger performed. Around four o'clock, Robeson took to the stage with "Let My People Go." According to Helen Rosen, armed men surrounded the concert from a ridge above, two of whom were kicked out by Robeson's security. Regardless, the concert was performed without incident, and Robeson left. When everyone else tried to follow, however, the armistice ended. As cars and buses began to move down the winding road back to town, they were met by hordes of townspeople who threw rocks and began to drag people out of their cars and beat them as the police stood by. The only action the police took, according to observers, was to join in, clubbing concertgoers and yelling things such as "Go back to Jew town—if we catch you up here again we'll kill you!" Back at the stage, the mob ensnared the union security forces, who had been prevented by the state police from taking cover in the buses that had brought them there.

One of the most dramatic recollections of what happened in Peek-skill that day comes from novelist Howard Fast, whose left-leaning works of historical fiction include *The Last Frontier* (1941), *Citizen Tom Payne* (1943), and, perhaps most famously, *Spartacus* (1951). An employee of the Office of War Information during World War II, where he wrote for Voice of America, Fast joined the American Communist Party in 1944 and, like Robeson, was called before the HUAC, where he refused to name names (and was eventually jailed for three months, in 1950).[24]

Fast wrote two memoirs, the second of which, *Being Red* (1990), included the events of Peekskill, based largely on the affidavit that he submitted during the famous red-baiting Foley Square trial, in 1952; his report to the Civil Rights Congress; and his essay entitled "Peekskill: A Personal Experience" (1951). In the affidavit, Fast recalls that the initial August 27 concert was "prevented from taking place by force and violence by hoodlums acting under police surveillance."[25] In his memoir, he writes that when he arrived at the Lakeland area, it quickly became apparent that entry was not going to be possible because of the throng of men equipped with "billies and brass knuckles and rocks and clenched fists, and American Legion caps." According to Fast, a group of local sheriffs arrived and prevented the mob from taking any more control. Fast engaged in a form of negotiation with them, emphasizing that his group merely wanted to attend a peaceful concert. As the mob re-amassed against those who came to see Robeson, Fast remembers a variety of chants coming from the multitude: "We'll finish Hitler's job! Fuck you white niggers! Give us Robeson! We'll string that big nigger up!" The chants were followed by another attack, during which the concertgoers tried to "hold the line," as Pete Seeger later outlined in his famous song about the incident. "Here were forty-two men and boys who had never seen each other before, and they were fighting like a well-oiled machine, and the full weight of the screaming madmen did not panic them or cause them to break," he remembered. "By sheer weight, we were forced back foot by foot, but they never broke the line." As night fell and the battle continued, police seemingly disappeared, and the FBI, Fast guessed, "watched calmly and took notes." With much of the area burned and many injured, a "demented campaign of anti-Communism" had occurred.[26]

At the rescheduled concert, Fast remembered watching Robeson sing and then trying to leave. As he made his way out, he "encountered an organized barrage of rock throwing." For the approximately five miles into Peekskill, he saw police—"sometimes Westchester County police, sometimes local police, sometimes state troopers"—standing alongside those hurling the stones. The police did "nothing to stop them"; indeed, the police took an active part in the offense:

> About one mile south of the golf course on North Division Street I saw a Westchester County policeman retrieve a rock that had bounded for a car and hand it to one of the hoodlums so that it might be thrown again. I saw a state trooper attack a car with his night-stick, smashing the windshield and fender. When another car directly in front of me, with windows smashed, with occupants bleeding badly attempted to halt, a Westchester County policeman drove them on smashing at the car with his night-stick and said, "Keep going, you dirty Jew bastards." I heard a state trooper say, "You deserve what you are getting—you dirty commie nigger lovers." . . . It was quite obvious to me from the actions of at least 50 policemen along the road which I have personally observed, that they were acting according to a central directive—that they had been instructed to allow the rock throwing to persist. There is no other explanation in my mind for the absolute uniformity of their actions, the boldness of the rock throwers and for the police insistence that badly wounded, badly bleeding people should have no relief or aid for their wounds and no action against their attackers.[27]

The legacy of the Peekskill Riot is complicated. The day after the violence, Robeson gave an emotional press conference in which he placed the blame on "police who were supposed to protect" but instead "attacked and assaulted us"; demanded a federal investigation; and pronounced that "we Negroes owe a great debt to the Jewish people, who stood there by the hundreds to defend me and all of us yesterday." Fanelli issued a report on the incident on September 7, absolving both the veterans' groups and the police officers; the governor concluded that "Communist groups obviously did provoke this incident." Later that fall, a grand jury reached a similar conclusion, placing the blame on Peekskill's summer residents and on Robeson.[28]

On September 4, 1999, a service entitled "A Remembrance and Reconciliation Ceremony" took place to mark the fiftieth anniversary of the Peekskill Riot. The observance brought together Seeger, Ossie Davis and Ruby Dee, Paul Robeson Jr., members of the ACLU and the NAACP, and an assembly of local activists. Sponsored by the Paul Robeson Foundation, the occasion was intended, according to Robeson Jr., to "use the anniversary of Peekskill to express [Robeson Sr.'s] abiding belief in peaceful relations among all people." Speaking at the event, Seeger recalled how the windshield of his car, in which he rode with his wife and children, was smashed by a series of rocks, which he later used to build a chimney in his home in nearby Beacon.[29]

"THOSE PEOPLE GATHER IN THE CRADLE OF LIBERTY"

No chimneys were to be built in Great Barrington, however, as the 1969 ceremony for Du Bois was a far cry from what occurred in Peekskill. As Gordon remembers, "We simply gathered in the field, did our thing, and left." However, for him, it was not an entirely different experience. "There was none of that kind of police activity," he says, "but there was a small contingent of VFW or American Legion around."

In order to ensure that the Du Bois dedication remained safe, security was visible, although not overwhelming. According to the *New York Times*, the ceremony had been threatened by "several men described by the local residents as 'rednecks' [who] circulated through the crowd drinking beer."[30] Simons thinks that it may have been the surrounding homeowners who intensified the level of hysteria regarding the event.

"The homeowners were concerned," he submits. "They may have been the ones to raise the red alert." Indeed, according to Gunn, there was only one family that welcomed those attending the ceremony, and even then, only for a profit. "As we were driving into the park, people were in front of their houses waving their hands—we couldn't park," she remembers. "But one family, farmers, decided to rent space for parking. So they charged us—not much, but they charged."

The *Berkshire Eagle* affirmed that although only a few uniformed police officers appeared at the event, four plainclothes state officers and one federal agent were also there to maintain peace. In addition, some forty sheriff's deputies, armed in riot gear—which had to be shipped in from Hartford, Connecticut—were on call in the town hall; the state police and a National Guard unit were on standby; and Fairview Hospital in Great Barrington had twelve extra nurses on duty and three ambulances on standby. As well, U.S. Army aircraft flew over the site several times throughout the ceremony. "We had arranged to meet any eventuality," police chief Emmett J. Shea said, although whether that meant protecting the ceremony participants from those who opposed the site or vice versa was not clear.[31]

Simons remembers well the police presence at the ceremony. When he arrived, excited because he was assigned to drive Ossie Davis to the airport at the conclusion of the ceremony, Shea approached him and "said he was glad I was there on behalf of law enforcement—he assumed I was one of the 'good guys.'" Because Simons worked as an assistant district attorney, it did not occur to the police chief that he was there as a member of the memorial committee. "He introduced me to an FBI guy who was there," Simons recalls. "They had great concerns of a riot, that 'those people' would come up from New York. He told me that there was a detachment of National Guard ready to respond nearby—they were not at the ceremony, but close enough. It was a feeling of hysteria, but it was hard to understand why." Gunn also found the event to be stressful, at least initially: "It was tense. We found out later that the police had gotten some firearms from Hartford and put them in the basement of the police station—they kept saying they were getting ready because the Panthers were coming. And there was a plane overhead, just kind of circling, and we found out that there were plainclothesmen in the crowd, and armed men in the attic of one of the abutters. These weren't local police, either."

Yet despite this attention to security and the apprehension about conflict, there were no disturbances. "It was such a beautiful day," continues Gunn. "People sat on blankets, Ossie Davis was the master of ceremonies, Julian Bond spoke, Pete Seeger sang—it was a beautiful dedication. We came quietly and left quietly." While the audience sat on their blankets, as well as on bales of hay and folding chairs, Walter Wilson spoke to the spirit of Du Bois: "Welcome back to the house of the black Burghardts." Dr. William Howard Melish, who had given the eulogy for Du Bois in Ghana, also spoke. Du Bois had been a neighbor of Melish's popular Holy Trinity Church, in Brooklyn, and wrote of the minister that he was "one of the few Christian clergymen for whom I have the highest respect . . . working honestly and without hypocrisy, for the guidance of the young, for the uplift of the poor and ignorant, and for the betterment of his city and his country." In 1949, Melish became embroiled in controversy when he joined the National Council of American-Soviet Friendship, causing a backlash in the community and forcing him to resign from his church. However, Du Bois argued in his autobiography that rather than being forced out because of his political beliefs, Melish, in what he calls "the most typical and frightening illustration of present American religion," was the victim of the "rich, white, 'respectable'" members of the congregation as a result of his reaching out to the "workers and Negroes" in the neighborhood.[32] Still other speakers at the dedication included local activist and memorial committee member David Gunn; Esther Jackson Davis of *Freedomways* magazine; Horace Bond; and playwright William Gibson, who read Du Bois's 1928 essay from *Crisis* about Great Barrington.[33]

Elaine Gunn and Ruth Jones had volunteered to pick up Julian Bond at the airport in Hartford, where they were stunned to see him get off the plane: "We were drooling, he was gorgeous. He had this huge Afro, and his bodyguard got off after him. Ruth had driven over, so she asked if I would drive back, which of course meant that she got to sit in the backseat with Julian and the bodyguard. We also picked up another guy who was also coming to the dedication. Kato was his name, that's all I remember. He didn't know where he was, or how he was going to get there, so we picked him up, too. He was from Cornell or something. It was a nice sixties thing to do."

Bond set the tone for the dedication ceremony early in the day, when he granted an interview to a local radio station, WBEC, to subtly address the opposition that had surrounded the remembrance. "I prefer to think of his [Du Bois's] whole life, not just the last couple of years," Bond said, "dedicated as no man's life perhaps has ever been to the abolishing of prejudice and injustice and of imperialism internationally."[34] In his keynote speech at the dedication, Bond affirmed Du Bois's understanding of the relationship between economics, subaltern struggle, and racial identity. He noted that Du Bois, in his famous observation that the "problem of the 20th century is the problem of the color line," was "summing up the failure of the white minority people of this world to share the wealth of the world with the colored majority." Speaking of the United States, Bond specified: "Violence is done when black children go to school for 12 years and receive five years of education. Violence is socialism for the rich and capitalism for the poor. Violence is the little tyrant of the Federal Bureau of Investigation who listens to your telephone conversations, and violence is the farmer who receives welfare payments of $25,000 for not planting crops." Until the end of this violence, Bond concluded, Du Bois's goal of "an end to the problems that beset man" would not be achieved.[35]

Shirley Graham Du Bois could not attend the ceremony, but, following Bond's remarks, a letter was read that she had written for the occasion: "No act of memory could have pleased him more. . . . I am sure his spirit hovers over the Berkshires Hills. . . . It was from this soil and the people of this community that his deep roots drew the strength, the courage and the dignity that shaped his character. He had absorbed into his being all the ideas and the tradition of New England, the cradle of liberty."[36] Although the dedication ceremony in the field ended the official program of events, according to Gunn, "That wasn't the end of the day. My Uncle David asked the minister of the First Congregational Church in Stockbridge if we could meet there, so Julian Bond and his father, and a small group of us went up there and met and Bond spoke again. His father sat in the front row, leaning forward, looking at his son, just listening and watching. I thought, wow. Wow."

The week following the dedication ceremony, the *Berkshire Eagle* ran a full-page photo special by local photographer Walter Scott, entitled "Footnote to History," featuring an array of moments from the dedication, including photographs of Gordon, Bond, Wilson, and Davis, as well as the Great Barrington police officers stationed at the event, the spectators scattered across the property, and members of the black news media documenting the dedication.[37]

Despite the apparent success of the dedication ceremony, the placement of the plaque on the ten-ton boulder did not take place. According to Wilson, there were no plans for the bronzed open book to be put on the stone until the local opposition to the park had somewhat subsided. "At this point, I wouldn't even leave folding chairs in the park overnight," Wilson said on the day of the dedication. "We put the chairs out this morning and we'll take them away after the ceremony."[38]

A QUESTION OF FOLLOW-THROUGH

Wilson's sarcasm was warranted. Just days after the dedication ceremony took place, the Board of Selectmen pursued its promise to prevent any future events at the park. Murtagh affirmed once again that the park violated the area's zoning but that the town had allowed the ceremony to take place out of respect for peaceful assembly. Now, however, the board decided to bring legal action against the memorial committee for violation of zoning bylaws.[39] The irony, of course, is notable: the board would not act on the claims of residents regarding zoning before the dedication, because technically nothing had yet been violated. But after the event, which the board itself had allowed, the claims against the creation of the park could go forward.

In anticipation of this action by the town, the memorial committee had contacted the NAACP Legal Defense Fund (LDF) for help. At that time, attorney Jonathan Shapiro was working for the LDF, specializing in land-use discrimination cases, and he was assigned to the case.[40] Shapiro, who would become famous in 1971 for working to reverse Muhammad Ali's conviction for draft evasion, was familiar with the Berkshires, having spent summers in nearby Cornwall Bridge, Connecticut, just south of the Massachusetts border in the Litchfield Hills. While he does not remember the zoning case, specifically, he does remember having attended the dedication ceremony with his wife, his two young children, attorney Margaret Burnham, who was working at the LDF with him at the time, and Burnham's husband, Max Stern, who went on to become Shapiro's partner.[41]

Little came of the zoning issue, for either side, and the memorial committee, considering the dedication a success, decided to take the movement to the next level. Early in 1970, Walter Wilson announced that the incorporators of the W. E. B. Du Bois Memorial Foundation would hold a meeting to plot their next move: to make the Du Bois park a national landmark. The committee picked an opportune moment to make such an announcement, as a new wave of interest in Du Bois began to surface. On the same day, Harvard University announced the creation of a ten-member committee to set up the W. E. B. Du Bois Institute of African and Afro-American Studies. Although the idea for the institute, as well as its name, had first been announced around the same time as the dedication of the Du Bois park in Great Barrington, this was Harvard's first actual step in making the program a reality. Wilson also worked to keep the public eye on Du Bois. Following his edited volume of Du Bois's works, that spring Wilson published, through Teachers College, Columbia University, *A Syllabus for the Study of Selective Writings by W.E.B. Du Bois*, which included a biographical overview, notes on selected writings, a topics review, and a series of appendixes. He also included the eulogy that Melish had given in Ghana after Du Bois's death.[42] Wilson felt that these examples of renewed interest in Du Bois indicated that the chances of getting the act of Congress required to create a national landmark were "very good." He also emphasized that unlike the process resulting in the national shrine to Booker T. Washington in Virginia, no additional funds were needed for the Du Bois site: the foundation would donate the land to the government.[43]

Wilson, however, had much on his plate that spring, as he was also creating a Shaker festival, which he hoped to make an annual event. As president of a newly formed nonprofit group, the Shaker Country Festival Inc., Wilson wanted to revive Shaker music and dance, and hoped to raise $100,000 in order to do so. At the center of the festival, Wilson wanted to stage an original play, *The Passionate Quest*, written by Music

Inn owner Philip Barber and based on Wilson's research on the Shakers. Wilson felt that the ideology of Shaker culture had much relevance for the contemporary period. "The ideas of the Shakers are just as alive and just as modern," he said, noting their antiwar stance, their emphasis on civil disobedience, and their focus on women's rights. He assembled a group similar to the Du Bois Memorial Committee (the Barbers and William Gibson among them) and used his old real estate development methods for encouraging people to get involved, promising that the affair would "bring tens of thousands of new visitors" to the area.[44]

However, Wilson's focus on the Shakers was not the only reason that the memorial committee seemed to be at somewhat of a standstill. Wilson had hoped that transforming the Du Bois site into a national shrine would be relatively simple, but the question of money became a bit more complicated. In the summer months, when more members of the committee were in residence in the Berkshires, the group announced that it needed $6,000 for both accrued expenses and future projects, and sent requests for donations to approximately four hundred people. While Wilson focused on getting money from the general public, Gordon sought financial support from academic circles, focusing on history and black studies departments. The letters they sent gave an explanation for the need: "To date, the cost of these several accomplishments is less than $10,000, of which sponsors and friends have contributed $3,887. The balance has been loaned by the two cochairmen and the Lenox Savings Bank, which holds the mortgage on the property." In terms of future needs, the letter specified that the committee would like to fence the park, install the plaque recognizing Du Bois onto the boulder, give scholarships and prizes, obtain a national designation for the park, and perhaps restore the Burghardt house that once stood on the plot.[45]

The announcement of the fund-raising campaign coincided with a widening spotlight on the Du Bois park in Great Barrington. In August, the park's dedication ceremony was televised on *Black Journal*, William Greaves's Emmy-award-winning program on National Education Television (NET).[46] Even more momentous, Du Bois's widow, Shirley Graham Du Bois, announced that she would visit the park during her upcoming trip to the United States.

The prospect of a visit from Graham Du Bois was not without controversy. She originally had planned on a trip to the United States that spring to speak at Fisk University, but the Justice Department refused to allow the State Department to issue her a temporary visa, because it said she was "affiliated with subversive organizations," making her ineligible.[47] Like her husband, whom she married the day before he was indicted as an "agent of an unnamed foreign power" because of his stance against nuclear weapons, Graham Du Bois had renounced her U.S. citizenship in 1961 and moved to Ghana. After president Kwame Nkrumah's government was overthrown, in 1967, she moved to Cairo.[48]

However, in a timely coincidence, the Black Academy of Arts and Letters announced the creation of a hall of fame to "provide recognition, encouragement and incentive" for those of the black experience in the United States, according to its president, C. Eric Lincoln, a professor at Union Theological Seminary. The hall's first inductees were to be W. E. B. Du Bois, historian Carter G. Woodson, and artist Henry O. Tanner. Shirley Graham Du Bois was invited to accept the honor for her husband that fall. In order to make it happen, Lincoln wrote attorney general John N. Mitchell to ask the Justice Department to overturn its previous denial of her visit. A representative from the Immigration and Naturalization Service of the Justice Department (INS) stated that Graham Du Bois had been "found to belong to some 30 subversive organizations which made her inadmissible under the law, and she did not advance sufficient reason to waive that inadmissibility." Lincoln responded that denying her a visa was a "direct slap at our youth," reiterating that the department needed to overturn its previous decision.[49]

In August, the Justice Department did just that, announcing in a letter to Lincoln that Graham Du Bois could enter the United States in September for up to a two-month period. In the letter, James F. Greene, associate commissioner of the INS, wrote, "In light of the reason for which Mrs. Du Bois now wishes to visit the United States, this service has concurred in the [Department of State's] recommendation."[50]

Although the focus of Graham Du Bois's visit was to be the hall-of-fame ceremony, as well as a number of speeches at various colleges, a trip to Great Barrington was included on her itinerary for October 17, the day before the one-year anniversary of the park's dedication. However, there was some question as to who was sponsoring the visit. According to Gordon, the Du Bois Memorial Foundation intended to hold a small ceremony, paid for with foundation funds, for both the park's anniversary and in celebration of Graham Du Bois. Wilson, however, stated that he did not believe the ceremony was an official event of the foundation, demonstrating perhaps that the Du Bois Memorial Committee had become a bit fractured in the time since the dedication, or perhaps that it wanted to keep its plans vague in order to prevent the controversy that descended upon the park's dedication the previous year. Gordon explained that the ceremony would be an "almost private affair" that would include, as the dedication had, Esther Jackson and William Howard Melish as speakers, and a reception at the nearby Cornwall Academy afterward. Yet despite the claim that the public was not invited, Gordon, who was to serve as master of ceremonies for the event, did say that Graham Du Bois was going to hold a small press conference at the site. And indeed, the *Berkshire Eagle* covered the event, printing with its story a large photograph of those who spoke at the ceremony.[51]

At the park, before some fifty people who had come together despite gray and cool weather, Graham Du Bois emphasized in her remarks how attached Du Bois had remained to Great Barrington, affirming her happiness at seeing the place "where little Willie lived and played and grew and was so happy." "He felt he was so fortunate to have been born in this valley," she continued, "the valley that represented the revolution of people who fought against tyranny." Du Bois, she said, had been proud of the fact that his great-great-grandfather Tom Burghardt had fought in the American Revolution, and that it added to his understanding of what both suffering and revolution meant as he traveled throughout the world.[52]

Graham Du Bois focused on her late husband's Great Barrington past, whereas both Melish and Jackson used the ceremony to make statements about the current state of affairs. Both made parallels between Du Bois's struggles with the U.S. government and more contemporary events, particularly the trial of black activist Angela Davis. Melish spoke of the consequences that Du Bois faced in 1950 because of his service as chair of the Peace Information Center, which led to his trial as an "unregistered foreign agent"; Melish concluded, "I feel sure he would feel identified with Angela Davis." Jackson, too, spoke of Davis, wondering why the United States government focused on a figure like her while failing to charge anyone in the Kent State killings.[53]

At the reception that followed the small ceremony, Walter Wilson gave Graham Du Bois a copy of his book *The Selected Writings of W.E.B. Du Bois,* and she gave him a portfolio of Charles White's drawings and thanked Wilson for his efforts in creating the park dedicated to her late husband, particularly in the wake of local opposition. Wilson responded that the park "was a community affair" and that the memorial committee "had more support from the community than most people realized."[54]

Yet after Shirley Graham Du Bois's visit to the park, there was little activity from the Du Bois Memorial Committee, and little talk about furthering the plan to gain national status for the memorial. Local historians were pleased at the findings of local journalist John O. LaFontana, who determined where on Church Street Du Bois had actually been born, before moving to the Burghardt house on the Egremont plain. LaFontana, who had written passionate letters to the editor during the height of the Du Bois controversy, made his discovery when looking through some old files, within which was a letter written by Du Bois presenting a biographical overview that identified which house he believed he had been born in. "I was born on Church Street 82 years ago in a small cottage belonging to Jefferson McKinley," the letter stated, "where my mother and father went to live after their marriage in Housatonic in 1867." Checking the registry of deeds, LaFontana found that McKinley had been a former slave from North Carolina, and he was able to determine where the house had been, as well as the fact that it had been torn down in 1900 in order to make room for the Stanley Insulating Company.[55]

Aside from this discovery, things remained quiet in regard to Du Bois in Great Barrington, and little was planned for the future of the park. One theory as to what happened speaks to the racial divide within the memorial committee, as well as the question of who was "local" and who was not. "The whole thing kind of frittered out," admits William Simons. "There was a need for this group of African Americans to take the lead, but it didn't happen. They were an out-of-county group, and there was no follow-through. We all ended up stopping in mid-effort, and handing everything over to the New York circle." When the group remained locally focused, Simons theorizes, it did well. But when the summer residents went home, there was little organization left to maintain interest. Likely, Simons thinks, the lack of involvement of Pittsfield residents—which became apparent in the days before the dedication ceremony, when members of the Afro-American Society of Pittsfield questioned the program—proved to be the movement's downfall. "It needed more people from Pittsfield to get involved," he says, "because a much larger black population was there." And finally, Wilson himself was problematic. "Not everyone in the New York group liked him," Simons affirms, echoing the feeling of Edmund Gordon. "I think it was because he was white."

By 1972, when the park still contained only a boulder without a plaque, and was overrun by weeds and grass, Wilson himself expressed frustration over the seemingly bleak future of the site for which he once had high aspirations, and thought that he had perhaps taken the movement as far as he could. That summer, the *Berkshire Eagle* ran a photograph of memorial committee member Ruth Jones standing in the park next to the boulder. Tall grass surrounds her, leveling off at her shoulders, and tall weeds populate the foreground, partially obscuring the boulder that had caused such an uproar in the community a mere four years earlier. In the accompanying article, Wilson promised that the grass would be mowed and the weeds taken out, but stressed that more local interest would be needed to develop the memorial any further. The park's future, he claimed, rested on the answers to two central questions: who would be able to coordinate the necessary improvements in the park, and to what use would the park be put in the future? Since its dedication, the only event to have taken place at the site was the ceremony honoring Shirley Graham Du Bois. Wilson felt that much more could happen in the future if the site could secure state or national recognition, and that an annual event centered on Du Bois could become a significant tourist attraction. "There should be a dedication every year, preferably during the Tanglewood season," Wilson said. "It would not be a hard job at all to promote." Wilson conjectured that such an event, perhaps a "Du Bois Day," could feature one of Du Bois's plays, and that the summer season would allow for a bigger draw from the pool of tourists visiting the Berkshires, particularly "many additional and needed blacks."[56]

Wilson's recognition that his own racial identity might be prohibitive to the park's future did not prevent him from having ideas about how to proceed, or from continuing to voice his disdain for the community's lack of interest in—or hostile opposition to—Du Bois. "This is a community opportunity for leadership such as newspapers, churches or historical activities to take over the park," he said. "This should be everybody's business, but in this case everybody's business is nobody's business." Two local residents—Jones, who lived in Great Barrington, and attorney Fritz Lord, who lived in nearby Stockbridge—were willing to serve as local directors of the park, but Wilson felt the community should provide support to them. The solution, according to Wilson, would be the creation of a part-time executive secretary for the Du Bois Foundation, someone who could volunteer time to the legal and administrative needs of the park. Among those needs were acquiring the national designation that "many less important sites" had; formalizing relationships both with the Black Caucus in Congress and with the University of Massachusetts, which hoped to obtain Du Bois's papers in the coming year or so; and creating a maintenance program for the park. However, the only tasks that the memorial committee felt it could achieve in the coming months were getting the grass mowed and perhaps putting up a fence.[57]

The erection of a fence revealed Wilson's optimism about the future of the park. When asked if future projects might garner the kind of hostile reaction from the local community that the creation of the park itself had sparked, Wilson claimed a change had taken place in the community regarding its famed native son: "I think a lot of the opposition to the park has disappeared as people have found out more about Du Bois. In fact, I think some of them have begun to take a little pride in him."[58]

Time would tell.

CHAPTER FIVE

A Prophet without Honor

Only now do I realize how fortunate I was in having been born in that
particular place, where my family had been for so many generations. I know
that I had enjoyed a free and happy childhood. All the woods, the hills, and
the river belonged to me and the companions of my own age. Not until I was
in high school was I dimly aware that my color made any difference.
—**W. E. B. Du Bois to Shirley Graham Du Bois, 1960**

W HETHER OR NOT THE BERKSHIRES had come to accept
Du Bois more willingly, the United States was moving out of its era
of hysterical Cold War anticommunism, particularly as Americans' beliefs regarding the conflict in Vietnam increasingly changed from somewhat blind patriotic support to skepticism and outright opposition. With
1968's Tet Offensive, a considerable turning point in terms of how Americans viewed what was happening in Southeast Asia, the war lost its
broadly based national backing, prompting President Johnson to opt out
of pursuing reelection. From the local perspective, it seemed that people
became far less worried about framing the memory of a black radical who
had once lived among their grandparents as a threat to their own well-
being. In 1971, peace activist and journalist Colman McCarthy, in honor
of Du Bois's birthday, wrote in the *Washington Post* of the controversy
over Du Bois that had enveloped the Berkshires in the past few years,
arguing that now that the park was in place, the members of the American Legion, the VFW, and the Knights of Columbus—those who had
opposed a park that honored "some wild revolutionary who renounced his
citizenship and became a Communist"—looked stupid. "The joke is on

the town fathers . . ." wrote McCarthy. "Not only was the park built, but Great Barrington is the same village where in August, 1774, rampaging citizens chased out of town the red-gowned royal judges of King George."[1]

Yet after the park's dedication, seemingly a victory for the Du Bois Memorial Committee, little else transpired in terms of Du Bois's role in Berkshire history. In 1973, in honor of his 105th birthday, Simon's Rock College (where key Du Bois Memorial Committee member Ruth Jones worked) held a series of events celebrating Du Bois. The relatively new college unveiled a portrait of him and dedicated its collection of black works to him, and it held an event honoring his legacy. The occasion included a series of speeches and a musical performance of "Look Down, Look Down That Lonesome Road," a spiritual that Du Bois had favored. The keynote was given by J. Saunders Redding, professor of American studies and humane letters at Cornell. In his lecture, Redding, who had known Du Bois well, stressed that Du Bois had left the United States for Ghana not because he was anti-American but because he was frustrated with the lack of American progress toward equality. Because he wanted "neither to Africanize America" nor "bleach his [own] Negro soul," the resistance to change pushed him to leave, creating "a consequence of his disillusion with his identity as an American." In a similar vein, Redding continued, Du Bois's act of joining the Communist Party was not a sign of disloyalty to his country but an indication that he had "changed vehicles" in his quest for civil rights when he felt that democracy had not accomplished what he desired.[2]

Redding was introduced at the Simon's Rock event by Walter Wilson, who characterized Du Bois as "the kind of man the early Greeks would have called 'earthshaking'" and reiterated that his memorial committee was going to try to get the Du Bois park a national designation. The president of Simon's Rock, Baird W. Whitlock, followed Wilson's speech, telling those gathered that recognizing Du Bois in the community was "long overdue," and that the outcry against the creation of a memorial to him had been a "sad element" for the area.[3]

"THE CHANGING OF THE SEASONS": AN AGE OF DU BOIS?

An event such as the one that took place at Simon's Rock, some four years after the creation of the memorial park, along with Wilson's consistent affirmations that efforts to turn the memorial park into a national site would not bring about another chorus of disapproval, would seem to symbolize a turn in the tide of local opposition to Du Bois. Wilson sold his interest in Berkshire Land Ventures to his partner, Philip Brent, which gave him more time to focus on his Du Bois activities.[4]

And indeed, there was much to focus on. By the summer of 1973, there seemed to be a Du Bois renaissance, as the University of Massachusetts made public that it was going to acquire Du Bois's papers for $150,000 from his widow, Shirley Graham Du Bois.[5] The announcement took place in the Crystal Suite of the Plaza Hotel in New York City, and the university, according to the *New Yorker*, had "sent down from Amherst everyone who had been closely connected with the transaction," including Michael Thelwell, a former member of SNCC who was chair of the W. E. B. Du Bois Department of Afro-American Studies. The papers, said Thelwell, were "one of the most important and historically significant collections acquired by any American university in recent times." Also present was Shirley Graham Du Bois, who expressed her delight that her late husband's papers would have a home in Massachusetts:

> Massachusetts—Great Barrington—was the birthplace of my
> husband. It was a section of the country that he loved dearly. Every
> fall after we were married, we would go to Massachusetts to see the
> trees in their brilliant colors. When we went to live in Africa, one of
> the things he dearly missed was the changing of the seasons. He had
> a happy childhood in Massachusetts—one that was unusual for a
> Negro in those days. One reason was that as he played with other
> boys in Great Barrington, and as they boasted of the great battles, like
> Concord, that their forebears had taken part in, he could boast that
> his grandfather had fought in the Revolutionary War, too. So the fact
> that the University of Massachusetts is making its library in Amherst
> a repository for his papers is a return, a full circle.[6]

Also speaking at the Plaza Hotel was Herbert Aptheker, described by the *New Yorker* as "a tall, white-haired man of fifty-seven, a Marxist historian and scholar, an old friend of Dr. Du Bois's and the custodian, until now, of the Du Bois papers." Aptheker noted that the size of the collection—some 75,000 letters, as well as lectures, interviews, photos, and mementos—indicated that Du Bois knew just how important he was going to be early on; the first document of the collection dated from when he was nine years old. As a historian, Aptheker said that the various pieces "constitute a collection for scholarship rivaling the papers of the Adams family." He continued:

> The Adams papers are perhaps the greatest collection in the United States. Other than that the Du Bois papers have no peer. What you have here are the papers of one of the outstanding figures of the twentieth century. There is no great Afro-American figure who was not influenced by Du Bois. There was no area of life he was not significantly connected to. In 1946, he suggested that many of his letters and papers be placed in my custody. I published a letter calling for letters and papers, and scores came to me. I combed the libraries and archives and found scores more. The University of Massachusetts will be a mecca for scholars in Du Bois lore for a long time. I can't say forever, because that is a word historians shy away from, but for a long time to come— as long as the University of Massachusetts lasts.[7]

During a question-and-answer session that followed the various speakers, Graham Du Bois was asked to elaborate on why she had chosen the University of Massachusetts to house the collection, rather than one of the historically black institutions in the South where her husband had taught, or even at Harvard, where he earned his doctorate. Graham Du Bois answered that she worried about the accessibility and safety of the papers, and preferred to place them in a public university in Du Bois's home state. Randolph Bromery supported her decision in his closing remarks. "The papers will be housed on the twenty-fifth floor of the new twenty-eight floor library," he said, "which is almost high enough to provide a view of Great Barrington across the Berkshire Hills."[8]

Still, the Du Bois collection at the University of Massachusetts had a bit of a road ahead of it. Upon its arrival on the twenty-fifth floor, which was kept to a cool sixty-eight degrees to aid preservation, the library found that the collection comprised more than seventy-five cubic feet of materials, all of which needed to be microfilmed and archived but none of which could be dealt with until the acid was removed from the paper in order to slow the aging process. The university received money from the National Endowment of the Humanities to help prepare the papers for public use, but it was to be a lengthy procedure.[9]

Moreover, although many people heralded the purchase, a series of all-too-familiar reactions made it evident that a general undercurrent of opposition to the memory of Du Bois remained. In western Massachusetts, the university's declaration renewed the fire against Du Bois, and not only in Great Barrington. In the city of Springfield, for example, which sits just a few minutes from the university's main campus in Amherst, the American Legion passed a resolution at its state convention censuring the school's purchase, noting that Du Bois's "left-wing tendencies" made the transaction particularly troubling. The Great Barrington American Legion staunchly supported the resolution; commander Rudolph Werner declared that he was "against glorifying [Du Bois] in any way." By purchasing his papers, Werner argued, the university was committing "a communist act."[10]

Theodore J. Handerek, the services officer of the Pittsfield American Legion and a member of the resolution committee, said that the resolution, which passed unanimously, had nothing to do with Du Bois's color but focused instead on his membership in the Communist Party, adding that because the university was public, the purchase had been made with taxpayers' money. However, John L. Phair, head of the Pittsfield Post, emphasized to the press that he had not voted for the resolution and, indeed, "was not in the hall when it passed." "Just because Du Bois was a Communist doesn't mean the university shouldn't acquire his papers," he said. "It's part of the history of the country."[11]

While the American Legion decided that its next step was to put the Du Bois question to a national vote at its convention in Hawaii later that summer, the University of Massachusetts stood by its decision to purchase the Du Bois collection for its library. "I don't believe any of his writings have anything to do with communism," said Mortimer H. Appley, dean of the Graduate School. "The fact that he was supposed to have turned Communist at age 90 is really irrelevant to our acquiring the papers. This university, like other universities, has to be open to all ideas."[12]

Whether Great Barrington was going to be open to all ideas remained to be seen. The W. E. B. Du Bois Memorial Foundation forged ahead, formally announcing, around Du Bois's 106th birthday the following February, that it planned to achieve national status for its small park.

Wilson again broadcast the intentions of the foundation, this time before approximately forty people at the dedication of a portrait of Du Bois given to Simon's Rock by the University of Massachusetts. Wilson said that his organization would ask senators Edward Kennedy and Edward Brooke to put legislation before Congress to grant the memorial park a spot in the National Register of Historic Places. Wilson also said that the group hoped to finally place the dedication plaque in the park later in the year.[13]

The following year, two federal representatives—Lucy Franklin and Lynne G. Graves, of the Afro-American Bicentennial Corporation, who were contracted by the U.S. Department of the Interior to distinguish sites of importance for black history—traveled from Washington, D.C., to Great Barrington to see the memorial park. Wilson met them at the airport in Hartford and took them to the library at Simon's Rock, where they explored the Du Bois collection, including two Du Bois scrapbooks that the college librarians had put together. Then, in pouring rain, Wilson escorted them to the park. Upon their return to Washington, Graves indicated that they would file in favor of giving national status to the Du Bois site, sending their recommendation to the National Park Service and to the advisory board of the secretary of the Department of the Interior. If the proposal received approval at these levels, the final decision would be made by the secretary of the interior.[14]

On May 11, 1976, a few months before the United States plunged into celebrations of its bicentennial, secretary of the interior Thomas S. Kleppe announced the approval of the Du Bois site as a National Historic Landmark.[15] It was not the first such designation for the Berkshires: Chesterwood, the country home of sculptor Daniel Chester French, in nearby Stockbridge, had become a National Historic Landmark in 1965. Hancock Shaker Village received the honor in 1968, as did the Mission House in Stockbridge, a 1739 building by John Sergeant, the first missionary to the Mohicans. Writer Edith Wharton's home, the Mount, in Lenox, entered the group in 1971.[16]

The W. E. B. Du Bois Boyhood Homesite, National Register number 76000947, now joined these sites, gaining its title as part of the Heritage Preservation Services. According to the National Park Service, which administrates Heritage Preservation Services, a National Historic

Landmark is a "nationally significant" historic area authorized as such by the secretary of the interior because it holds "exceptional value or quality in illustrating or interpreting the heritage of the United States."[17] It is a place that forges "a common bond between all Americans." The National Park Service acknowledges that although "there are many historic places across the nation, only a small number have meaning to all Americans."[18]

The National Park Service's "statement of significance" for the Du Bois site reads as follows: "Only ruins mark the site of the boyhood home of prominent sociologist and writer William Edward Burghardt Du Bois. A major figure in the African-American civil rights movement during the first half of the 20th century, he helped found the NAACP. He authored more than 20 books and several hundred articles. He was the first African American to receive a Ph.D. degree from Harvard, and his dissertation, 'The Suppression of the African Slave Trade,' became the first volume in the Harvard Historical Studies."[19] According to the *Berkshire Eagle*, the designation marked "the success of a seven-year effort on the part of former NAACP 'Man of the Year' Walter Wilson." The newspaper praised the cochair of the W. E. B. Du Bois Memorial Park Foundation for having bought the site, thereby preventing anyone else from building on it. Of his foresight, Wilson said, "I just wanted to be damn sure we had the property."[20]

Preparations to put the new national landmark in order began that spring. Wilson set June 14, 1976, as a day to clean up and landscape the site, and he hoped to schedule some kind of "black" observance of the bicentennial, as well as, undoubtedly, to prepare for some kind of ceremony to mark the national landmark honor.[21] However, as these efforts began, tensions grew between those who had worked to achieve the national designation and others. Wilson, for example, never one to avoid a storm, launched accusations of racism at local historical groups regarding their lack of participation in activities at the Du Bois site, asking, "Is it a white bicentennial?" In response, Donald Smith, executive director of the Berkshire Historical Society (which was in the process of restoring Herman Melville's home, Arrowhead), indicated that his organization was not participating in Du Bois activities because no one had asked it to. Paul Ivory, chair of the Great Barrington Historical

Commission and curator of Chesterwood said that his organization, too, had not been asked, but that it had assisted the memorial committee in other endeavors. Wilson, however, had no patience for what he considered to be racist mind-sets veiled in community ennui. "We are individuals," he retorted. "We have no staff and we have no money. Why is it our job to ask people who ought to be more interested than we to join in?"[22]

As part of the effort to rebuild interest in Du Bois after several years of relative quiet, the *Berkshire Eagle* spotlighted Du Bois in a feature article in its magazine, *Berkshires Week*. In a four-page spread, the article detailed the civil rights leader's legacy in the community and probed into the backlash that had emerged in the late 1960s. Entitled "Black Sheep of the Native Sons," and written by freelancer Steve Turner, formerly of Great Barrington, the piece summarized the creation of the National Historic Landmark honoring Du Bois, noting that "the whirlwind of controversy that existed in the life of W.E.B. Du Bois continues to swirl through his home town," and arguing, however subtly, that the storm had an undeniable racial aspect to it: "Small country towns, as a general rule, have memorials to their world-famous native sons. But when the town is mostly white and the native son is black, and a brilliant black radical at that—a racial organizer as well as a scholar, educator, novelist, poet and diplomat, a leader in the attempt to unseat powerful social and economic elites and an early advocate of black pride—then the rule meets an exception. Add a touch of declared membership in the Communist party, and the rule just . . . What rule?"[23] Turner observed that after the community protested the idea to memorialize "this renowned black man" with "every device short of violence," there had been little progress in the eight years that followed. Describing the other Berkshire landmarks as "structurally splendid places," Turner noted that because of the lack of buildings and signage, making the site difficult to locate, "the Du Bois site comes up a little short," with only the cellar hole and crumbled chimney remaining of the house where Du Bois spent some of his childhood. But the lack of development of the site, he continued, belied its historical significance. The homestead represented the family of Du Bois's mother as well as of the famed civil rights leader, descendants of one whose good turns in the American Revolution gave him his freedom and put his roots in Great Barrington with the earliest of its settlers. The site represented early African American New England, a community that helped create the first black doctorate graduated from Harvard. And Du Bois remembered that community, Turner continued, burying his first wife and child in the town's cemetery, and hoping to someday renovate the home of his boyhood for his retirement, a hope prevented only by a lack of money.[24] As for the controversy over Du Bois as "a longtime proponent of socialism," "a contradiction developed," Turner argued. "The country might happily offer monuments and cultural tributes to infamous crooks such as Blackbeard and Jesse James, not to mention an enormous clutch of anti-democratic financiers, robber barons and renowned racists; but a memorial to a left-wing black hero was unacceptable."[25]

Turner called the year in which the Du Bois Memorial Committee formed—1968—the most riotous in the area since Shays's Rebellion. He claimed that in addition to the town's attempt to close down the park because of zoning, there were "at least 30" threats to blow up the park, and that many members of the committee were also threatened. An article in the *Berkshire Courier,* Turner pointed out, advised opponents of the park to boycott the dedication ceremony and "leave the monument to those who will undoubtedly take out their wrath on it in weeks to come." Such vitriolic opposition came from somewhere, but Turner determined that no one would admit what really stood at the core: race. In an interview with George Francis, editor and publisher of the *Courier,* Turner asked why the hostility had grown to such levels. "The black thing didn't enter into it at all," Francis answered. "A lot of us were duped into the Vietnam war then. It hadn't been proved to be such a monstrous waste of men and materials. And with us losing people in Vietnam, it seemed like the wrong time to put up a monument to a Communist." Walter Wilson, however, dismissed Francis's rationale, affirming that race had always been the central motive against memorializing Du Bois in Great Barrington. "He was the most important man ever born in the Berkshires, but he was being ignored here long before he joined the party," Wilson countered. "The Communist issue is not pertinent at all."[26]

Turner fell in line with Wilson's riposte: those who had been opposed to Du Bois had conflated racial issues and communism. But he also found that people were perhaps beginning to separate the different aspects of Du Bois's life. "Some people may agree with him and some may not," said Paul Ivory. "But his deeds and publications had an impact on American history, and that's the measure for recognition." Even Francis, who once led a segment of the campaign against the memorial committee, seemed to have come around somewhat. "Attitudes have changed," he admitted, perhaps considering his own change of heart. He felt that the announcement of the national landmark status would not stir up much, if any, controversy. "I don't think there'll be any opposition at all," Francis continued. "The Watergate thing and the war kind of took the wind out of [the opposition's] sails. They're not so willing to wave the flag any more and say 'My country, right or wrong.'"[27]

Walter Wilson gave the bulk of the credit for the shift in attitude to the work of the memorial committee: "We did conduct a pretty good educational campaign, and if we haven't done anything more we have enlightened the county about the Civil Rights Movement and this great leader." Yet Wilson was not done, revealing that a new fund-raising program would begin in order to landscape the site and rebuild the house. "We can't yet project the cost, but cost is really not an object," Wilson predicted. "We always count on a lot of voluntary help. We're just going to get it done."[28]

However, there were factors that indicated that Wilson was not going to be able to get this project done as quickly or as easily as he imagined. One response to Steve Turner's piece in *Berkshires Week* indicated that much remained the same. In a letter to the editor, Gerard Chapman of Mill River, which lies on the southeast border of Great Barrington, in the town of New Marlborough, took issue with Turner's piece, because "the burden of his theme is racial": "I do not believe that the indifference, and even violent opposition, to a memorial to . . . Du Bois is based on racial animosity, but to the fact that he 'went over to the enemy' in the last years of his life. . . . In 1968 the timing was wrong for erecting a Du Bois memorial. The war in Vietnam was indeed unpopular, with many killed and maimed and with lives and families disrupted, and to attempt to sanctify one who had so openly cast his lot with the Communists—our enemies in Vietnam at the time—was almost bound to arouse opposition."[29] Chapman considered himself something of a local historian. A retired research chemist, he worked as a boutique publisher and frequently wrote for the *Berkshire Eagle* in the "Our Berkshires" section, a column on the op-ed page written by a selection of local residents on a variety of Berkshire topics.[30] He did acknowledge that the intense opposition to the Du Bois memorial had died down since the Vietnam era, but unlike Turner, he found that resistance remained. This remaining antagonism was not indicative of the particular historical moment, according to the writer, but rather of Du Bois himself:

> I think there is still a lingering feeling that Du Bois was a fool and worse for going over to the communists; a person I know is implacably opposed to memorializing Du Bois, and his feeling is not racial but political. Du Bois "blew it." Unquestionably, he was a man of great abilities and accomplishments, and some day he will be recognized for them. But Russia is still our enemy, despite cultural exchanges and détente, and until Russia throws its power on the side of peace and civilized behavior, those who embraced it will be out of popular favor. Yes, Du Bois blew it; he was so discouraged over the lack of progress from his efforts to ameliorate the lot of blacks that his emotions got the better of his critical faculties, perhaps because of his advanced age. He undid much of what he had accomplished. There are many blacks in this country who have suffered discrimination but who have been smart enough to know that for all its faults, the United States is gradually approaching acceptance of "ethnic" minorities. . . . Russian solicitude for minorities is an illusion. Russia makes a great show of accepting them for education, but actually such minorities are kept under wraps most of the time, to be trotted out for propaganda purposes on occasion. Du Bois, in his dotage, did not perceive this, and that, rather than his being black, was—and is—the reason for lack of interest in his memorial.[31]

Thus, whereas Wilson and others hoped that the campaign of the memorial committee had created an age of enlightened responses to Du Bois, Chapman diametrically disagreed. The problem with Chapman's stance was that at the time of the national landmark designation, the United States was only outwardly distanced from Vietnam; and civil rights, in spite of the Civil Rights and Voting Rights acts, had hardly been accomplished by or for anyone. Thus, singling out Du Bois's late-in-life political affiliations as the only important tenet of opposition was to greatly gloss over the inner workings of the larger historical moment.

THE DIVINATION OF THE FBI: COINTELPRO AND HOMEGROWN HATRED

Both Turner and Chapman understood, albeit with different conclusions, just how important the historical context of the creation of the Du Bois park was to understanding the passion of both sides of the debate. This became even more critical after the national landmark designation was secure, when the anticommunist tenor that had greeted each step the memorial committee took transcended local opposition and became part of the larger, national forum, in which Du Bois was condemned as an enemy of the state, or at least an enemy of democracy. Amid rumors that had circulated for almost a decade that the FBI had been concerned about the efforts in Great Barrington to herald Du Bois, evidence began to emerge in 1977 that lent some truth to the seemingly absurd claims. It began with *Boston Globe* journalist Thomas Oliphant, who had been doing research in FBI files and discovered that the organization had played a role in stirring up the opposition to the creation of a Du Bois park. Oliphant was well acquainted with civil rights controversy, as he had supervised the turbulent desegregation of the Boston school system, which garnered the *Globe* a Pulitzer Prize in 1975.[32]

According to *Berkshire Eagle* staff writer Stephen Fay, Oliphant found a memo in the files that confirmed FBI activity in 1968 and 1969 designed to inflame locals against the Du Bois memorial project. As part of the broader counterintelligence program (COINTELPRO) that the FBI had conducted since 1956 under J. Edgar Hoover, targeting communist and black radical activity in particular, the FBI claimed that it had planted two articles in the *Berkshire Eagle* in October 1968, one of which was the story regarding the radio poll indicating that 78 percent of Berkshire residents were opposed to the Du Bois memorial. According to Fay, "a reading of the *Eagle*'s clipping files on Du Bois from 1966 to 1968 failed to turn up any news stories that bore apparent earmarks of a plant," although he admitted that at least some of the many letters to the editor that stormed against the proposed memorial could have been FBI-generated.[33]

Frank McCarthy, who was county editor of the *Eagle* at the time the FBI claimed it had infiltrated the paper, said that the agency had never contacted him directly, and Oliphant admitted that it was his understanding that the FBI often made false claims in order to pad their files. However, he also said he found FBI documentation that local veterans' organizations had been given information about Du Bois in order to get them involved in the controversy. Harold Beckwith, who had been commander of Post 8348 of the Veterans of Foreign Wars in 1968, countered that his group had received no influence from any outsiders, including the FBI, and that his organization had independently decided to "strongly oppose" the memorial.[34]

At a request from the *Berkshire Eagle*, and using the Freedom of Information Act, United Press International (UPI) examined photo reproductions of original FBI files to find out whether or not previously published reports that the FBI had tried to plant a story in the *Eagle* in 1968 regarding the memorial movement were true. The UPI reported a few weeks later that the Boston office of the FBI had considered a number of strategies both to bring doubt on Du Bois's reputation and to prevent any kind of memorial to him from taking place. One such strategy, as Oliphant had revealed, was to plant a story in the *Eagle* in 1968 focusing on Du Bois's membership in the Communist Party. According to the UPI, an FBI memo dated February 13, 1969, and addressed to Hoover, stated, "Consideration was given by the Boston office to contact of news sources [*sic*] at The Berkshire Eagle." However, the FBI rethought its strategy, apparently taking into account the *Eagle*'s tendency toward open-minded politics and charging it with a bias toward those who visited the Berkshires in the summer months: "This paper has not at all times been favorable to the bureau and it has a liberal reputation and a tendency to avoid criticism of the academic elements which moves in [*sic*] for summer residence." The memo speculated that the future of the memorial, without the intervention of the FBI, seemed questionable because of the "furor" raised by the various local veterans' groups. According to the memo, the announcement of the memorial project

brought an immediate and outraged opposition on the part of local
citizens, led principally by the American Legion and the V.F.W.
posts. . . . This opposition appealing to both sources established that
the veterans' groups were thoroughly briefed concerning Du Bois'
Communist Party background. . . . [Deleted] were of the opinion the
American Legion and Veterans of Foreign Wars had complete source
material concerning Du Bois and said there were elements in both
groups who had become so heated over the matter that any attempted
erection of a memorial would be dismantled overnight. . . . Both
cautioned against open contacts by this office, suggesting many
local "hotheads" who opposed the Du Bois Memorial would welcome
an affiliation with the FBI and might attempt to publicize any overt
interest for their own purposes.[35]

Perhaps most significant, the FBI attributed the strong opposition to
the allegedly well-informed front put on by the VFW. The memo indicated that the FBI had at least two agents working in the Berkshires,
both of whom concluded that because of the VFW's success in its efforts
to thwart the memorial plans, the FBI's own strategies—delineated in
a deleted paragraph of the memo, but likely including planting stories
in the *Eagle*—were not needed. "This opposition," the memo continued, "appealing to both sources established that the veterans' groups
were thoroughly briefed concerning Du Bois' Communist Party background." This report begs the question, of course, of who had "briefed"
these groups as to Du Bois's Communist Party credentials. The UPI concluded that one possible source was a pamphlet entitled *W.E.B. Du Bois
Clubs of America, an Expose*, which, according to a memo from Hoover
dated February 28, 1967, demonstrated the "connections" between the
Du Bois Clubs and the Communist Party.[36] The February 13 memo indicated this to be true and further detailed the degree of success that
the veterans' opposition likely had in deferring any successful memorial effort.

The degree of FBI activity in the Berkshires, though somewhat clar-
ified by the UPI, remained a bit of a mystery. The FBI's understanding
of the opposition to the Du Bois park was expressed in enough detail to
demonstrate that the Boston office had, indeed, been following it quite
closely. Further, as William Simons confirmed, at least one agent was at

the dedication ceremony in 1969. "They were there," he remembers, "because somebody thought there was going to be a riot." Thus, at the minimum, the FBI had a cursory relationship with the Great Barrington Police Department, a fact that demonstrates the near-atomic detail that Hoover's COINTELPRO program went into, and that exemplifies the degree to which a group of people—even one from a small, rural town in Western Massachusetts that wanted merely to set aside five acres to honor a local son—could be defined as threatening to the nation.

For Edmund Gordon and his New York circle, the workings of the FBI came as no surprise, particularly in the aftermath of the McCarthy era and the persecution of Du Bois. "The black academic community was one that the FBI took a position against. Once it opposed Du Bois, people fled. Those that stayed with him, knew what it was," he remembers. "The FBI was very active following all of us—[they pursued] pure speculations, but it gave the media enough negative imagery to fuel it. All they needed to do was make an inquiry to set off the media." Gordon finds the speculation of the agency's involvement in Great Barrington to be familiar: "I suspect that the FBI informed local people that this was coming—drove local groups, drove the media—all they needed to do was inquire." William Simons agrees: "Somebody riled up the Great Barrington people."

For Stephen Fay, the "last laugh" in the "FBI's purported shenanigans" would have to go to Hoover himself. Although the *Eagle* staff, he argued, had "been having a hell of a good time lately deriding the FBI and its tricksters and speaking ill of the bureau's late director," as well as learning about "the coals-to-Newcastle aim of the FBI to stir up trouble in Great Barrington," he understood that the overarching story of the conflict about a memorial to Du Bois was, in the end, simply not funny. When retracing the chronology of the Du Bois controversies in Great Barrington, Fay reminded his readers, it was important to remember that the FBI was not at the helm of the initial opposition to the memorial park. "The anger, opposition and outrage was [*sic*] our own natural, homegrown product," Fay wrote, "not an import from the Boston office of the FBI." Nevertheless, the recently released FBI documents—some 53,000 pages—revealed that the FBI was guilty of *wanting* to act in an unethical manner, by planning to plant a newspaper story biased against

Du Bois; the idea of "perverting freedom of the press" was there, and that idea was considered "virtuous" by the agency. "And that's sick," Fay concluded.[37]

Although the FBI's plans to incite disfavor against Du Bois, as well as its hopes to disrupt the dedication ceremony, never came to fruition, the mission of the memorial committee had not yet been fully achieved. "The happy ending," Fay observed, "is still a long way off." The site itself looked to be abandoned, filled with weeds and the still-unadorned boulder that had been selected to showcase the memorial plaque. There had been no bicentennial activities in conjunction with the site, as Wilson had hoped there would be, and none of the local historical societies had included the newly established park in any of their programming. Fay asked,

> What chances are there in 1977 that the town of which Du Bois was
> so fond will endeavor to ensure that he will not be forgotten? What
> chance is there that Du Bois, who is a major figure in the history of
> black consciousness, will be remembered in 20 years . . . in 10
> years? Indeed, how many residents of the Berkshires are aware that
> he was born here? How many, indeed, are aware that he lived?
> What the hell, maybe we're wrong to laugh at the presumption of the
> FBI agent who claimed in 1969 that the drive to memorialize Du Bois
> was a dead issue. That guy is starting to look like a prophet.[38]

The Memorial Committee, which had originally planned to have a celebration of the national landmark status in the summer of 1976, in conjunction with the bicentennial, delayed its plans to the following August so that the celebration could be held at the nearby Barrington Fair Grounds, enabling the group to expand the plans for the event. However, those dates, too, came and went. Indeed, as Fay suspected, despite the national designation of the memorial, the plans of the memorial committee, and the importance once granted to Du Bois by the FBI, Du Bois yet again seemed to fade again into the background of Berkshire history.

In 1978, while Du Bois's 110th birthday "went unnoticed in his native Berkshire County," the United Nations held a celebration to mark the occasion, and Wilson, according to the *Berkshire Eagle*, attended the event. Many mentions of Great Barrington were made throughout the affair, and numerous people expressed interest in visiting the site. "As

I sat for hours under the spell of the occasion," Wilson said, "I felt more confident than ever that we are just entering the age of Du Bois. . . . I'm convinced that besides New York and Washington, Great Barrington is now the most well-known American community in Africa."[39] In a letter to the editor of the *Eagle*, Wilson wrote of the great honor that he felt, as founder of the Du Bois memorial, to have been invited to such an affair and to sit among representatives of "at least half of the world's people," all of whom had gathered to praise the gifts of Du Bois, deemed the father of civil rights, the father of Pan-Africanism, and, in the words of civil rights activist and U.S. congressman Andrew Young, "the father of us all." In contrast, Wilson later rued, "in 1978 W.E.B. Du Bois was not honored in the Berkshires by radio stations, newspapers, churches, history societies, or local governments or by the county's private and public schools." Perhaps, he hoped, "individuals might just stand a few moments in silent tribute."[40]

EMBRACING DU BOIS: THE NATIONAL HISTORIC LANDMARK CEREMONY

As Wilson wished, a proper tribute, and one none too silent at that, came to fruition, with the planning and execution of the ceremony to celebrate the Du Bois site as a National Historic Landmark. On May 2, 1979, the Du Bois Memorial Committee announced that the landmark would be dedicated on October 20 of that year, with a ceremony at Tanglewood featuring a series of celebrated figures who would speak in honor of Du Bois. The dedication ceremony, the *Berkshire Eagle* argued, in conjunction with the purchase of Du Bois's papers by the University of Massachusetts, would help intensify the spotlight on Du Bois, perhaps finally granting him his due in the place where he spent the first eighteen years of his life.[41]

Walter Wilson, however, according to Elaine Gunn, had grown increasingly weary in his campaign to commemorate Du Bois, a task that he once had thought would have an obvious conclusion. From Gunn's perspective, in the decade since the park's dedication, Wilson had not only gotten ten years older, he had also become somewhat resigned: "Walter was determined—he didn't care what people were saying—he felt this was something that should happen and you had to give him credit for what he believed was the right thing. And he did—you could see it. He talked about the park, about putting a bench there where people could think about Du Bois, and feel his presence, and read about him. He had a vision about it. And when it didn't happen, he was really, well, it just didn't happen the way he thought it was going to happen. He talked Du Bois all the time, and it didn't happen. He kept thinking that it *had* to happen, it was *right*, but it still didn't."

Gunn also speculates that Wilson was unhappy about the location of the national landmark ceremony. In 1969, she remembers, "the folks in Barrington at one of the last meetings before the dedication said they should try to have it at Tanglewood, and Walter thought it would defeat the whole purpose—why have it at Tanglewood when Du Bois was here in Great Barrington? Later on, people said that if they'd had it at Tanglewood in the first place, there wouldn't have been any hullabaloo."

Wilson remained involved in his cause, but he did not play as central a role in planning the ceremony. According to Gunn, the event was organized primarily by Homer Meade, "with Walter's input." Meade worked with Ruth Jones at Simon's Rock. Meade was a longtime resident of the Berkshires, a member of the Du Bois Memorial Committee, and an English teacher at Monument Mountain Regional High School, in Great Barrington.[42] The day before the ceremony, Meade published an op-ed piece in the *Berkshire Eagle* regarding the upcoming ceremony and the decade-long controversy that preceded it. He began his exposition judiciously:

> Ambassadors, statesmen, leaders, citizens from afar and little children came unto him; and yet those about him remained silent. Ceremonies which will officially dedicate the Du Bois Memorial Park in Great Barrington as a National Historic Landmark will be held tomorrow on the Tanglewood grounds in Lenox. But, surprisingly, it seems that rather than voice support and encouragement, the long-term residents and the natives of Berkshire County are witness to a curious phenomenon as concerns the county's attitude toward this honored son. We of Berkshire County have been told over and over again of the Great Barrington birthplace of W.E.B. Du Bois. We have had detailed in newspapers, on radio, recently in books and also in some county

classrooms, the accomplishments and achievements of Mr. Du Bois. We in the county have heard more often than some can count that Mr. Du Bois had not only local importance but helped shape the world to a degree which very few individuals without benefit of government finance and military power have ever been able to accomplish.[43]

And yet, Meade pointed out, the residents of the Berkshires, for the most part, persisted in their "curious lethargy" regarding the important ceremony about to take place. He argued that this lethargy was a "Cassandra complex," alluding to a failure on the part of the local citizenry to "believe that it should be a thing of great pride to lay claim to Mr. Du Bois." It was not a failure because of their condemnation of or apathy toward Du Bois, but rather a failure to understand that Berkshire County "was a victim, as in fact Mr. Du Bois was a victim, of a vicious, well-organized plot of malicious innuendos and outright lies, planted and nourished by members of the highest echelon of government."[44] Meade, then, located the failure to recognize Du Bois within the Cold War battles of the U.S. government.

But this statement did not preclude Meade from making the thoughtful conclusion that the Cold War crusade had serious racial implications: the "innuendos and lies came from those who wished to strengthen their own racist megalomania and to destroy those who challenged their positions of power so wrongfully held." In the face of the "tools of influence" that figures such as J. Edgar Hoover used, Meade argued, residents of the Berkshires were faced with a herculean task, because "to embrace Mr. Du Bois is no small act":

> We must admit that for over 25 years we had been presented a false image fostered by those in trusted positions. They misused the trust given them, and their claims of knowledge were really perpetrations of their own illusions tainted by ignorance and bigotry. . . . The truth is that Mr. Du Bois believed truth needed to be voiced regardless of the threat of personal danger. For this, he was made a victim of the misplaced desires of those who were less educated, less intelligent, less truthful but more egotistic than he. At the mention of his name, and the National Historic Landmark dedication in his honor, representatives of African governments across the Atlantic Ocean and from nations across the Pacific respond and send representatives.

At the mention of his name, representatives from national organizations send representatives to speak in his behalf. And yet from only a few in Berkshire County does there come an encouraging word. Why? Berkshire County has become victim of the Cassandra complex. We have not admitted the truth of the warnings and insights pointed out and spoken by one of our own.[45]

Meade's piece spoke volumes regarding the makeup of the audience at the dedication ceremony. And on October 20, a day that the *New York Times* described as "vivid with the blush of autumn," some nine hundred people attended the ceremony to designate the Du Bois park a National Historic Landmark.[46] Infused with performances by the Elma Lewis National Center of Afro-American Artists (NCAAA)[47] and the Voices of New Africa House of the University of Massachusetts (now the W. E. B. Du Bois Department of Afro-American Studies), the ceremony at Tanglewood lasted 3½ hours, and featured fifteen speakers who, according to the coverage in the *Berkshire Eagle,* described Du Bois as "a prophet largely without honor in his own home and time."[48]

The first of the speakers was David Graham Du Bois, the adopted son of Du Bois and the son of Shirley Graham Du Bois, who—along with her brother Lorenzo—was in attendance but did not speak. At the time of the dedication, David Du Bois was living in Cairo, Egypt, where he worked as a college instructor and a journalist. In his remarks, Du Bois explained how he took on the "full responsibility," in the African sense, of the role of the son to the father, and that his father should be remembered for his "dignity, commitment and militancy." Other speakers included Alex Quaisin-Sackey, ambassador to the United States from Ghana, Du Bois's adopted homeland, and a close friend of Du Bois's; Xie Qime, who read a letter from Chinese ambassador Chai Zemin, who knew Du Bois from his days as the Chinese ambassador to Ghana and had planned on attending but could not; Medoune Fall, Senegal's ambassador to the United Nations; Herbert Aptheker, literary executor of Du Bois's estate; Margaret Bush Wilson, chair of the board of the NAACP; and former University of Massachusetts chancellor Randolph Bromery, who noted that he—as well as a few others in attendance—had turned down an invitation to attend the dedication of the John F. Kennedy Presidential Library and Museum to be at the Du Bois event.[49]

The last speaker of this distinguished list was Walter Wilson, who observed that "when we honor Du Bois, we honor ourselves." Wilson drew applause for denouncing FBI director J. Edgar Hoover as the United States' "leading racist," a reference, undoubtedly, to the belief that the FBI had spurred on local protest to the memorial park in 1969. According to Gunn, placing Wilson as the final speaker was not a good idea. "He was the last speaker, but somebody forgot that Walter never lets go, never stops talking about Du Bois. Never," she says. "That day, he talked and talked about Du Bois, and finally—I was sitting down in front—Ruth [Jones] whispered to me, 'I have to get Walter to stop talking.' So she did. Pete Seeger hadn't even sung yet!"

Once Wilson took his seat, the program concluded with Seeger, who was on crutches because of a foot injury, leading a sing-along of "We Are Climbing Jacob's Ladder," with new verses written especially for the occasion. The addition of Seeger to the program was likely Wilson's idea, as "Jacob's Ladder" had often been used by labor organizers as a union song in the 1930s in the South, the time that Wilson was there working for the ACLU.

For many attendees, the highlight of the day was keynote speaker Julian Bond, who had accepted the invitation to attend only a month earlier. Bond positioned the dedication within what he described as the broader problems of African Americans, especially in education and employment, ensuring that, according to the *Boston Globe*, "there was joy tempered by some social reality" in the ceremony.[50] In the post–civil rights moment, Bond described the national prospects for black America as worsening, noting that although integration efforts in public schools in the South had made great strides, the North had "stubbornly resisted" change. Du Bois, he said, would be "surprised and shaken" to see the lack of progress in racial equality in the period since his death: "He would be shocked to find Southern schools mostly integrated while Northern cities stubbornly insist on maintaining segregation. He might quickly conclude that the 25 years since Brown v. the Board of Education have been almost more painful than the results have been fruitful. [He would] be alarmed that in 1978 more blacks dropped out of high school than enrolled in college."[51] Bond continued with his bleak picture, citing statistics regarding the elderly black poor, the high percentage of black families that relied on public assistance, the infant mortality rate in black families, the decrease in black teachers, the racial inequities in professional salaries, and the high death rate from hypertension in the black community. The mission that Du Bois had framed with the Niagara Movement back in 1905, Bond concluded, remained largely the same in 1979: working against injustice and toward full political participation to ensure equality.

Although the crux of Bond's speech focused on the ability Du Bois would have as a leader in the contemporary moment, he also discussed the need for black input into U.S. foreign policy. After the speech, Bond was asked if he supported Jesse Jackson's idea that the United States should open negotiations with the Palestine Liberation Organization. Bond definitively stated that he was not a Jackson supporter, yet he did voice his support for President Carter to talk with Yasir Arafat.[52]

According to the *Eagle*, Bond's statement regarding U.S. foreign policy "was one of only two to refer to the militant side of Du Bois." The other was made by his cousin Jean Carey Bond, who at the time was managing editor of *Freedomways*, one of the central publications of civil rights movements. Carey Bond argued that, were he still alive, Du Bois would support the ratification of SALT II, encourage relationships between the United States and socialist nations, and support the Palestine liberation movement.

However, the dedication ceremony remained largely celebratory, "call[ing] up images of Du Bois as patriotic, dignified, committed, visionary, global, agitating and troublesome," according to the *Eagle*.[53] The program culminated in the presentation of the National Historic Landmark plaque, presented by Gerald Wallette, a White House staffer, to the key members of the memorial committee—Ruth Jones, Walter Wilson, and Edmund Gordon.

For many, the ceremony at Tanglewood presented an opportunity to highlight the achievements of other influential blacks. The University of Massachusetts, for example, used the day to announce its acquisition of Horace Bond's papers and the naming of its Horace Mann Bond Center for Equal Education.[54]

The ceremony also had a broader effect on the community, even on those who could not attend. Florence Logan, for example, who was ninety years old when the landmark dedication took place, had graduated from the Searles High School in 1906, some twenty years after Du Bois. The dedication ceremony stirred fond memories of "Will" for her, especially his return to the Berkshires to speak to the Searles High School Alumni Association on July 10, 1925, at the Red Lion Inn in Stockbridge, an event that served somewhat as a precursor to latter battles over his memory. Some 180 people had attended the event to hear Du Bois's speech, "What Great Barrington Means to Me." Other residents were not as pleased with his arrival. According to the *Berkshire Courier,* "A fiery cross emblem of the Ku Klux Klan was reported to be seen burning over East Rock [in Great Barrington] on Saturday evening. . . . the cross burned for nearly an hour." The newspaper ran an editorial condemning the "pitifully misguided residents" who had committed the racist deed, and hailed the return of Du Bois in its coverage of the alumni event.[55]

> Dr. William E.B. Du Bois, editor of the magazine 'The Crisis,' made the principal address of the evening, taking for his subject 'What Does Great Barrington Mean.' Dr. Du Bois today one of the most prominent men of his race in the United States graduated from the Great Barrington high school but said that he had not been to town for about 25 years. He said that upon returning he had found that despite his long absence it was the only town where he could call folks by their first name and that here in this valley he found a sense of detachment from the ordinary course and many unforgettable phases of human life. His ancestors back over a period of 250 years, veterans of the Revolution and War of 1812, lie buried here. He knew the town intimately and felt qualified to handle the subject which he selected.[56]

"He had an elegant Van Dyke beard and he was very handsome," Logan remembered. "He spoke beautiful English. We all turned out to hear a political speech, and he talked about the possibility of cleaning up the Housatonic River." Logan felt that the recognition of his birthplace was a worthy event, regardless of the controversy that surrounded him. "It's all to the good," she concluded. "He was brilliant. I'm sorry he became a Communist, but a 90-year-old man couldn't do much harm."[57] Logan expressed sincere admiration for Du Bois—calling him "brilliant," for example—yet she also relied on stereotypically problematic admiration—her observation, for example, that he "spoke beautiful English."

By and large, however, her comments reflected pride that a fellow alum was being honored in such a grand manner.

The Tanglewood ceremony proved valuable to the Berkshire tourism industry, as Wilson had predicted that such an event would. Leaders such as Xie and Quaisin-Sackey, as well as members of the Chinese embassy, toured nearby attractions such as Chesterwood, having their photographs snapped while they looked at replicas of various sizes of the Lincoln Memorial.[58] As well, it extended the reach of Du Bois's locality; radio stations in Amherst, Massachusetts (WFRC), and Albany, New York (WAMC), broadcast the taped Tanglewood ceremony for their listeners.[59]

For Elaine Gunn, however, the ceremony could not compare to the one they had held in the field ten years earlier:

> The one in 1969 was a far more important event, it was groundbreaking. It is where the cellar hole is, it's where he was born. He was not born in Lenox, he was not born at Tanglewood. The impression that many of us had was that 1969 was a problem because we made it happen here. And Walter knew that—he knew it was important. And he didn't back down. It was his land, and he didn't understand why more people weren't as enthusiastic as he was. Why didn't more people come forward? But I was surprised by some who did. People surprised us in terms of who showed up. We all had been meeting, so it was nice to stand there and see who came that was different.

A PROPHET WITHOUT HONOR

The Tanglewood ceremony, grand as it was, marked an end to the recognition of Du Bois, rather than the beginning that memorial committee members hoped it would. "Several hundred people were there, and it was quite a dedication," recalls Gunn. "Walter was quite pleased, and I think he felt that this was the beginning of something, and it just didn't happen." However, she notes, "Tanglewood was not his vision." He had imagined that such a ceremony would be held in the memorial park itself. "Between '69 and '79 people would occasionally go out there, we would pick the weeds, etcetera. But that was it."

In the period that followed the dedication ceremony, grand plans continued for the new National Historic Landmark. The *Eagle* reported that

New York architecture firm Bond Ryder and Associates wanted to design a Du Bois memorial on the site that would include a reconstruction of the "House of the Black Burghardts."[60] According to Edmund Gordon, the company got involved because one of the partners, Max Bond, was the husband of Jean Carey Bond, who had been involved in the national landmark campaign. Gordon remembers that when Shirley Graham Du Bois handed her late husband's papers over to the University of Massachusetts, there had been an arrangement that the college would help rebuild the site. When Gordon and Wilson eventually gave the deed for the property to the university, they had a similar understanding. But those plans never came to fruition; nothing was ever commissioned by the Du Bois Foundation or the University of Massachusetts for Bond to build there.

In the summer of 1980, a group of fifty people visited the park to witness the installation of the Department of the Interior plaque, which stated, "W. E. B. DuBois Boyhood Homesite has been designated a National Historic Landmark. This site possesses national significance in commemorating the history of the United States of America." The event took place beside the boulder that had originally been designated for the Du Bois commemoration plaque designed by the memorial committee. Wilson led the ceremony, alongside other members of the committee, and playwright William Gibson read "The House of the Black Burghardts" to commemorate the occasion.[61] However, the ceremony was merely that—ceremonial—according to Gunn, because they did not leave anything on the site for fear that it would be stolen.

Within a few years, the Eagle noted, Du Bois yet again remained "largely ignored within the community where he was born and raised." Despite the seemingly ever-increasing awareness of the significance of his work in the larger community of scholars and historians, eventually only a handwrought white sign stating "W.E.B. Du Bois U.S. Historic Site," so plain that no one could want to steal it, designated the landmark.[62]

For William Simons, the movement died largely because of a lack of racial diversity at the local level, as well as the continued split between the local set and the New Yorkers. "That whole thing kind of frittered out. . . . There came the need to turn it over to African-Americans to head up the situation . . . [but] there was no follow-through," he says.

"There also was a need for this group of African Americans to take the lead, but it didn't happen." Further, says Simons, the fact that the majority of the black members of the memorial community were "an out-of-county group" greatly isolated it from neighborhood politics. "When it was locally focused, it was quite respected, with the Gunns, for example," he says. "None from Pittsfield, though, which hurt the movement. They needed people from Pittsfield to get involved because a much larger black population was there." In the end, he concludes, the fact that Wilson was white remained a factor, because members of Gordon's New York group still would not acknowledge his efforts.

But although the site itself saw little improvement and the memorial committee grew relatively quiet, the dedication ceremonies seemed to have some sort of an impact on residents, particularly members of the black community. The curriculum of the local schools had avoided Du Bois in the past, according to Horace Smith, a graduate of Du Bois's alma mater in Great Barrington. "There was nothing about him in high school," Smith said. "The first time I learned about W.E.B. Du Bois was when I returned from the service in 1969 and they were dedicating the memorial."[63] However, since the campaign to commemorate Du Bois began, that seemed to have changed. Elaine Gunn, for example, taught a unit on black Americans to her third-grade classes that included the history of Du Bois, and her daughter went to the superintendent of schools to petition for a black studies course at Monument Mountain High School. The superintendent, says Gunn, told Gunn and her daughter to write a proposal and he would put it through the school board, which he did. He then hired Homer Meade to teach the courses on black literature and history that the students had asked for.

This inclusion of Du Bois in some programs of study marked a change of sorts, but it was a change at the hands of a few active black educators and students, rather than a curricular revolution. Du Bois did not receive special attention in U.S. history courses, John Beacco, chair of the Monument Mountain history department said, because there was simply too much other material to cover. However, the *Eagle* speculated, the old, now-familiar reasons might be at the root of the continued omission of Du Bois from Berkshire classrooms: his status as a communist and his self-expatriation to Ghana.[64]

In Ghana, Du Bois's legacy continued to grow. *Berkshire Eagle* writer Stephen Fay lamented how, "in his hometown, in the Bay State and in the United States," Du Bois remained "an obscure figure," whereas Ghana, calling itself Du Bois's adopted home, dedicated a national monument honoring Du Bois and his work on August 27, 1986.[65]

While the Ghanaians prepared to celebrate Du Bois, interest in the Du Bois projects in the Berkshires continued to lie fallow. Less than a decade after the National Historic Landmark dedication ceremony, the *Eagle* observed, "The 5-acre site near the Egremont town line is overgrown with weeds and brush," reflecting how in the Berkshires, as compared especially to Ghana, Du Bois remained "largely without honor in the nation where he lived and worked." The *Eagle* somewhat inexplicably explained the disregard in pseudopsychological terms, determining that it could be attributed to "the bitterness and loneliness that characterized the later years of his life," but an interview with Homer Meade by *Eagle* reporter Stephen Fay provided what was now a familiar explanation as to why Du Bois had become ostracized by his birthplace. "Two years before his death and in the wake of 50 years of government surveillance and an arrest, at the age of 83, for treason, Du Bois joined the Communist Party," Meade explained. "But the act was regarded by many as ceremonial, occasioned by U.S. harassment."[66] Fay then outlined the familiar series of events that led to Du Bois's leaving the United States: the War Department's surveillance of him in 1919 for lecturing on equal rights; his indictment in 1951 because of his refusal to register as an agent of a foreign power as chair of the Peace Information Center; and the State Department's confiscation of his passport until 1958. These entanglements, Fay concluded, left Ghana to honor the civil rights leader but ensured that for the citizens of his birthplace, Great Barrington, Du Bois was to remain "a prophet without honor in his own land."[67]

CHAPTER SIX

An Uncertain Legacy

We have no right to sit silently by while the inevitable seeds are sown for a harvest of disaster to our children, black and white.
—**W. E. B. Du Bois,** *The Souls of Black Folk*

WALTER WILSON DIED IN 1991, just over a decade after his dream of having Du Bois's birthplace get the national recognition that he felt it deserved became realized. The legacy of that dream since the Du Bois memorial park attained official national landmark status has been chaotic at best; the citizens of Great Barrington—and Berkshire County at large—have continued to vacillate over their relationship with the famous and controversial native son.

Without question, the battle over Du Bois began, visibly and vigorously, in the late 1960s, when people expressed their fury over a small ceremony furnished with lawn chairs and bales of hay in a nondescript field. The reduction of Du Bois to a communist seemed to overshadow most anything else he had done, indicating that the escalating Cold War forced many to perceive Du Bois in only the narrowest of views. A town that had once prided itself (quite rightly, considering the racial politics of the era) for its foresight in supporting the young Du Bois felt that he had deserted it in his later years, perhaps ungrateful for all that the townsfolk, or at least their forebears, had provided him with. Their liberal tolerance of an exceptional young black man in their midst had deteriorated into a feeling that the latitude provided by their generous open-mindedness had never been repaid. The town cast Du Bois as an ingrate, one who bigheartedly had been chosen—allowed, even—to pursue the American dream, but who had instead chosen a path that seemed to fly in the face of the community that had provided him the opportunity.

Du Bois's critiques of the United States' democratic system and his increasing support of global socialism, which culminated in his joining the Communist Party, greatly confused perceptions of him at the local level. He had once been seen as a victim of the circumstances of his race, which propelled the town to help him in his early years. Certainly, Du Bois had always been a *black* neighbor, but Great Barrington prided itself on the fact that he had been, indeed, a *neighbor*. But his latter political stances and writings were seen by many in his hometown to be a refutation of their grandparents' attempts at integration. Moreover, his opting to leave the United States seemed to invalidate all that the town had done for him, despite what he had endured throughout his own life and sought to change for the lives of others.

The way Great Barrington had treated Du Bois in his youth unquestionably was important to him. In his many autobiographical writings, he often described how others regarded him, indicating that personal conduct played a large role in how he formed his nuanced perspectives of various peoples and countries. How a passerby dealt with him on the street, for example, often served as a gauge by which he judged a society as a whole. This process dealt little with what anyone thought about his views, but rather with how he was thought of as a person, giving him a means by which to determine a nation's level of civilization:

> The Soviet Union seems to me the only European country where
> people are not more or less taught and encouraged to despise and
> look down on some class, group or race. I know countries where race
> and color prejudice show only slight manifestations, but no white
> country where race and color prejudice seems so absolutely absent.
> In Paris, I attract some attention; in London I meet elaborate
> blankness; anywhere in America I get anything from complete
> ignoring to curiosity, and often insult. In Moscow, I pass unheeded.
> Russians quite naturally ask me information; women sit beside
> me quite confidently and unconsciously. Children are uniformly
> courteous.[1]

AN UNCERTAIN LEGACY

Given that Du Bois wrote often of his appreciation for Great Barrington neighbors such as Frank Hosmer, his high school principal, he undoubtedly would have been disappointed—although likely not surprised—by the inattention to his legacy in the years that followed the national landmark designation of his boyhood home. The national status was, indeed, an achievement, yet Walter Wilson, for one, had hoped for much more. Before his death, he outlined a series of ambitious plans. In 1978, in his role as cochair of the W. E. B. Du Bois Foundation, he guided two California documentary filmmakers, John Simmons and Carlton Moss, through Great Barrington, where they set up shots of key sites from Du Bois's youth, including Searles Middle School, Searles Castle, and the town hall. Wilson hoped that the documentary could be a centerpiece at a W. E. B. Du Bois museum, which he wanted to establish. Wilson planned on raising thousands of dollars to build the museum, which would feature materials from the Du Bois collection at the University of Massachusetts each summer. However, even Wilson understood just how grand his plans were. Although he spoke of constructing a "Civil Rights Hall of Fame" at the park, he understood that before such plans could begin, more pressing tasks, such as getting people "to clear the weeds from the lot," should likely be his main concern.[2]

That the parcel of land once at the center of a heated debate had so rapidly come to disrepair exemplified just how quickly Du Bois's visibility faded after the hard-fought battle to recognize him had seemed to be won. An op-ed piece in the *Berkshire Eagle* in 1980 reviewed a bit of Du Bois's early history in Great Barrington, emphasizing the support that he garnered from his community at that time and speculating as to what his legacy in the Berkshires should be in the contemporary moment. "From what I read in newspapers," the piece observed, "it seems that most people hereabouts think of W.E.B. Du Bois as primarily a political figure." They were most likely to recognize Du Bois for his work as a civil rights activist, "and for that they either revere or deplore him." Further, there were those who "cannot forgive him for making common cause with communists in his later years." What people were missing about "one of Berkshire County's most brilliant, and controversial, sons" was his life as a writer and scholar, particularly for his works *The*

Philadelphia Negro and *The Souls of Black Folk.* "Together," the piece concluded, "the two works form a unity that delineates the man: proud, intelligent and fierce in his determination to better the lives of black people here, there, everywhere."[3]

Not everyone ignored Du Bois, of course. The University of Massachusetts, now housing Du Bois's papers in its library, maintained a healthy interest in him in a variety of ways. Perhaps most notably, on October 5, 1994, the school's board of trustees voted to rename the main library on the Amherst campus after Du Bois, declaring, "As we march into the Twenty First Century we feel that it is time to go beyond the colorline and appropriately name the tower library in honor of one of the finest heroes, not only of Massachusetts but of the world—William Edward Burghardt Du Bois."[4] The actual dedication took place in February 1996, with a series of events devoted to Du Bois's accomplishments, including readings from *The Souls of Black Folk*, a lecture by Du Bois biographer David Levering Lewis, and a convocation that included the granting of honorary degrees to Herbert Aptheker, Rachel Robinson, and Randall Robinson.

The University of Massachusetts' interest in Du Bois was twofold: he was a figure of both local and global importance, and had to be recognized as such by the largest public institution of higher learning in the state. The renaming of the library, the manuscript collection that it archived, and the Afro-American Studies Department, also named in his honor, provided such recognition. As well, the university granted an honorary degree to Shirley Graham Du Bois at its commencement ceremonies in 1973.[5]

But it was the Department of Anthropology, in conjunction with the Afro-American Studies Department, that maintained the closest relationship with local aspects of Du Bois, as it viewed the site of his boyhood home to be of significant anthropological interest. The Burghardt homestead, in the eyes of UMass anthropological scholars, represented an ideal place to study African American home life in New England, given that the extended Burghardt family had occupied it from the early nineteenth century until the mid-twentieth century. As early as 1981, UMass researchers pushed for the university to purchase the site in order to begin archaeological excavation. (It eventually did so, in 1988.)[6]

The UMass anthropology department launched a series of studies of the site in 1983, uncovering some ten thousand artifacts and taking oral histories from Burghardt descendants.[7] This project was one of the few things that gave Du Bois any kind of profile in the years that followed the national recognition of his boyhood home. Occasionally, events emerged that focused on Du Bois as a local figure of prominence, but, as Wilson had feared, such happenings occurred infrequently, at best. Simon's Rock of Bard College, for example, held a series of lectures in 1983 to commemorate the eightieth anniversary of the publication of *The Souls of Black Folk* that included David Graham Du Bois as a speaker, but little else took place.[8]

However, the UMass anthropology project sustained a focused interest. In the summer of 1984, UMass anthropologist Robert Paynter, for example, gave a lecture, sponsored by the New Marlboro Historical Society, about the work going on at the Burghardt family home. According to Paynter, the site was of "high integrity" in terms of historical archaeological investigation, and was the center for summer fieldwork projects, which focused on nineteenth-century settlement patterns. The homestead served as an example of what he called a poor, non-Yankee family, and findings from it were compared to a similar study ongoing in Deerfield, Massachusetts (in neighboring Franklin County), of a wealthy, Yankee family.[9] "One of the truly important education values of the site," said Paynter, "is to alert people to the presence of Afro-American communities in New England back into the 17th century—in areas where whites, and black people too, I'll hazard, tend to think there were only white folks."[10]

At the time of Paynter's initial work, the university maintained a relationship with the property, although not in terms of direct ownership. However, when the town of Great Barrington went after the site for back taxes, in 1985, the university was listed as the home of the Du Bois Memorial Foundation. According to town tax collector John P. Boddie, the property would be taken on August 14, 1985, because the foundation owed approximately $5,500 in property taxes dating back to 1981. Homer Meade, who served as a liaison between UMass and the foundation, stated that the town was wide of the mark in its attempt to take the land, because its National Historic Landmark status, granted in 1976, ensured that the property was tax-exempt.[11] A resolution was reached when the chair of the town assessors, Robert G. Guidi, determined that the foundation misunderstood how tax-exempt status operated: a national landmark designation did not automatically make a property tax-exempt; the foundation had to apply for that status. If the foundation cooperated and did so, an abatement would be granted and the town would not take the property. "We will give them [the foundation] every consideration as we can," said Guidi. "We want to be as cooperative as we can to help them."[12]

Although the town did not take the land, its attempt demonstrated both its disregard for the past efforts of those involved in commemorating Du Bois and the instability and disorganization of the movement itself. Further, the coverage of the brief skirmish demonstrated the degree to which Du Bois remained an outsider to his birthplace, as local news stories of the tax disagreement tended to end with a brief explanation of who he was: "Du Bois (1868–1963) was a black civil rights leader, scholar, philosopher and—very late in life—communist."[13] The Great Barrington of Reagan's Cold War era, it seemed, not only needed to identify the founder of the NAACP but also needed to know the political affiliation that seemed to keep him from joining the pantheon of historic figures so proudly heralded in the Berkshires.

An attempt to change that perception came, again, from the University of Massachusetts, which, in cooperation with the Berkshire Museum, located in Pittsfield, launched a series of events to mark Du Bois's 121st birthday and, quite self-consciously, to resurrect him as a local figure of global significance. "Though the career and contributions of Du Bois are barely and rarely recognized in the town and county of his birth," observed the *Berkshire Eagle*, "efforts by scholars and admirers indicate that the long lapse in local recognition may soon come to an end." Among the events comprising the birthday celebration were talks by Williams College professor David Smith and esteemed historian John Hope Franklin; a moment of remembrance by local ministers; and a luncheon at the University of Massachusetts with·ambassadors from Germany, Ghana, and the Soviet Union. The capstone event was an announcement, delivered by UMass chancellor Joseph Duffy and Massachusetts Office of Travel and Tourism representative Deborah First, that a new Du Bois memorial would be built on the site of his childhood home. Duffy declared that the memorial, which would consist of a pavilion, benches, weatherproof plaques, and perhaps an audio system to play some of Du Bois's speeches, would combine "history and technology" and would demonstrate "who Du Bois was and what he taught."[14]

The birthday celebration compelled the *Berkshire Eagle* to examine the status of Du Bois in the Berkshires once again. The newspaper yet again found him to exist in relative anonymity and wondered why a figure of such historical importance "remains a somewhat obscure figure in the county of his birth."[15] An *Eagle* survey of Berkshire high school history teachers, for example, provided "a mixed picture of Du Bois' place in a high school curriculum." The *Eagle* found that students at Monument Mountain High School, in Great Barrington, read portions of *The Souls of Black Folk,* and seventh- and eighth-graders at Searles Middle School studied Du Bois in their local history unit. John A. Beacco Jr., who then served as chair of social studies at Searles, explained his school's approach to teaching Du Bois: "We don't single him out and focus on him for [a] week, but he's certainly mentioned. There's just too much to cover in terms of American history to spend a whole lot of time on any one figure." A further challenge, according to those interviewed, was that Du Bois was not in any of the textbooks that they used. Thus, concluded Beacco, "There's nothing other than what teachers themselves might drag into the curriculum."[16] One person, it seemed, was willing to "drag" Du Bois into the curriculum, but it was not a teacher. A senior, Anne Carman, at Mount Greylock High School, located in the northernmost tier of Berkshire County, had seen an exhibit on Du Bois while visiting the University of Massachusetts, and arranged for its traveling counterpart to come to her school as part of a broader celebration of Martin Luther King Jr.'s birthday.[17]

Other developments helped to ensure that Du Bois's profile would maintain a degree of visibility within his hometown. "It's time to give Du Bois his due and the recognition he deserves," observed the Reverend Esther Dozier, who lived in Great Barrington for more than three decades and served as pastor of the Clinton African Methodist Episcopal Zion Church, which Du Bois had occasionally visited. "There's been resistance to Du Bois, but the truth always stands. . . . And now, the momentum is growing."[18] At the Visitor Information Center in Great Barrington, tourists occasionally came to the town "looking to discover W. E. B." Joy Lyon, the manager of the center, said that at one point it was not easy to help these people, but with the 1994 installation of historic plaques by the Great Barrington Historical Society at the site of Du Bois's birthplace and in Mahaiwe Cemetery, it has become easier.[19]

In 2002, a garden at the entrance of Great Barrington's Housatonic River Walk, an initiative of the Great Barrington Land Conservancy that opened in 1992 after countless hours of volunteer cleanup labor, was dedicated to the memory of Du Bois, an effort spearheaded by River Walk coordinator Rachel Fletcher.[20] Du Bois had featured the "golden river" in a speech to his fellow high school alumni when he returned to Great Barrington in 1930:

> What has happened? The thing that has happened in this valley has happened in hundreds of others. The town, the whole valley, has turned its back upon the river. They have sought to get away from it. They have neglected it. They have used it as a sewer, a drain, a place for throwing their waste and their offal. . . . And so I have ventured to call to the attention of the graduates of the Searles High School this bit of philosophy of living in this valley, urging that we should rescue the Housatonic and clean it up as we have never in all the years thought before of cleaning it, and seek to restore its ancient beauty: making it the center of a town, of a valley, and perhaps—who knows? of a new measure of civilized life.[21]

Club Helsinki, a popular music café in the town, has held several events as part of its Du Bois Concert Series. Local historian Bernard Drew, who, along with Fletcher, has been a key figure in propagating the history of Du Bois in the area, put together *Fifty Sites in Great Barrington Associated with W.E.B. Du Bois,* available at the Visitor Information Center. Area colleges have gotten into the act also, with conferences focusing on Du Bois held at Williams College and the Massachusetts College of Liberal Arts in North Adams. At the University of Massachusetts, the Special Collections and University Archives Department of the library includes on its Web site a page dedicated to Du Bois, the "W.E.B. Du Bois Boyhood Homesite," with links to photographs, narratives, and even a short film of the 1969 dedication ceremony in the field, narrated by Ossie Davis.[22] And in January 2004, the Upper Housatonic Valley African American Heritage Trail Advisory Council emerged, founded by Fletcher, bringing together many of the people who had been proponents of Du Bois in various ways for a number of years, and producing a "trail guide" that lists the Du Bois homestead as one of forty-eight sites of African American interest in the area.[23]

WHAT'S IN A (COMMUNIST) NAME?

These efforts, among others, have worked to heighten the history of Du Bois in his hometown, and have undoubtedly educated many—both within and outside Great Barrington—but it was yet another firestorm that brought any kind of intense focus back on the civil rights leader. In June 2004, at a meeting of the school committee of the Berkshire Hills Regional School District, Bernard Drew publicly raised the idea of naming a local school for Du Bois.[24] The lengthy and, at times, heated debate that followed Drew's suggestion rang all too familiar to those who had been part of the movement to honor Du Bois some thirty-five years earlier. Yet again, Du Bois exemplified how history is generated and re-created at the most local and personal of levels, by people passionately determined for their voices—and thus their ways of remembering—to be heard.

The naming of schools for figures of historic note has been a quietly controversial practice for some time in the United States. The decision to name a library, for example, after a past president or a past civil rights figure often has had more to do with the location of the library (Is it in a *black* neighborhood?) than with the figure him- or herself. In the American South, for example, the legacy of the Confederacy, which frequently rears its head with issues such as the Georgia state flag (Does it symbolize slavery? Does it stand for something called states' rights?), has become a question for schools. According to the National Center for Education Statistics, there are nineteen public schools below the Mason-Dixon line named for Robert E. Lee, nine for Stonewall Jackson, and five for Jefferson Davis. J. E. B. Stuart, Turner Ashby, and George Edward Pickett all have at least one school named for them. Many speculate that the naming of schools for these figures has been an attempt by a white power elite to have the last word in the battles that emanated from the 1954 *Brown v. Board of Education* decision, and the decades of school integration efforts—or, in the spirit of massive resistance, lack thereof—that followed. Some schools have taken steps to remove the Confederate legacy from campuses, whether by barring students from wearing clothing that bears Confederate symbols or by renaming the schools themselves. Louisiana's Orleans Parish School Board, for example, voted to change the name of any school that bore the name of a former slave owner, meaning that George Washington Elementary, for one, became Dr. Charles Richard Drew Elementary.

In Hampton, Virginia, in 2003, a battle emerged over Jefferson Davis Middle School when Erenestine Harrison, an alumna of Hampton's segregated system, launched a petition drive to rename her alma mater. "If I were a kid . . . I would be ashamed to tell a friend that I went to Jefferson Davis," argued Harrison. One of her supporters, Julian Bond, agreed. "If it had been up to Robert E. Lee, these kids wouldn't be going to school as they are today," he pointed out. "They can't help but wonder about honoring a man who wanted to keep them in servitude."[25] Petersburg school superintendent Lloyd Hamlin, whose jurisdiction, approximately 80 percent black, includes Jefferson Davis Middle School (as well as two other schools named for Confederates), countered that the name of a school is not the point. "It's not the name on the outside of the building that negatively affects the attitudes of the students inside," Hamlin responded. "If the attitudes outside of the building are acceptable, then the name is immaterial."[26]

Back in Great Barrington, after Drew's proposal to rename Searles Middle School for W. E. B. Du Bois, the debate began to take up space in letters to the editor of the *Berkshire Eagle,* much as the furor over Walter Wilson's idea for a park had done decades earlier. Unlike the earlier era, though, many of these letter writers favored the idea of naming a school for Du Bois. Sally Harris pointed out that Du Bois's "fond feeling for the town where he was born and grew up, testifies to the way he must have been treated here at a time when race relations in other places were far from just or kind."[27] For Harris, by honoring Du Bois, the town would also be honoring itself, just as Wilson had said at the Tanglewood event, acknowledging the racially progressive nature of Great

Barrington's forebears. Rachel Fletcher wrote a letter that offered highlights of Du Bois's life, as well as his relationships in and connections to the local area. "Schools and entire school districts are named for Du Bois in Baltimore, Cincinnati, Brooklyn, Fresno and Detroit," Fletcher wrote. "Surely here in Great Barrington, home of the schools he first attended and where his remarkable abilities were recognized and allowed to grow, we can find it in our hearts to lend his name to a school of our own."[28] Barbara Bartle, a history professor at Berkshire Community College and a member of the Upper Housatonic Valley African American Heritage Trail Advisory Council, pointed out Du Bois's affection for the area: "From his writings, we know that he clearly loved his birth place in the Berkshires Hills and . . . the area's natural beauty and its people were a catalyst for his later successes."[29]

Some letters, however, launched familiar accusations at his memory. One writer opened by revealing that she was "sickened" at the idea of naming a school for Du Bois, and she hoped that "his expatriation [would] not be forgotten." Although she acknowledged his work as a civil rights leader, she contended that Du Bois "became the very thing this nation has risen above, fought against and triumphed over since its inception: a communist." Schools, she pointed out, were built "with taxes generated by our capitalist economy." She likened naming a school for Du Bois to naming one for "Mussolini, Stalin or Hussein—figures who, like Du Bois, hated America and that for which it stands," and she offered other "honorable black Americans" as alternatives, such as Frederick Douglass, Harriet Tubman, and Elizabeth "Mum Bett" Freeman; or someone such as Daniel Pearl (who began his journalism career at the *Berkshire Eagle*) or a local who had died fighting in Iraq.[30]

A subsequent letter to the editor, dismissing these points, found that "likening [Du Bois] to Stalin and Saddam Hussein is unjust and deeply offensive," and argued that the same U.S. government that once persecuted Du Bois had since then created two postage stamps in his honor.[31] Other letters suggested that controversy simply be avoided by naming the new school complex for the surrounding area, Monument Mountain, just as the high school is named.[32] One letter noted that the high school had been named after a contest was held to let the public decide on a name.[33] Still another commended the idea of retaining the appellation

"monument" in some form, arguing that rather than use the school to commemorate "the best-forgotten W.E.B. Du Bois," the community should
"turn even the elementary schools into Monuments to the fallen," because in "the never-ending war on terrorism . . . it is important to indoc-
trinate all our children into this great cause as early as possible."[34]

Naming the school after a less controversial local figure or after a
natural feature of the area would miss the point, according to Katharine
Bambery and Daniel Allentuck in their second letter to the editor regarding the issue. The lack of celebration for Du Bois in Great Barrington was "scandalous," as was the suggestion that Du Bois's association
with communism made him ineligible for honor. "We wonder if any of
these self-appointed guardians of the status quo have actually taken the
time to read Du Bois' books and articles," they challenged.[35]

But avoiding controversy appeared to be exactly what the Berkshire
Hills Regional School Committee intended to do, officially recommending that the new elementary and middle school complex should not be
named for any one person; should reflect the entire area; and should not
have any reference to specific racial or ethnic groups. This recommendation, according to a *Berkshire Eagle* editorial, was a "cop-out":

> Since when do we elect our officials to spare us controversy? Are we
> children, that we need to have our choices limited to our favorite
> rock, hill or stream? If people want to name the schools for Nathaniel
> Hawthorne or Herman Melville, two of our greatest dead white men,
> let them propose it. If others object to naming the school for Mr.
> Du Bois because he was black or a communist in later life, let them
> say so. The School Committee, which purports to be in the education
> business, should not timidly limit the terms of public debate.[36]

The school committee scheduled a meeting for October 21, 2004, at
which the naming of the new school complex would be discussed. As
the meeting drew closer, letters to the editor of the *Eagle* continued to
flow. The Reverend Kathy Duhon, of the Unitarian Universalist Meeting
of South Berkshire, asked that people attend the meeting. "The rules
that are being considered exclude every name I've heard suggested so
far, and may have been constructed to avoid controversy and contention,
but also to avoid a chance to do something meaningful and perhaps

justice-serving in naming our schools," she wrote. From her point of view, either Du Bois or Catherine Maria Sedgwick should be considered, and not only for their contributions to "the world in education, social reform and brilliant thought": "That they happen to come from two groups of people who are not often appropriately honored for their achievements— African Americans and women—should make us especially proud to lift up their names and strike a blow against racism and sexism."[37] Another writer made a playful plea for folks to get involved in the naming discussion, pointing out that by naming everything after Monument Mountain, "mail delivery could be a problem." But, the writer continued, to name the schools after a person could be even more dangerous:

> No doubt about it—naming schools after people is risky business.
> Famed eighteenth-century Stockbridge educator John Sergeant would
> be ruled out. He has a militaristic last name. And local Native
> American sachem Konkapot's name might suggest violent drug use!
> I suppose there is no hope for my two personal favorites—the Howard
> Stern Middle School and Ferris Bueller's Day Off Elementary School.
> Perhaps it's best to develop an acronym for use as a school name.
> For example, Welcome Education By Developing Unusually Bold
> Optimistic Idealistic Students, or W.E.B.D.U.B.O.I.S. for short.[38]

According to Berkshire Eagle writer Ellen Lahr, when the school committee meeting finally took place, "a delicate détente, sealed with apologies and handshakes among offended parties, followed a tense exchange."[39] After many voiced the opinion that the school committee's naming criteria had brought "a racially offensive tenor to the discussion," committee member John Grogan put forth a motion to get rid of the restrictive measures. "It's not our job to restrict name submissions or prevent controversy; the discussion goes on whether [or not] we choose a fancy parliamentary way of doing things," Grogan said. "We can take as many options and choices as people want."[40] After being held at a stalemate 4–4, the committee finally voted 5–3 in favor of Grogan's motion. The committee announced that it would accept name suggestions for the schools until December 20, but it made clear that the decision regarding a name would be left solely to the committee itself and would be announced in January. At the conclusion of the meeting, it seemed that both sides regretted the tone that the debate had taken. Many apologies were offered: by the school committee, for unintentionally putting forth an offensive recommendation regarding the naming process; and by community members—including Rachel Fletcher and Bernard Drew, both of whom spoke passionately at the meeting—who emphasized that they were deeming racist not the school committee members but the wording of the recommendation policy.

Over the next few months, various folks submitted forty-three names to the school committee, sixteen for the new elementary school and twenty-seven for the new middle school. A special school committee meeting scheduled for January 18, 2005, at Monument Mountain Regional High School would reveal the committee's decision. According to committee chair Stephen Bannon, despite the fact that the special session would be open to the public, the committee was ready to act. "We've accepted public comment," he said. "And I don't anticipate taking any more comment at the meeting." Further, he said that the number of times a particular name had been submitted would have no bearing on the committee's final decision. "I've said this several times, this is not a popularity contest."[41]

The names that had been submitted for both schools ranged in focus from specific natural sites in the local area to famous individuals (despite the school committee's fairly public stance that it did not want to go in the latter direction) such as Norman Rockwell, George Washington, Horace Mann, John F. Kennedy, Elizabeth Freeman, and—of course—W. E. B. Du Bois. A final plea in support of Du Bois—who was the only individual suggested for the elementary school—came from Rachel Fletcher and her colleagues on the Advisory Council for the Upper Housatonic Valley African-American Heritage Trail. Fletcher urged that the school committee realize that Du Bois, "more than any other alumnus of this school district, exhibits the promise of public education."[42] But the appeal, in the form of a letter to the editor of the *Berkshire Eagle*, came a day too late. At a special session, the Berkshire Hills Regional School District, after what the *Eagle* described as "40 minutes of thoughtful debate," announced the unveiling of the Monument Valley Regional Middle School and the Muddy Brook Regional Elementary School. At the meeting, Bannon expressed his concern over the amount of attention that had been given to the naming process. "I wish the print media would look more at what goes on inside these schools," he said. Committee member Richard Coons concurred, describing the naming procedure as a "media circus."[43]

As an "olive branch" to those who were undoubtedly disappointed by the failure of the committee to recognize Du Bois, the school committee requested that the libraries of the two schools be named—"at the appropriate time"—for specific individuals from the local area. "I think W.E.B. Du Bois is long overdue to be celebrated in this community," committee member Alan Wilkins said. "But maybe a library within one of the schools should be named after him." Further, he noted that support for Du Bois had come from area residents, rather than students, who tended to favor names that revolved around the natural environment.[44]

An editorial in the *Berkshire Eagle* expressed disappointment in what seemed to be a weak and somewhat cowardly compromise, as well as in the school committee's suggestion that the newspaper had played a role in blowing the issue out of proportion. Not only had the committee named the schools "after innocuous features of the local landscape," but "respected members of the community and *The Eagle* have been unduly scolded for arguing for a name that actually means something to the education of the district's children." The refusal to name a school for Du Bois came across as "typical small-town public behavior: Avoid any controversy that might cause trouble at re-election time and blame the media for rocking the boat." As for the proposal to name the library for Du Bois, the *Eagle* saw it as insulting, concluding that Du Bois "would not have appreciated tokenism."[45]

Letters to the editor agreed. One noted that the "lovely new lunch room" of the new school complex served things like "Nacho Chips & Cheese Sauce" and "String Cheese and Cereal" as main courses to school children who were suffering from a national epidemic of obesity, reflecting "an education that ignores deeper facts and analysis in favor of the superficial, the industrial, the readily palatable." Such thinking, the letter continued, "afflicted the debate and recent decision on the naming of the two schools," noting that anyone who knew anything about Du Bois must agree that "his public school education in Great Barrington was an absolute and undeniable triumph of the American democratic spirit and principles." This writer asked her community to see him as a "profoundly original and independent thinker—a man who literally shaped American history."[46] Other letters noted the irony that, coming on the tail of county and nationwide celebrations of the birth of Martin Luther King Jr., the decision of the school committee was "not only a slap in the face to the black community of the Berkshires, as well as other members of the surrounding communities, but also dishonors the memory of Dr. King and everything he stood for."[47]

A SON WITHOUT HONOR

Nearly forty years after the initial controversy, it appeared that Du Bois's legacy simply could not move beyond his identity as a communist. As David Blight has argued in his study of how race has influenced the way in which the Civil War has been remembered, Americans make choices about what to remember and what to forget about the past, and public memory "serves as a site in which these choices are made." In his research, Blight found that themes of reconciliation, rather than emancipation, run through the historical context of the Civil War, casting it as a tale of reunion above all else.[48] Just so, Great Barrington chose to see Du Bois as a communist rather than the founder of the NAACP—a person who tried to rip America apart, rather than one who tried to make it better. The community approved of his story only when it was one in which he accepted its help and went to college, reflecting a generous move of the town, but one that exemplified the politics of patronage from all sides. Thus, Great Barrington as a whole continues to be unable to reconcile Du Bois's late political leanings with his earlier civil rights contributions, never understanding how the two tales might fit together but instead continually pushing the "bite the hand" question: Whom did we send to college? What did our racial tolerance create?

But perhaps the story of nineteenth-century Great Barrington's relationship with Du Bois has a bit of hold left. Less than a month after the school committee chose nature themes for the names of its new schools, the Great Barrington selectmen seemingly settled on a way to finally deal with the issue of Du Bois's commemoration, voting 4–1 to put a nonbinding referendum question on the upcoming spring town election ballot as to whether or not signs celebrating Great Barrington as the birthplace of Du Bois should be erected. Yet from the get-go, the idea of the signage seemed to be problematic, beginning with how the town should decide the issue. According to selectwoman Judith Keefner, several residents wanted to vote on the matter, including some who were not in favor of it. "I have gotten calls from people who have defended this country and died, and there is nothing for them," she said (with apparently no one questioning just how these particular people used the phone). Why, she asked, should signs be put up for Du Bois when there was nothing in the town—"except for a small *park* on Main Street"—commemorating inventor William Stanley (who had been born in Brooklyn, but later lived in Great Barrington)? The issue had to be put to a vote, she concluded, so that more public participation could occur.

Other residents wanted to wait until the annual town meeting to issue a warrant article concerning the signage. Planning board member Anthony Blair questioned why there needed to be public debate over such signs at all, arguing that the Department of Public Works should just do it. "It's a fact that [Du Bois] was born here," he said. "No one can argue that. Why not just put up the signs?"[49]

An editorial in the *Berkshire Eagle* observed that the signage debate was another opportunity "to watch Great Barrington wrestle with the legacy of native son W.E.B. Du Bois." In agreement with Blair that the town would be well within its rights to just post the signs, the editorial noted that the selectmen instead had opted "to toss this hot potato to the voters." Hopefully, it concluded, voters would be "upfront" about their opinions of Du Bois, rather than hide behind a figure such as Stanley.[50]

In the midst of this tide of conversation, David Graham Du Bois, son of Shirley Graham Du Bois, died in Northampton, Massachusetts, about an hour or so away from Great Barrington. As W. E. B. Du Bois's stepson, who had retired as visiting professor of African-American studies and journalism at the University of Massachusetts Amherst in 2001, he was familiar with Great Barrington, and had recently spoken at the dedication of the Du Bois garden at the Housatonic River Walk, in 2002. With his death, both the school naming debate and the discussion regarding signage in Great Barrington received further local attention, particularly as the prominent obituary that the *Berkshire Eagle* devoted to David Graham Du Bois explained both situations.[51]

The writer of a letter to the editor found the death of Du Bois's step-son—as well as that of Ossie Davis, who had died on February 4—to be further impetus for the raising of signs commemorating Du Bois's birth in Great Barrington. In agreement with Anthony Blair that it was an issue that needed no vote, the writer argued that "placing signs in proud proclamation of the fact at the entrance to the town would seem a minimal effort, at the very least." Another writer, protesting against the secret vote of selectmen rather than an open forum, quoted Du Bois's autobiography on what he once had learned at a Great Barrington town meeting: "Gradually as I grew up, I began to see that this was the essence of democracy: listening to the other man's opinion and then voting your own, honestly and intelligently." The letter urged town officials—including members of the school committee—to read the autobiography, in the hope that by doing so, "they may better understand why many people want Du Bois' association with Great Barrington memorialized in some fitting way."[52]

As the town election drew closer, Du Bois made the front page of the *Berkshire Eagle* in a lengthy piece that thoroughly explored why, exactly, Great Barrington continued to go back and forth on the legacy of its famous resident. "Although W.E.B. Du Bois is internationally known and, in some places, revered, questions and confusion about his life continue to swirl about town," reporter Derek Gentile began. Gentile summarized why such debate had enveloped the town regarding the posting of signs designating the place of Du Bois's birth, and why his late belief in communism and residence in Ghana still permeated his public image.

The question of the signs, which was scheduled as a nonbinding referendum on the ballot (meaning that regardless of the vote, the selectmen still held the power to decide the fate of the signs), had yet again galvanized Du Bois supporters, who held a meeting in early April at the Claire Teague Senior Center in Great Barrington to discuss the details of the debate and decide how to combat the anger that the public still held over Du Bois's joining the Communist Party. Gentile covered the meeting. "I can't understand why a town would hold something against a man who made this decision at the end of his life," commented Rev. Esther Dozier. "[Du Bois] never said a thing against the United States, but he is without honor in Great Barrington. There are none so blind as those who will not see."[53] For Rachel Fletcher, the misunderstandings stemmed from the pieces that the *Berkshire Courier* ran against Walter Wilson and his initial project to create a memorial ceremony in honor of Du Bois. Fletcher also lamented the spurious belief that when he moved to Ghana, Du Bois officially renounced his U.S. citizenship, a story often confused with the fact that the State Department rescinded his passport. "W.E.B. Du Bois never renounced his homeland," Fletcher told the *Eagle.* "David [Graham Du Bois] had letters from Du Bois to the family lawyer insisting that he retain dual citizenship. But that story just never goes away."[54]

Gentile continued thinking about the debate in an op-ed piece a few weeks later that cemented what was at stake in the upcoming Great Barrington vote on signage, regardless of how "binding" the resolution was. Du Bois had been under constant government watch and scrutiny, Gentile argued, not because he was a threat to the state but "because he had, throughout his adult life, advocated for equal rights for himself and his fellow black Americans," a stance that had been "considered seditious." Some people had forgiven Du Bois for his communism, understanding that it was his final attempt at finding a way of living that embraced blacks within its ranks. "For the most part, history has forgiven him this alleged trespass," Gentile observed. "There are schools and buildings named after Du Bois in various parts of the state and, in fact, two commemorative stamps issued with his likeness on it." But in Great Barrington, he continued, Du Bois has remained "either forgotten or deliberately ignored" largely because the specter of communism remains. Gentile saw the opposition as being of an older nature, speculating that those who were not of age during the height of the Cold War might have trouble understanding just how fearsome the "red menace" had been and to what degree Cold War battles had saturated everyday American life. Gentile thoughtfully positioned Du Bois as a victim of Cold War rhetoric. He had not wanted to revoke his U.S. citizenship; the State Department took his passport *after* he left for Ghana, leading to the widespread, but wrongheaded, belief that he had rejected America, rather than vice versa. But like so many other figures in history, concluded Gentile, realities about Du Bois have often taken a backseat to his public image: "In the end, the most interesting thing about the Du Bois controversy is that the true, real information about him is not too difficult to find. There are plenty of reasons to honor this man as a son of Great Barrington."[55]

Great Barrington voters finally consented, agreeing by a two-to-one margin (850–431), with 29.9 percent participation, that signs commemorating Du Bois should be posted throughout the town.[56] Shortly afterward, the board of selectmen voted 4–1 in agreement with the voting public, authorizing the Department of Public Works to place signs noting Great Barrington as the birthplace of Du Bois at, minimally, four entrances to the town. The sole dissenting voice on the board was the chair, Margaret Beckwith, who argued that because of the low voter turnout, the selectmen should not authorize the move. Her dissenting vote, she said, was "procedural" rather than "personal."[57]

Others did not attempt to couch their opposition with Great Barrington's decision in technical terms. One letter to the editor of the *Eagle* agreed that Du Bois needed to be memorialized, but more in the manner of the way Benedict Arnold is remembered in American history. "The message to be drawn from the life of W.E.B. Du Bois is that all his earlier work, which deserves respect, was overshadowed by his later denunciation of America, and his espousal of Soviet Communism," the letter argued. "The fact that the new schools are not named for him, and why that is so, is a lesson which our kids should learn, along with all the positive aspects of his life."[58]

Green signs, which officially declare Great Barrington the "Birthplace of W. E. B. Du Bois," now greet visitors and residents alike at many of the entrances into the town. They are an innocuous compromise, signaling just how very deep the debate over Du Bois has become embedded within Great Barrington. Participants in the discussions regarding his commemoration understand the consequences of their actions, knowing that any recognition of Du Bois will etch his presence in the community forever. Just as Maya Lin's minimalist design to remember Vietnam has "proved to be the perfect medium for the debate to continue," in the words of scholar David Simpson,[59] so too are the signs in

Great Barrington: the fact that they offer only a bit of information about Du Bois ensures that no decision regarding his legacy has been reached.

Whether or not the presence of the signs will help secure Du Bois firmly within Great Barrington's embrace remains to be seen; but, if nothing else, the road it took to put them there has exemplified that acts of commemoration are, indeed, for the living. Even one of the signs' advocates, Randy Weinstein, who founded the Du Bois Center for American History in a space adjacent to his shop of rare and used books, has somewhat sanctioned Du Bois's confused legacy. "Let there be no mistaking the fact that from the vantage point of the 21st century, Du Bois' politics, at times, appears naïve, even wrongheaded," Weinstein wrote in a letter to the editor of the *Berkshire Eagle*. "Yet politics aside, his contribution to the 20th century's civil rights movement was righteous, global and indelible."[60]

Of course, there can never be a "politics aside" in any kind of historical understanding of a figure such as Du Bois. Yet Weinstein's burgeoning Du Bois Center looks to be a central place for the local celebration of Du Bois's legacy. On February 1, 2006, an esteemed panel composed of David Levering Lewis (New York University), David Blight (Yale University), and John Y. Simon (Southern Illinois University) marked the center's grand opening as part of a larger program intended to widen the visibility of both Du Bois and those who support the local celebration of his memory. The panel, held at the St. James Episcopal Church on Main Street in Great Barrington, where Du Bois once worshipped, drew almost four hundred people and was taped by C-SPAN. Blight remembered first coming to Great Barrington in the 1980s in search of Du Bois, asking people where the memorial to him was, only to find that no one knew. Years later, Blight found the small plaque on Church Street that the Great Barrington Historical Society had installed in 1994 noting his birthplace. Lewis, after giving an extensive overview of Du Bois's youth in Great Barrington, weighed in on recent local politics, deeming it "passing strange" that "Barringtonians chose to name one of their schools after a geological formation rather than Du Bois, who was a 'mountain of a man' in his own right."[61] Two weeks later, on February 25, 2006, Great Barrington again came out in droves, this time to celebrate Du Bois's 138th birthday in the Clinton African Methodist Episcopal

Zion Church, with an evening of music and a keynote by William Strickland, director of the Du Bois Papers at the University of Massachusetts.[62]

The University of Massachusetts may have the last word in regard to how Great Barrington needs to forge ahead. After a series of conversations with the revamped Friends of the Du Bois Homesite, chaired by Elaine Gunn herself, the school has now pledged a $20,000 planning grant to revamp the Du Bois family homestead. The grant, along with anonymous matching funds, builds on a $50,000 gift from the university to renovate the homestead; thus far, it has built a parking lot, a walking trail, and a few interpretive signposts.[63] Thus, visitors must still search for the unremarkable sign on the road that notes the national landmark site, but once they have found it, they are able to reach the site of the homestead and Wilson's boulder, something not easily possible just a few years ago.

Whether the Du Bois Center, the revamped W. E. B. Du Bois Memorial Committee, the signs, or the various Du Bois events that continue to find their way into the local calendar will lead to a more permanent home for W. E. B. Du Bois in Great Barrington's history cannot yet be determined. For the townspeople of Great Barrington, Du Bois became, to borrow a phrase from historian Paul Boyer, a "litmus test of patriotism."[64] Thus, the story of his story remains somewhat the same: anticommunist, often racially expressed sentiment seems to meet each step of commemoration that Du Bois's relatively small group of supporters takes, much in the manner that it greeted Walter Wilson's dream for a small piece of field to be made special. Wilson's era could be construed as far different from the contemporary landscape, and, of course, it was. The onus of hostility created at the height of the Cold War, when the specter of the Soviet Union converged with the most militant moments of civil rights actions, mushrooming countercultures, and the increasingly violent actions in Vietnam, was placed on Du Bois by those who claimed that they did not want to commemorate his many merits because of what they considered to be un-American—even seditious—behavior. Du Bois, in the late 1960s, gave the so-called silent majority—those who elected Richard Milhous Nixon to the White House in a time deemed radical—something they did not need to be silent about. To Walter Wilson and the many who worked beside him, the silent majority turned their attempt to commemorate a figure of the civil rights movement into an act of civil rights itself, ensuring that the more Great Barrington tried to forget Du Bois, the more important his memory became. It was the opposition, perhaps, that made creating a memorial seem all the more important. It was the opposition that made Du Bois more visible in Great Barrington than he ever had been.

The opposition, of course, does not remain silent, for, as David Blight has observed, "all memory is prelude."[65] As the Cold War becomes grounded in the past, the sentiments and actions it created slide almost seamlessly into the post-9/11 era. Binaries of "us versus them" exist in amorphous yet devastating ways; someone—on behalf of and for the good of the general public—is continually trying to figure out who the "us" is, since the "them" remains part of an imaginary state of emergency, albeit one with very real ramifications, as it continues to drive U.S. foreign policy in much the same way that it did in the Vietnam era.

Thus, the legacy of disavowal that continues to surround Du Bois in his hometown, in the wake of and regardless of signs and ceremonies, ensures that we must continually push to understand how national and global situations continue to be digested and dealt with at the most local of levels. Then, perhaps, we can better expose the power of racial enmity hidden in efforts that proclaim to be focused on security and well-being, and well masked in patriotic language that seems available to only a few who are lucky enough to reside in America's quintessential small towns, yet feel compelled to take on the battles of the world. Only then can we learn just how silent we actually are, for only after the debate is over—regardless of how long or how loud it is—can we see how very little came of all that noise.

Acknowledgments

WITH SO MANY TO THANK, I should start with those who were willing to return my calls. Although I avoided approaching this project from the angle of an oral history, there are a few folks with whom I had lengthy conversations in order to piece much of this story together, particularly since Walter Wilson left no records of any kind. Thanks, first, to Dr. Edmund Gordon, who took the time to sit down with me to work through his involvement in the Great Barrington Du Bois project in the late 1960s as well as his friendship and partnership with Wilson. Thanks to the Honorable William Simons, whose wise and ample memory provided the real turning point in my research on Wilson, allowing me to get as close to him as I think I possibly could. And many thanks to Elaine Gunn. My time with her, arranged through Randy Weinstein at the Du Bois Center in Great Barrington, I will always treasure. I doubt she could understand how special it was to me to take a look into the past through her eyes.

For archival research, there was no greater help to me than Grace McMahon, formerly of the *Berkshire Eagle*. The amount of time she was willing to spend with me, the access she granted me, and the seemingly perfect archives she maintained are the main reasons I was able to get this project off the ground and running; I cannot thank her enough. When Grace left the newspaper, the wonderful and wondrous Jeannie Moschino took her place; her help in obtaining many of the images for this book, as well as the permission to reprint them, was simply astonishing. I am forever grateful for the generosity of the *Berkshire Eagle*. Thanks also to the head of special collections at the library at the University of Massachusetts Amherst, William Thompson, and also to Robert Paynter of the anthropology department there.

There are many to thank at the University of Minnesota Press. My editor, Richard Morrison, knows well what a long journey this book has been. His feedback, his close readings, his humor, and his promise of a lovely dinner when it was completed ensured that we forged ahead. Thanks, too, to his assistant Adam Brunner, especially for his endless patience on matters that ranged from digital photography to pesky paperwork. Copy editor Tammy Zambo has made me appear to be a much better writer than I am.

Matthew Frye Jacobson continues to be my professional hero—such generosity, such wisdom, such humor. I cannot imagine putting anything to press without his eyes upon it (sometimes more than once), and I am incredibly lucky that he remains a valued part of my world. Appreciation also goes to Grant Farred for his detailed and supportive reading of an early draft; his comments and suggestions made this a much better book.

Many others asked about this project along the way and offered support, feedback, and suggestions where and when needed (and sometimes they simply told me that yes, of course they'd like to read it someday). Particular thanks to Sarah Tynan, Beth Vihlen MacGregor, Nikhil Pal Singh, Jodi Melamed (who shared pieces of her dissertation with me), Roblyn Rawlins, Nereida Segura-Rico, and Nick Smart. And thanks to dean Richard Thompson, who helped me to obtain financial support from both The College of New Rochelle Faculty Fund and the National Endowment for the Humanities summer grants program.

On a personal level: thanks to Alana Ruptak for helping to take care of me and mine when we needed it most. My brother, Michael, and my sister, Elissa, are as close as one could hope, so to them, Donna and Joe, and the gang of Sam, Summer, Emily, Max, and Jake, big hugs. My parents, Ruth and Milton Bass, have their own legacy in the Berkshires, one that I am proud to crow about endlessly. They are always interested in what I'm doing, yet with this project they have been tireless—hunting down information, answering my endless questions, reading draft after draft, finding photographs, taking photographs, and making all of the suggestions that their knowledge of the Berkshires and their esteemed writing abilities allow. They provided the genesis for this book and were there for all stages of its follow-through, whether trekking through the woods with me to "find Du Bois" or producing many of the images that grace these pages. For all of that—and just about anything and everything else—I thank them.

Evan Klupt continues to lovingly feign interest in what I do, as well as assure me that there are far more important things in life than writing a book, for which I thank him. Finally, I am pleased to thank Hannah Lena Klupt, a project coauthored by Evan and me, who has done as much as she could to stall the book but did not prevail. She came into this world anything but silent, and my hope for her is that she may continue to yell for all the right reasons. With that in mind, I dedicate this book to her.

Notes

INTRODUCTION

1. I refer to civil rights movements in the plural, as I have in my previous publications, to make the point that the fight for civil rights was not a singular cohesive movement, regardless of the many common goals those involved with civil rights had. To situate a group such as the Black Panthers under the same heading as the Southern Christian Leadership Conference, for example, does a disservice to the very different strategies each group meticulously designed and attempted to execute. Furthermore, to refer to *the* civil rights movement pinpoints a closed time framework—generally from the *Brown* decision to the assassination of Martin Luther King Jr. Such a structure negates the early work of the NAACP, particularly efforts of activists such as Charles Hamilton Houston, and, perhaps more important, gives the movement closure, as if equity and human rights have been definitively accomplished.

2. Philip Pettijohn, quoted in Stephen Fay, "Barrington's Du Bois: Dead and Gone?" *Berkshire Eagle*, August 27, 1988.

3. Philip Pettijohn, quoted in Susanna Cooper, "Blood of W. E. B. Du Bois Still Flows in Berkshires," *Berkshire Eagle,* September 5, 1989.

4. Elaine Gunn, interview with the author, Du Bois Center for American History, May 13, 2006.

5. Ibid.

6. Cedric J. Robinson, "W.E.B. Du Bois and Black Sovereignty," in *Imagining Home: Class, Culture, and Nationalism in the African Diaspora*, ed. Sidney J. LeMelle and Robin D.G. Kelly (London: Verso, 1994), 145, 147. Indeed, Robinson uses Du Bois's ideas regarding Americo-Liberia in the early twentieth century as a way to demonstrate "a set of characterological weaknesses in his [Du Bois's] historical social consciousness," particularly when juxtaposed with the likes of C. L. R. James, Frantz Fanon, and Amilcar Cabral. See Robinson, 155.

7. Quoted in Stephen Fay, "Du Bois, Harassed in Own Country, to Be Honored by Nation of Ghana," *Berkshire Eagle,* July 28, 1986.

8. Ghana Department of Tourism, http://www.ghanatourism.gov.gh/regions/highlight_detail.asp?id=11&rdid=20 (accessed June 16, 2004).

9. David Levering Lewis, *W. E. B. Du Bois: Biography of a Race, 1868–1919* (New York: Holt, 1993), 4–5, 10.

10. In his final autobiography, Du Bois briefly describes his grandfather's life in New Haven, writing, "He and certain other Negroes with property were permitted to buy lots at the rear of the new Grove Street Cemetery, opposite the Yale campus. Years later when this cemetery was enlarged, those Negro lots lay on the center path. Here my grandfather lies buried and here I shall one day lie." *The Autobiography of W. E. B. Du Bois: A Soliloquy on Viewing My Life from the Last Decade of Its First Century (New York: International, 1968),* 67.

11. Lewis, *Du Bois: Biography of a Race,* 12.

12. Du Bois, *Autobiography,* 63. Du Bois erroneously lists the date of the gift as 1930.

13. Bernard A. Drew, *Great Barrington: Great Town, Great History* (Great Barrington Historical Society, 1999), 16–17.

14. Du Bois, *Autobiography,* 64.

15. Ibid., 92.

16. David Graham Du Bois, quoted in Richard T. Delmasto, "Du Bois's Vision for Future Is Theme of Talks at College," *Berkshire Eagle,* February 5, 1983.

17. Susanna Cooper, "Du Bois Memorial Planned," *Berkshire Eagle,* February 24, 1989.

18. Harold J. Beckwith, quoted in Douglas Robinson, "W.E.B. Du Bois Hometown in the Berkshires Angers Residents," *New York Times,* May 16, 1969.

19. See Jorge Luis Borges, "Funes, His Memory," in *Borges: Collected Fictions,* trans. Andrew Hurley (New York: Penguin, 1999).

20. Quoted in Linton Weeks, "Maya Lin's 'Clear Vision,'" *Washington Post,* October 20, 1995.

21. Marilyn B. Young, "Dangerous History: Vietnam and the 'Good War,'" in *History Wars: The Enola Gay and Other Battles for the American Past,* ed. Edward T. Linethal and Tom Engelhardt (New York: Holt, 1996), 200.

22. David Simpson, *9/11: The Culture of Commemoration* (Chicago: University of Chicago Press, 2006), 76; parentheses in the original.

23. Marita Sturken, *Tourists of History: Memory, Kitsch, and Consumerism* (Durham, N.C.: Duke University Press, 2007), 5.

24. Ibid., 273.

25. Ibid., 292. See Edward T. Linethal, "Anatomy of a Controversy," in Linethal and Engelhardt, *History Wars.*

26. Monroe W. Hatch to Martin Harwit, September 12, 1993, Enola Gay Archive, Air Force Association, http://www.afa.org/media/enolagay/09-12-93.asp (accessed March 20, 2008).

27. Linethal and Engelhardt, *History Wars,* 2.

28. Alison Landsberg, *Prosthetic Memory: The Transformation of American Remembrance in the Age of Mass Culture* (New York: Columbia University Press, 2004), 3.

29. Conversely, it is important to remember, as Marc Augé observes, that "official memory needs monuments." See Marc Augé, *Oblivion* (Minneapolis: University of Minnesota Press, 2004), 88.

30. Kirk Savage, *Standing Soldiers, Kneeling Slaves: Race, War, and Monument in Nineteenth-Century America* (Princeton: Princeton University Press, 1997), 4.

31. David Levering Lewis, *W. E. B. Du Bois: The Fight for Equality and the American Century, 1919–1963* (New York: Holt, 2000), 571.

32. Savage, *Standing Soldiers, Kneeling Slaves,* 7.

33. James Williams, quoted in Fay, "Barrington's Du Bois."

1. DU BOIS IN GREAT BARRINGTON AND BEYOND

1. Berkshire Visitors Bureau, "The Berkshires," http://www.berkshires.org/ (accessed December 16, 2003).

2. Southern Berkshire Chamber of Commerce, http://www.southernberk shires.com/ (accessed December 16, 2003).

3. Du Bois, *Autobiography,* 128 (cited in text in remainder of chapter 1).

4. For an excellent overview of the history of these houses, see Carole Owens, *The Berkshire Cottages: A Vanishing Era* (Stockbridge, Mass.: Cottage Press, 1984). Owens, a resident of Stockbridge, lives in one of the nineteenth-century estates that fall into this category.

5. Massachusetts Department of Housing and Community Development, "Community Profile: Great Barrington," http://www.state.ma.us/dhcd/iprofile/ 116.pdf (accessed January 16, 2004).

6. Michael Ballon, quoted in Christina Tree, "A Berkshires Hug That's a Magnet for New Yorkers," *Boston Globe,* August 24, 2003. Tree, who lives in Boston, coauthored (with William Davis) *Massachusetts: An Explorer's Guide,*

3d ed. (Woodstock, Vt.: Countryman, 2000), and *The Berkshire Hills and Pioneer Valley of Western Massachusetts: An Explorer's Guide,* 2d ed. (Woodstock, Vt.: Countryman, 2007).

7. Quoted in Tara Mandy, "Summer 2002 Getaways: Great Barrington, Massachusetts," *New York,* June 3, 2002.

8. W. E. B. Du Bois, "House of the Black Burghardts," *Crisis* 35, no. 4 (April 1928): 133–34.

9. Drew, *Great Barrington,* 375.

10. Lewis, *Du Bois: Biography of a Race,* 11.

11. Ibid., 11–12.

12. According to Lewis, Borghardt also spelled his name Coonrad Borghardt and Conraed or Conrad Burghardt. Ibid., 13–14.

13. The Trustees of Reservations, "Ashley House," http://www.thetrustees .org/pages/252_ashley_house.cfm (accessed January 7, 2004).

14. Lewis, *Du Bois: Biography of a Race,* 14.

15. Jodi Melamed, "W. E. B. Du Bois's UnAmerican End: A Soliloquy of Race against U.S. Empire," *African American Review* 40, no. 3 (2006); Lewis, *Du Bois: Biography of a Race,* 28; Manning Marable, introduction to W. E. B. Du Bois, *Darkwater: Voices from within the Veil* (New York: Dover, 1999), v. Indeed, there are both similarities and differences between *Darkwater* and the *Autobiography,* which were written decades apart. Using one more prominently than the other is, likely, just as problematic as using them equally, given they were obviously written for very different purposes and at very different times in Du Bois's life. In many ways, *Darkwater* is far more about the moment in which Du Bois wrote it than about his past; as Marable notes, "One cannot read and understand *Darkwater* outside of its immediate historical context" (introduction, vi). For my own purposes, I have used the *Autobiography* as the standard in regard to how Du Bois remembers his first eighteen years, and have added pieces from *Darkwater* only when they offer further insight into a particular moment.

16. Marable, introduction, vi.

17. Herman Melville, quoted in Morgan Bulkeley Sr., "A Whale in the Berkshires," in *Berkshire Stories: History, Nature, People, Conservation* (Great Barrington, Mass.: Lindisfarne Books, 2006), 205; Jonathan Sternfield, *The Berkshire Book: A Complete Guide* (Great Barrington, Mass.: Berkshire House Publishers, 1986), 85.

18. The idyllic scene that Du Bois describes here was not always so in his memory. Although he uses the image of the golden river in a similar opening in

Darkwater, he goes on to explain that it is so "because of the woolen and paper waste that soiled it." See *Darkwater,* 6.

19. Robert Paynter, cited in Drew, *Great Barrington,* 16–17. The land was actually divided into two plots, one 1.78 acres and the other 2.71 acres. The University of Massachusetts anthropology department led digs on the site in 1983, 1987, and 2003.

20. Carl Nordstrom, "The Truth Shall Make You Free," *Berkshire Eagle,* February 13, 1980.

21. Paynter, quoted in Drew, *Great Barrington,* 16–17.

22. Drew, *Great Barrington,* 323–25.

23. Du Bois, *Autobiography,* 86–87; Drew, ibid.

24. Quoted in Drew, *Great Barrington,* 375.

25. Lewis, *Du Bois: Biography of a Race,* 53.

26. Ibid.

27. Du Bois, quoted in Lewis, ibid., 545.

2. EVOLUTION OF A PROGRESSIVE MIND

1. Lewis, *Du Bois: Biography of a Race,* 56.

2. Du Bois, *Autobiography,* 105–6.

3. Ibid., 106.

4. Ibid., 108.

5. Ibid., 110.

6. Lewis, *Du Bois: Biography of a Race,* 65.

7. Ibid., 84.

8. Ibid., 193. First published in 1899, *The Philadelphia Negro* is considered to be the first sociological study of African Americans in an urban setting.

9. Ibid., 228.

10. Ibid., 251.

11. Du Bois, *The Souls of Black Folk* (1903; repr., New York: Signet Classic, 1969), 227, 229, 230.

12. Ibid., 44.

13. Lewis, *Biography of a Race,* 345.

14. Lewis, *Du Bois: Fight for Equality,* 545. Du Bois also buried his daughter Yolande in the Mahaiwe Cemetery, in 1961, but never had a stone erected to mark the site.

15. W. E. B. Du Bois, "I Bury My Wife," in *Writings by W. E. B. Du Bois in Periodicals Edited by Others,* vol. 4, *1945–1961,* ed. Herbert Aptheker

(Millwood, N.Y.: Kraus-Thomson, 1982), 155. The *Chicago Globe* first published the piece on July 15, 1950.

16. Gunn, interview.

17. Du Bois, *Autobiography*, 120, 121.

18. Carol Anderson, *Eyes Off the Prize: The United Nations and the African American Struggle for Human Rights, 1944–1955* (Cambridge: Cambridge University Press, 2003), 52.

19. Ibid., 166.

20. See Paul Buhle and David Wagner, *Hide in Plain Sight: The Hollywood Blacklistees in Film and Television, 1950–2002* (New York: Palgrave Macmillan, 2003); Buhle and Wagner, *Radical Hollywood: The Untold Story behind America's Favorite Movies* (New York: New Press, 2003); and Gerald Horne, *The Final Victim of the Blacklist: John Howard Larson, Dean of the Hollywood Ten* (Berkeley: University of California Press, 2006).

21. Although the racial genocide of Jews and others in Hitler's "final solution" are well documented and well known, the racial aspects of the Pacific theater of war remain in the shadows of World War II history. See John Dower, *War without Mercy: Race and Power in the Pacific War* (New York: Pantheon, 1986).

22. See John D. Skrentny, *The Minority Rights Revolution* (Cambridge, Mass.: Harvard University Press, Belknap Press, 2002).

23. Anderson, *Eyes Off the Prize*, 276.

24. Mary L. Dudziak, *Cold War Civil Rights: Race and the Image of American Democracy* (Princeton: Princeton University Press, 2000), 48.

25. Melamed, "Du Bois's UnAmerican End."

26. Manning Marable, *Race, Reform, and Rebellion* (Jackson: University Press of Mississippi, 1991), 49.

27. Walter White, *A Rising Wind* (1945), quoted in Dower, *War without Mercy*, 177–78.

28. Robin D. G. Kelley, "'But a Local Phase of a World Problem': Black History's Global Vision, 1883–1950," *Journal of American History* 86, no. 3 (December 1999): 1075–76.

29. Brenda Plummer, *Rising Wind: Black Americans and U.S. Foreign Affairs, 1935–1960* (Chapel Hill: University of North Carolina Press, 1996), 4; Mary L. Dudziak, "Desegregation as a Cold War Imperative," in *Critical Race Theory: The Cutting Edge*, ed. Richard Delgado (Philadelphia: Temple University Press, 1995), 110–21.

30. Melamed, "Du Bois's UnAmerican End."

31. Dudziak, *Cold War Civil Rights*, 49, 50.

32. Ibid., 54–55.

33. Julian Bond, quoted in Clayborne Carson, *In Struggle: SNCC and the Black Awakening of the 1960s* (Cambridge, Mass.: Harvard University Press, 1995), 135.

34. Baruch A. Hazan, "Sport as an Instrument of Political Expansion: The Soviet Union in Africa," in *Sport in Africa: Essays in Social History*, ed. William J. Baker and James A. Mangan (New York: Africana, 1987), 253–55, 259, 265; Penny Von Eschen, *Race against Empire: Black Americans and Anticolonialism, 1937–1957* (Ithaca, N.Y.: Cornell University Press, 1997), 265.

35. George Lipsitz, "'Frantic to Join . . . the Japanese Army': Beyond the Black-White Binary," in *The Possessive Investment in Whiteness: How White People Profit from Identity Politics* (Philadelphia: Temple University Press, 1998), 94.

36. Linethal and Engelhardt, *History Wars*, 6.

37. See Penny Von Eschen, *Satchmo Blows Up the World: Jazz Ambassadors Play the Cold War* (Cambridge, Mass.: Harvard University Press, 2004).

38. Dudziak, *Cold War Civil Rights*, 67.

39. Lewis, *Du Bois: Fight for Equality*, 517. Rather than create a defense for the Scottsboro Boys, who had been falsely accused of gang-raping two white women, the NAACP shied away from the case out of concern over the consequences of defending alleged rapists. The Communist Party, which saw an opportunity to recruit both southern blacks and northern leftists, established a hard-hitting defense with its International Labor Defense arm. Late in the game, the NAACP, assured of the innocence of the accused, moved in to take the case from the ILD, eventually getting famed attorney Clarence Darrow to take the case on the NAACP's behalf. See James E. Goodman, *Stories of Scottsboro* (New York: Vintage, 1995).

40. Arthur Schlesinger Jr., quoted in Lewis, *Du Bois: Fight for Equality*, 526.

41. Max Yergan, quoted in Von Eschen, *Race against Empire*, 115.

42. Von Eschen, *Race against Empire*, 115.

43. Max Yergan, quoted in Dudziak, *Cold War Civil Rights*, 56–57.

44. Quoted in Dudziak, *Cold War Civil Rights*, 57.

45. The idea that communism must be "contained" came from George F. Kennan's "X article," which he anonymously published in 1947, in *Foreign Affairs*, as "The Sources of Soviet Conduct." The policy of containment dictated that rather than try to defeat communism, the United States would isolate it,

preventing a "domino effect." According to Kennan, by encouraging nations to choose the Western system of capitalism over the Soviet system of communism, communism would eventually fade into oblivion. For the classic treatment on containment policy, see John Lewis Gaddis, *Strategies of Containment: A Critical Appraisal of American National Security Policy during the Cold War* (New York: Oxford University Press, 2005).

46. Quoted in Dudziak, *Cold War Civil Rights*, 61.

47. Martin Duberman, *Paul Robeson: A Biography* (New York: New Press, 1995), 340–42.

48. Lewis, *Du Bois: Fight for Equality*, 544–45.

49. U.S. State Department, quoted in Dudziak, *Cold War Civil Rights*, 62.

50. William Patterson, quoted in Dudziak, *Cold War Civil Rights*, 63–64. See also William Patterson, *The Man Who Cried Genocide: An Autobiography* (New York: International, 1991).

51. The State Department was quoted in the *New York Times*. See Dudziak, *Cold War Civil Rights*, 66.

52. The *Afro-American* is quoted in Von Eschen, *Race against Empire*, 116; Anderson, *Eyes Off the Prize*, 103.

53. Lewis, *Du Bois: Fight for Equality*, 530–31.

54. Du Bois, quoted in ibid., 532.

55. Von Eschen, *Race against Empire*, 117–18; Lewis, *Du Bois: Fight for Equality*, 534.

56. Arthur B. Spingarn, quoted in Anderson, *Eyes Off the Prize*, 144.

57. Lewis, *Du Bois: Fight for Equality*, 536.

58. Ibid., 568.

59. Du Bois, *Autobiography*, 16.

60. Melamed, "Du Bois's UnAmerican End."

61. Du Bois, *Autobiography*, 58.

62. Du Bois was one of many black intellectuals who espoused what can be called classical African Marxism, rooted in previous decades of Pan-Africanism but definitively articulated by Du Bois, C. L. R. James, Frantz Fanon, George Padmore, and Kwame Nkrumah. Using the specific examples of the Algerian and Guinean revolutions, this form of Marxism argued that European colonialism had to be permanently pushed out of Africa. See Ntongela Masilela, "Pan-Africanism or Classical African Marxism?" in LeMelle and Kelly, *Imagining Home*, 309.

63. W. E. B. Du Bois, *Black Reconstruction in America, 1860–1880* (1935; repr., New York: Free Press, 1998).

64. Melamed, "Du Bois's UnAmerican End."

65. Thomas Borstelmann, *Apartheid's Reluctant Uncle: The United States and Southern Africa in the Early Cold War* (New York: Oxford University Press, 1993), 161.

66. Dean Acheson, Du Bois, and William Foley are all quoted in Lewis, *Du Bois: Fight for Equality*, 546–47.

67. Walter White, quoted in Anderson, *Eyes Off the Prize*, 173.

68. Lewis, *Du Bois: Fight for Equality*, 547–53.

69. Subversive Activities Control Board, quoted in Von Eschen, *Race against Empire*, 134.

70. Lewis, *Du Bois: Fight for Equality*, 555.

71. Von Eschen, *Race against Empire*, 183.

72. Lewis, *Du Bois: Fight for Equality*, 567.

73. Du Bois, quoted in ibid.

74. Von Eschen, *Race against Empire*, 183–84.

3. HER PROUDEST CONTRIBUTION TO HISTORY

1. Fay, "Du Bois, Harassed in Own Country."

2. Carlin Romano, "Memoir of 'Growing Up Niebuhr' Starts from Timeless Prayer," *Philadelphia Inquirer*, February 22, 2004. The "Serenity Prayer" is this: "God, give us grace to accept with serenity the things that cannot be changed, courage to change the things that should be changed, and the wisdom to distinguish the one from the other." See Elisabeth Sifton, *The Serenity Prayer: Faith and Politics in Times of Peace and War* (New York: Norton, 2003). Niebuhr died in 1971 at his home in Stockbridge and is buried in Stockbridge Cemetery.

3. John W. P. Mooney, quoted in Fay, "DuBois, Harassed in Own Country."

4. Elaine Gunn, interview by the author, Du Bois Center for American History, Great Barrington, Massachusetts, May 13, 2006. All subsequent citations of Gunn refer to this interview.

5. "The Hard-Nosed Idealist," *Berkshire Eagle*, March 9, 1968. Wilson also claimed to have worked on the screenplay for the 1925 film *Hell's Highroad*, which starred Robert Edeson, Julia Faye, and Leatrice Joy, was directed by Rupert Julian, and was based on Ernest Pascal's novel by the same name. He is not credited in the film, although that does not mean he did not work on it in some capacity. See Edward J. Farrell, "Realtor Wilson Founding Publishing Firm in Lenox," *Berkshire Eagle*, November 18, 1966.

6. William Simons, interview by author, Pittsfield, Massachusetts, July 16, 2004. All subsequent citations of Simons refer to this interview.

7. Simons played a large role in the establishment of the W. E. B. Du Bois Memorial Committee but has no remaining files of his work; they were lost in the many moves he made throughout his career as an assistant district attorney, a civil lawyer, and a Superior Court judge.

8. *The Fight for Civil Liberty, 1930–1931,* annual report of the American Civil Liberties Union, New York, June 1931, http://debs.indstate.edu/a505f54_1931.pdf, p. 3 (accessed June 13, 2005).

9. Ibid., 4.

10. Ibid., 33–34.

11. American Civil Liberties Union, *Eternal Vigilance: The Story of Civil Liberty, 1937–1938* (New York, June 1938), 27, 85, 88.

12. "Fannie Wilson," obituary, *Berkshire Eagle,* January 13, 1988. Fannie died on January 3, 1988, leaving two brothers, Abe and Max Sher. Upon her death, she donated thirteen pieces of Shaker furniture to the Old Chatham Shaker Museum, in Chatham, New York. Simons is not alone in his affection for Fannie. To a person, anyone asked about her had a similar reply: she seemed to be unilaterally adored in the community.

13. "Hard-Nosed Idealist."

14. "Farm Property Sold," *Berkshire Eagle,* June 2, 1952. For more on Bellefontaine, see Owens, *Berkshire Cottages.*

15. Wilson's involvement in Wheatleigh, which was owned and occupied by Philip and Stephanie Barber in this period, cannot be confirmed. For an index of reviews of Wheatleigh, see http://www.wheatleigh.com/reviews_detailed.html#harpers02. For more on Alice's Restaurant, see "Youths Ordered to Clean Up Rubbish Mess," in *This Is the Arlo Guthrie Book* (New York: Macmillan, 1969), 39; and Saul Braun, "Alice and Ray and Yesterday's Flowers," in *Playboy's Music Scene* (Chicago: Playboy Press, 1972), 122–25. For understanding the legacy of Music Inn, there are many sources, including my own father, who "ran" with the Music Inn crowd in its heyday of the late 1950s and early 1960s. The Barbers founded Music Inn in 1950, and remodeled the Wheatleigh barn into the Berkshire Music Barn in 1955, where they hosted the likes of Louis Armstrong, Duke Ellington, Ella Fitzgerald, Sarah Vaughan, Count Basie, the Weavers, and Mahalia Jackson. The Modern Jazz Quartet's recordings with Sonny Rollins took place on the barn's stage, and Dave Brubeck's family lived in the guesthouse on the property. The famous School of Jazz opened in 1957 and ran for three years, inspired by the series of roundtables on jazz that the

Barbers had held at the inn from the beginning; its students included Ornette Coleman and Don Cherry. There are several projects in progress documenting the important history of the Music Inn.

16. Hawthorne lived in "the Little Red House," directly across from Tanglewood, the former Tappan family estate, which was given to the Boston Symphony Orchestra in 1936 by Mrs. Gorham Brooks and Miss Mary Aspinwall Tappan. Hawthorne's house burned in 1891, but the Federated Music Clubs of America built a replica in 1948 that can be visited today.

17. The Stockbridge School became the DeSisto School, a residential place of learning for emotionally disturbed children, which closed in 2004 after the Massachusetts Office of Child Care Services found "serious risks" to student safety. The school has since moved to Mexico. See Jessica Bennett, "'Serious Risks' Cited at School for Teens," *Boston Globe,* February 23, 2004.

18. "Walter Wilson Starts New Development around Bowl," *Berkshire Eagle,* August 22, 1959. Of those who lived in Wilson's developments on the Bowl, Ghitalla and Kapuscinski are perhaps best known. Ghitalla, who passed away in 2001, is known not only for his twenty-eight-year career playing with the Boston Symphony Orchestra, where he was principal for fifteen years, but also for his teaching. He served on the faculty of Boston University, the Hartt School of Music (Hartford, Connecticut), and the New England Conservatory (Boston), among other schools, and, of course, taught at the Tanglewood Institute. Kapuscinski mentored many of the great contemporary cellists at the Oberlin Conservatory and was principal cellist for the Baltimore Symphony Orchestra.

19. *Berkshire Eagle,* October 3, 1964.

20. Walter Wilson, quoted in ibid.

21. Andrew L. Clarke, "Apostle of a New Industry," *Berkshire Eagle,* August 14, 1965.

22. "3,000 Acres in Hill Towns Proposed for Development," *Berkshire Eagle,* February 10, 1966; Edward J. Farrell, "Vacation Homes Planned for Peru," *Berkshire Eagle,* February 19, 1966.

23. Walter Wilson, quoted in "Broker Urges County-Wide Survey to Assess Impact of Second Homes," *Berkshire Eagle,* December 16, 1967.

24. "'Interior Land Is Worth More,' Wilson Asserts," *Berkshire Eagle,* November 2, 1966.

25. Edward J. Farrell, "Developer Proposes New Land-Use Plan," *Berkshire Eagle,* July 1, 1967; Richard K. Weil, "An Enigma Develops," *Berkshire Eagle,* August 13, 1966.

26. "Richmond Land Case Creeps On," *Berkshire Eagle*, November 20, 2971; "Court Awards $17,500 to Berkshire Land Co.," *Berkshire Eagle*, November 24, 1971.

27. "Greenberg Suing Wilson for Fees," *Berkshire Eagle*, July 9, 1971; "Greenberg Suing 2 Principals of Land Ventures Co.," *Berkshire Eagle*, July 13, 1971.

28. The final straw between Wilson and Simons happened in the late 1970s, when a group of people, including Eli Wallach, Tom Lehrer, and Phil and Stephanie Barber, formed a limited partnership for investment purposes. Simons joined the group, of which Wilson was the general partner and the rest were limited partners. Simons felt that Wilson, in a variety of unethical dealings, had become "greedy," and felt he had to protect the other investors from Wilson. Soon afterward, in 1979, Simons was appointed to a superior court bench and Wilson went to a series of other lawyers for representation.

29. Wilson, quoted in Weil, "Enigma Develops."

30. Weil, "Enigma Develops."

31. "Hard-Nosed Idealist."

32. Walter Wilson to Lawrence K. Miller, October 5, 1946, Sketch B File, Du Bois, *Berkshire Eagle*.

33. Amy Bess Miller and her husband first became interested in the Shakers in 1933, when they received a Shaker table as a wedding present. At the auction that followed her death, in 2003, the table sold for $25,312.50. Jackie Sideli, "The Amy Bess Miller Estate Sale," *Maine Auction Digest*, December 2003, http://www.maineantiquedigest.com/articles/dec03/bess1203.htm (accessed June 27, 2005). The Hancock Shaker Village now boasts the Amy Bess and Lawrence K. Miller Library, which has a wide-ranging collection of primary and secondary materials on the Shakers. See http://www.hancockshakervillage.org/. Artifacts from Amy Bess Miller's collection provide a core of the museum's holdings.

34. Wilson, quoted in "Hard-Nosed Idealist."

35. Weil, "Enigma Develops."

36. Farrell, "Realtor Wilson Founding Publishing Firm."

37. "Du Bois State Memorial Proposed," *Berkshire Eagle*, February 12, 1968.

38. Drew, *Great Barrington*, 378.

39. Gordon is the John M. Musser Professor Emeritus of Psychology at Yale University and the Richard March Hoe Professor Emeritus of Psychology and Education. He currently serves as the director of the Institute of Urban and Minority Education at Teachers College, Columbia University, in New York City.

One of the key leaders in developing a series of innovations in American education, including Head Start, he has written a wealth of scholarship in his illustrious career—some 175 articles and 15 books. In 2004, when the Education Testing Service (ETS) created the Edmund W. Gordon Chair for Policy Evaluation and Research, Eleanor Horne, ETS vice president, eloquently summarized Gordon's contributions in a press release: "Dr. Gordon has been a tireless champion for equity and social justice in education during his distinguished career as a minister, psychologist, author, educator, and research scholar. His seminal work on issues of affirmative development and minority achievement is world renowned and has changed the face of education in the United States." According to a January 2003 *New York Times* article, Gordon "could reasonably be called one of the leading psychologists of our era and the premier Black psychologist." Educational Testing Service, "News and Media: Feb. 4, 2004" (press release), http://www.ets.org/news/04020302.html (accessed June 28, 2004); the *New York Times* article is quoted in the press release.

40. Edmund W. Gordon, conversation with the author, June 23, 2004, Columbia University, New York. All subsequent citations of Gordon refer to this conversation.

41. D. Robinson, "W.E.B. Du Bois Hometown."

42. "Hard-Nosed Idealist."

43. Gunn greatly emphasizes the influence of Jones, who worked at Simon's Rock College and was the daughter of Raleigh Dove, pastor of the Clinton A.M.E. Zion Church, on the memorial movement, although she says Wilson maintained the more public face of the activism.

44. See *Berkshire Eagle* issues dated February 26, 1960; November 25, 1961; February 19, 1963; August 28, 1963; and March 9, 1965.

45. "Great Barrington's Illustrious Son," *Berkshire Courier*, February 23, 1950.

46. Russell G. Willcox, letter to the editor, *Berkshire Courier*, reprinted in "Planned Du Bois Memorial Criticized in Great Barrington," *Berkshire Eagle*, February 21, 1968. The writer also sent an almost identical version of the letter to the *Eagle*, which published it the day after the *Eagle* ran the article, on February 22, 1968.

47. Martin Luther King Jr., quoted in David Levering Lewis, "Exit Strategy," *Crisis*, July–August, 2003, http://www.findarticles.com/p/articles/mi_qa 4081/is_200307/ai_n9240656 (accessed June 28, 2005).

48. "Martin Luther King Backs Du Bois Project," *Berkshire Eagle*, February 26, 1968.

49. Volpe was governor of Massachusetts from 1961 to 1963 and again from 1965 to 1969. During his administrations, he banned racial inequity in education and opened the door for a more open policy regarding contraception. Criticized for raising the state sales tax, he resigned midterm in 1969 to accept President Nixon's appointment to run the Department of Transportation. Under Volpe's leadership there, Amtrak was founded.

50. "Du Bois State Memorial Proposed."

51. Cecil E. Brooks, quoted in "Brooks Backs Anti–Du Bois Stand by VFW," *Berkshire Eagle*, March 5, 1968.

52. Michael S. Sherry, "Patriotic Orthodoxy and American Decline," in Linethal and Engelhardt, *History Wars*, 99.

53. John W. Tynan Jr., "Barrington VFW Acts," *Berkshire Eagle*, February 29, 1968.

54. Leonard R. Spencer, letter to the editor, *Berkshire Eagle*, March 18, 1968. Spencer cites 83d Cong., 1953–1954, H. Report 2681.

55. William F. Bell, "Prophet Not without Honor: A Special Report," *Berkshire Eagle*, March 2, 1968.

56. Polly Pierce, letter to the editor, *Berkshire Eagle*, March 6, 1968.

57. G. Albert Sauer, letter to the editor, *Berkshire Eagle*, March 6, 1968. Vidkun Quisling, known by some as "Norway's Benedict Arnold," served as the president of Norway during World War II while the elected government remained in exile in London. At the end of the war, Quisling, a fascist, was found guilty for high treason and executed.

58. Spencer, letter to the editor.

59. Editorial, *Berkshire Courier*; reprinted in *Berkshire Eagle*, March 7, 1968.

60. "County NAACP Expected to Back Memorial," *Berkshire Eagle*, March 9, 1968.

61. "Du Bois Memorial Is Endorsed by National NAACP," *Berkshire Eagle*, April 16, 1968.

62. Mrs. Robert F. Nielson, letter to the editor, *Berkshire Eagle*, March 20, 1968.

63. "Three More Organizations Oppose Du Bois Memorial," *Berkshire Eagle*, March 7, 1968; "Legion Opposes Memorial to W.E.B. Du Bois," *Berkshire Eagle*, March 9, 1968; "Dalton VFW Opposes Du Bois Memorial," *Berkshire Eagle*, March 13, 1968.

64. "County Legion May Enter Du Bois Issue," *Berkshire Eagle*, March 6, 1968; "County Legion, Curtiss Join Memorial Foes," *Berkshire Eagle*, March 18, 1968.

65. "Senator Hammond Opposes W.E.B. Du Bois Memorial," *Berkshire Eagle*, March 14, 1968; "County Legion May Enter Du Bois Issue"; "County Legion, Curtiss."

66. Edward W. Brooke, quoted in "Brooke Praises Du Bois, Defends Memorial Project," *Berkshire Eagle*, March 30, 1968. Brooke, a graduate of Howard University and Boston University Law School, served as attorney general of Massachusetts before getting elected to the U.S. Senate in 1966, where he served until his second reelection bid proved unsuccessful, in 1978. "Biographical Directory of the United States Congress, 1744–Present," http://bio guide.congress.gov/scripts/biodisplay.pl?index=B000871 (accessed June 3, 2004). See also Edward Brooke, *The Challenge of Change: Crisis in Our Two-Party System* (Boston: Little Brown, 1966); and John Henry Cutler, *Ed Brooke: Biography of a Senator* (New York: Bobbs-Merrill, 1972).

67. "7 More Negro Celebrities Support Du Bois Memorial," *Berkshire Eagle*, March 26, 1968.

68. "Bonneville Heads Group Opposed to Memorial," *Berkshire Eagle*, March 15, 1968; "7 More Negro Celebrities"; "New Group Opposes Du Bois Park," *Berkshire Eagle*, September 26, 1968.

69. John W. Tynan Jr., "Wrong Town, Wrong Time," *Berkshire Eagle*, March 9, 1968.

70. W. E. D. Stokes Jr., letter to the editor, *Berkshire Eagle*, February 29, 1968.

71. Henry A. Kittredge, letter to the editor, *Berkshire Eagle*, March 6, 1968.

72. Walter Wilson, "How the Du Bois Idea Was Born," letter to the editor, *Berkshire Eagle*, March 7, 1968.

73. Savage, *Standing Soldiers, Kneeling Slaves*, 6–7.

74. National Park Service, "Saratoga National Historical Park," http://www .nps.gov/sara (accessed July 7, 2005).

75. Wilson, "How the Du Bois Idea Was Born."

76. Ibid.

77. Ibid.

78. Ibid.

79. C. W. Kirkpatrick, letter to the editor, *Berkshire Eagle*, March 9, 1968.

80. Clarence Dohoney, letter to the editor, *Berkshire Eagle*, March 9, 1968.

81. Ruth H. Olsen, letter to the editor, *Berkshire Eagle*, March 6, 1968.

82. Agnes S. Majewski, letter to the editor, *Berkshire Eagle*, March 6, 1968.

83. William Muller, letter to the editor, *Berkshire Eagle*, March 9, 1968.

84. "Bonneville Heads Group."

85. Wilson, quoted in "Hard-Nosed Idealist."

86. Wilson, quoted in D. Robinson, "W.E.B. Du Bois Hometown."

87. Douglas Robinson, "Berkshires Park Named for Du Bois," *New York Times,* October 19, 1969, http://search.nytimes.com/books/00/11/05/specials/dubois-park.html (accessed June 12, 2001).

88. Walter Wilson, "Du Bois's Motives," letter to the editor, *Berkshire Eagle,* March 27, 1968.

89. Editorial, *Nation,* April 1, 1968, 429.

90. It is not surprising that Elizabeth "Lib" Blodgett Hall supported the movement to memorialize Du Bois, as her life was marked by progressive accomplishments and goals. Born in New York City, Elizabeth Blodgett Hall moved to Great Barrington in 1922, when her father purchased Great Pine Farm. She married Harvard law professor Livingston Hall in 1930, and, after completing her college work at Radcliffe as an adult, she took a position as chair of the history department at Concord Academy in 1948. The school named her headmistress a year later, and under her leadership it became one of the top private schools in the country. She returned to Great Barrington in 1963 to take care of her parents, and began to work on the creation of a new school. Hall founded Simon's Rock, which is now part of Bard College, in 1964, with land donated by her mother, Margaret Kendrick Blodgett, as well as the resources of the Blodgett Foundation, with the mission of establishing America's first "early college," meaning that most students begin their education at the institution while still of high school age.

91. Lawrence Larson and the *Courier* editorial are quoted in "Barrington Cleric Rapped for 'Insinuating Bigotry,'" *Berkshire Eagle,* April 11, 1968.

92. Alfred E. DeFreest, letter to the editor, *Berkshire Eagle,* April 11, 1968.

93. Dwight P. Campbell, letter to the editor, *Berkshire Eagle,* August 19, 1968.

94. John S. Steele, letter to the editor, *Berkshire Eagle,* March 28, 1968.

95. John O. LaFontana, letter to the editor, *Berkshire Eagle,* April 18, 1968.

96. Ibid.

97. Ibid.

4. WHERE WILLIE LIVED AND PLAYED

1. "Du Bois Memorial Group to Offer Books to Library," *Berkshire Eagle,* May 1, 1968.

2. Quoted in "Courier Offers New Plan," *Berkshire Eagle*, April 25, 1968.

3. Du Bois, *Souls of Black Folk*, 54.

4. "Site Work to Commence," *Berkshire Eagle*, March 26, 1968; "Work Bee Set for May 18 on Du Bois Memorial Site," *Berkshire Eagle*, April 30, 1968; "Du Bois Memorial Site Cleanup," *Berkshire Eagle*, May 17, 1968; "Dozen Workers Begin Cleanup," *Berkshire Eagle*, May 20, 1968.

5. "Dedication Planned for Du Bois Park," *Berkshire Eagle*, June 18, 1968.

6. "Group Questions Zoning at Du Bois Memorial Site," *Berkshire Eagle*, May 28, 1968. Murtagh was a local, born in Great Barrington in 1916 and admitted to the bar in 1952 after serving a stint as captain in the U.S. Air Force from 1941 to 1946. He served as town counsel from 1962 to 1985, and as town moderator from 1969 to 1990. His firm, which calls itself the "oldest and most prestigious" in Great Barrington, still bears his name and is housed in William Cullen Bryant's former home.

7. "Radio Poll Finds 78% Opposed to Du Bois Memorial," *Berkshire Eagle*, October 5, 1968.

8. "Group Renews Opposition to Du Bois Plans," *Berkshire Eagle*, September 23, 1968; "New Group Opposes Du Bois Park," *Berkshire Eagle*, September 26, 1968.

9. "Dedication Delayed," *Berkshire Eagle*, October 2, 1968. Richardson served as attorney general of Massachusetts from 1967 to 1969, when he became undersecretary of state and then secretary of health, education, and welfare in the Nixon administration. In January 1973, Nixon appointed him secretary of defense, an office he served in for just five months, resigning in October after refusing to fire a Watergate special prosecutor at Nixon's demand. He filled posts in both Ford's and Carter's administrations before returning to his law practice.

10. Walter Wilson, quoted in "DuBois Memorial Group Will Launch Fund Drive," *Berkshire Eagle*, February 28, 1969.

11. "Publication Planned for Du Bois Works," *Berkshire Eagle*, September 18, 1969. See Walter Wilson, ed., *The Selected Writings of W.E.B. Du Bois* (New York: New American Library, 1969). Stephen J. Wright wrote the introduction to the book.

12. "Work on Site Begins for Du Bois Memorial," *Berkshire Eagle*, June 10, 1969.

13. "Julian Bond, GA Legislator, to Speak," *Berkshire Eagle*, July 18, 1969.

14. "BSO Offers Shed for Dedication of Du Bois Park," *Berkshire Eagle*, July 18, 1969.

15. Robert Parrish, quoted in Doane Hubick, "Delay Ordered in Du Bois Rites," *Berkshire Eagle*, October 15, 1969.

16. "Du Bois Park Transferred to Foundation Ownership," *Berkshire Eagle*, September 17, 1969.

17. "Du Bois Foundation Holds to Its Dedication Plans," *Berkshire Eagle*, October 16, 1969.

18. William P. Murtagh, quoted in "Selectmen Allow Du Bois Rites," *Berkshire Eagle*, October 17, 1969; D. Robinson, "Berkshires Park Named for Du Bois." Robinson's piece was news itself, as the *Berkshire Eagle* printed a story on it: "DuBois Memorial Subject of Feature in New York Times," *Berkshire Eagle*, May 16, 1969.

19. "MCAD Checks for Racial Bias in Du Bois Dedication Ban," *Berkshire Eagle*, October 16, 1969.

20. "Ossie Davis Will Emcee Du Bois Rites," *Berkshire Eagle*, October 14, 1969.

21. Allen H. Nolan and Walter Wilson are both quoted in "City Afro-American Leader Raps Du Bois Rites Plans," *Berkshire Eagle*, October 13, 1969.

22. William E. Bell, "Controversial Du Bois Park Scene of Quiet Dedication," *Berkshire Eagle*, October 20, 1969.

23. Quoted in Duberman, *Paul Robeson*, 364. The account of the Peekskill incidents that follows is from pp. 364–70.

24. Upon release from prison, Fast was blacklisted and had to publish under a variety of pseudonyms, including E. V. Cunningham, and through his own press, Black Heron. He ran for Congress for the American Labor Party in 1952, and received the Stalin Peace Prize in 1954; he split from the Communist Party that same year, writing about his decision in *The Naked God* (1954). In 1974, Fast moved his family to Los Angeles, where he settled into a career writing for television, including *How the West Was Won*, and he published his immensely popular series *The Immigrants*, which became a two-part television series. For an overview of Fast's life, see Alan Wald, "Howard Fast," in *Encyclopedia of the American Left*, ed. Mari Jo Buhle, Paul Buhle, and Dan Georgakas (Urbana: University of Illinois Press, 1992). See also Andrew MacDonald, *Howard Fast: A Critical Companion* (New York: Greenwood, 1996).

25. Howard Fast, "Peekskill Affidavit," *Daily Worker*, September 13, 1949, http://www.trussel.com/hf/plots/t624.htm (accessed June 30, 2004).

26. Howard Fast, *Being Red: A Memoir* (New York: Houghton Mifflin, 1990), 226–39.

27. Fast, "Peekskill Affidavit."

28. Duberman, *Paul Robeson*, 370–71.

29. "Ceremony Marks 50th Anniversary of Peekskill Riot at Paul Robeson Concert," *Half Moon Press*, September 1999, http://www.hudsonriver.com/half moonpress/stories/0999robe.htm (accessed June 30, 2004). *Half Moon Press*, now defunct, was a newspaper that served a consortium now called the Historic Hudson River Towns, formed by some fifteen municipalities that dot the east bank of the Hudson River, including Peekskill.

30. The *New York Times* article is cited in D. Robinson, "Berkshires Park Named for Du Bois."

31. Bell, "Controversial Du Bois Park"; Emmett J. Shea, quoted in "Du Bois Rites Occasioned Strong Security Measures," *Berkshire Eagle*, October 25, 1969.

32. Du Bois, *Autobiography*, 416–17; "War in Brooklyn," *Time*, February 7, 1949, http://www.time.com/time/archive/preview/0,10987,799798,00.html (accessed July 27, 2005).

33. Bell, "Controversial Du Bois Park."

34. Ibid.

35. Julian Bond, quoted in D. Robinson, "Berkshires Park Named for Du Bois."

36. Shirley Graham Du Bois, quoted in Bell, "Controversial Du Bois Park."

37. Walter Scott, "Footnote to History," *Berkshire Eagle*, October 25, 1969. A short film of the dedication ceremony, narrated by Ossie Davis, can be viewed at http://www.library.umass.edu/spcoll/collections/dubois/index.htm.

38. Walter Wilson, quoted in D. Robinson, "Berkshires Park Named for Du Bois."

39. "Barrington Unrelenting on Du Bois Park," *Berkshire Eagle*, October 21, 1969; "Board Gives Warning on Du Bois Issue," *Berkshire Eagle*, November 19, 1969.

40. "NAACP Assigns Lawyer to Du Bois Case," *Berkshire Eagle*, October 18, 1969. Shapiro graduated from Harvard Law School in 1961 and then worked in Mississippi as part of the Lawyers' Committee for Civil Rights under Law, to ensure that the civil rights laws of the 1960s were enforced. He joined the LDF in 1968.

41. Jonathan Shapiro, phone interview by author, July 20, 2005. As well as his work on the Ali case, Shapiro successfully argued Supreme Court cases such as *Ham v. South Carolina*, in 1973, and *Ponte v. Real*, in 1985. Today, he is a founding partner of Stern Shapiro Weissberg & Garrin, which identifies itself as "a litigation firm with a reputation for superb and effective advocacy."

For more of Shapiro's professional biography, see http://www.sswg.com/text/ john.html.

42. "Syllabus on Du Bois Is Published," *Berkshire Eagle*, May 14, 1970.

43. "Du Bois Foundation to Lay Plans for National Shrine" and "Harvard Committee Named to Design Du Bois Institute," both in the *Berkshire Eagle*, March 30, 1970.

44. "Shaker Festival Planned as Annual Area Art Event," *Berkshire Eagle*, May 9, 1970; "Music and Dance Drama about Shakers to Be Presented," *Berkshire Eagle*, September 16, 1969.

45. "Du Bois Group Issues Appeal for Funds," *Berkshire Eagle*, June 3, 1970.

46. "Du Bois Park Rites on Television Tonight," *Berkshire Eagle*, August 31, 1970. NET was an important forerunner to the Public Broadcasting Service (PBS). Established in 1952, NET was principally funded by the Ford Foundation, but when it eventually clashed with the younger PBS, it transferred its programming, including *Sesame Street* and *Mister Rogers' Neighborhood*, to public television.

47. "Du Bois Widow Is Barred from U.S.," *Berkshire Eagle*, May 5, 1970.

48. For more on Shirley Graham Du Bois, see Gerald Horne, *Race Woman: The Lives of Shirley Graham Du Bois* (New York: New York University Press, 2000).

49. C. Gerald Fraser, "Black Academy Names 3 Leaders to Hall of Fame," *New York Times*, July 14, 1970.

50. C. Gerald Fraser, "Mrs. W.E.B. Du Bois to Visit U.S. Next Month," New York Times News Service, reprinted in the *Berkshire Eagle*, August 17, 1970; "Mrs. Du Bois Comes to U.S. Next Tuesday," *Berkshire Eagle*, September 9, 1970.

51. "Widow of W.E.B. Du Bois to Visit Great Barrington," *Berkshire Eagle*, October 8, 1970; William F. Bell, "Mrs. W.E.B. Du Bois's Visit to Mark 1st Anniversary of Husband's Memorial," *Berkshire Eagle*, October 10, 1970.

52. William F. Bell, "Du Bois's Love for Great Barrington Is Stressed by Widow on Visit to Park," *Berkshire Eagle*, October 19, 1970.

53. Ibid.

54. Ibid.

55. "Du Bois's Birthplace Pinpointed by Newsman," *Berkshire Eagle*, July 15, 1971.

56. James E. Overmyer, "Weeds Replace Furor at Du Bois Park," *Berkshire Eagle*, August 18, 1972.

57. Ibid.

58. Ibid.

5. A PROPHET WITHOUT HONOR

1. Colman McCarthy, "The Black Genius of W.E.B. Du Bois," *Berkshire Eagle*, February 23, 1971, reprinted from the *Washington Post*.

2. "Simon's Rock Will Honor Du Bois," *Berkshire Eagle*, January 18, 1973; "Simon's Rock Honors Du Bois," *Berkshire Eagle*, February 24, 1973. Redding, who died in 1988, taught at a number of places, including Morehouse College, before becoming the first African American faculty member at Brown University, in 1949. He published *To Make a Poet Black* in 1939, followed by *No Day of Triumph* (1942), *Stranger and Alone* (1950), *They Came in Chains* (1951), *On Being Negro in America* (1951), *An American in India* (1954), and *The Lonesome Road* (1958).

3. "Simon's Rock Honors Du Bois."

4. "West Stockbridge May Sue Developer," *Berkshire Eagle*, August 1, 1973.

5. "UMass Buys Papers of Dr. Du Bois," *Berkshire Eagle*, June 5, 1973.

6. Shirley Graham Du Bois, quoted in "Memorabilia," *New Yorker*, July 16, 1973, 23.

7. Herbert Aptheker, quoted in "Memorabilia," 23–24.

8. Randolph Bromery, quoted in "Memorabilia," 24.

9. "Papers of W.E.B. Du Bois Await Fixing to Make Them Permanent," *Berkshire Eagle*, February 7, 1974; "$69,942 Allotted for Du Bois Papers," *Berkshire Eagle*, July 31, 1975.

10. "Legion Blasts UMass Buying of Du Bois Papers," *Berkshire Eagle*, July 16, 1973.

11. John L. Phair and Rudolph Werner, quoted in ibid.

12. Mortimer H. Appley, quoted in "Legion Blasts UMass Buying."

13. "Du Bois Foundation Seeks Federal Status for Park," *Berkshire Eagle*, February 28, 1974.

14. Stephen Fay, "Du Bois Park Eyed as Historic Site," *Berkshire Eagle*, September 25, 1975. The secretary of the interior changed often in this period. At the time of the visit to the Du Bois site for review, the secretary was former Wyoming governor Stephen K. Hathaway, a member of Gerald Ford's cabinet, who resigned after a short stint for health reasons. President Ford replaced him with Thomas Kleppe in October 1975.

15. "Du Bois Site Landmark Status Made Official," *Berkshire Eagle,* May 29, 1976.

16. Two other National Historic Landmark designations in the Berkshires came after that of the Du Bois park: Crane and Company Old Stone Mill Rag Room, in Dalton (1983), and the Jacob's Pillow Dance Festival, in Beckett (2003). See http://tps.cr.nps.gov/nhl/.

17. National Park Service, http://www.cr.nps.gov/nhl/ (accessed June 22, 2004). The designation of National Historic Landmark is one of five allotted by the Department of the Interior; the others are American Battlefields, Historic Buildings, Historic Landscapes, and Tribal Communities. Today, there are fewer than 2,500 places that bear the designation National Historic Landmark.

18. National Historic Landmarks Program, http://www.cr.nps.gov/nhl/whatis .htm (accessed June 22, 2004).

19. "W.E.B. Du Bois Boyhood Homesite," National Historic Landmarks Program, http://tps.cr.nps.gov/nhl/detail.cfm?ResourceId=1623&ResourceType= Site (accessed June 22, 2004).

20. Walter Wilson, quoted in "W.E.B. Du Bois Site Received Approval as National Landmark," *Berkshire Eagle,* April 14, 1976.

21. "Cleanup Set at Du Bois Homesite," *Berkshire Eagle,* May 28, 1976.

22. Walter Wilson, quoted in "Du Bois Admirer Prods White History Group," *Berkshire Eagle,* June 9, 1976.

23. Steve Turner, "Black Sheep of the Native Sons," *Berkshires Week,* August 26, 1976, 6 (ellipsis in original).

24. Ibid.

25. Ibid., 8.

26. George Francis and Walter Wilson, quoted in ibid.

27. Paul Ivory and Francis, quoted in Turner, "Black Sheep of the Native Sons," 9.

28. Wilson, quoted in Turner, "Black Sheep of the Native Sons," 9.

29. Gerard Chapman, letter to the editor, *Berkshire Eagle,* August 25, 1976.

30. Drew, *Great Barrington,* 122.

31. Chapman, letter to the editor.

32. Among the highlights of Oliphant's career, he obtained the Pentagon Papers for the *Boston Globe* in 1971, and his reporting on the Wounded Knee occupation in 1973 garnered him several awards. He served as the analyst for PBS during the impeachment trial of Bill Clinton, in 1999. In 1989, he published *All By Myself,* an account of the 1988 presidential campaign. He published his last column in the *Globe* in 2005 but remains a popular "talking head."

33. Stephen Fay, "FBI Takes Credit for Opposition to Du Bois Barrington Memorial," *Berkshire Eagle*, November 30, 1977.

34. Ibid.

35. "FBI Eyed, Dropped Story Plant in Eagle," *Berkshire Eagle*, December 2, 1977.

36. Ibid.

37. Stephen Fay, "Prophetic Snoops," *Berkshire Eagle*, December 3, 1977.

38. Ibid; ellipsis in the original.

39. Walter Wilson, quoted in "U.N. Ceremony Commemorates Birthday of W.E.B. Du Bois," *Berkshire Eagle*, February 24, 1978.

40. Walter Wilson, "Marking Du Bois' Birthday," *Berkshire Eagle*, February 22, 1979.

41. Steve Moore, "Recognition of Du Bois Advances on Two Fronts," *Berkshire Eagle*, October 18, 1979.

42. Meade went on to complete his PhD at the University of Massachusetts and taught in the W. E. B. Du Bois Department of Afro-American Studies there. He has served as a trustee of the Berkshire County Day School, where he helped create the W. E. B. Du Bois Curriculum Project. He presented a paper on the Great Barrington memorial efforts at the William College conference "Souls of Black Folk: W.E.B. Du Bois and the Century of the Color Line," November 6–8, 2003, Williamstown, Massachusetts.

43. Homer L. Meade II, "Du Bois: Honored Prophet," *Berkshire Eagle*, October 19, 1979.

44. Ibid.

45. Ibid.

46. Sheila Rule, "Two Pioneering Black Scholars, Du Bois and Bond, Are Honored," *New York Times*, October 22, 1979.

47. Founded in 1968 in Boston by Dr. Elma Lewis, the NCAAA is a private nonprofit organization "committed to preserving and fostering the cultural arts heritage of black peoples worldwide through arts teaching, and the presentation of professional works in all fine arts disciplines." It built upon the foundations Lewis created in 1950 with the Elma Lewis School of Fine Arts. See http://www.ncaaa.org/ncaaa.html for more information (accessed June 8, 2004).

48. Steve Moore, "900 Turn Out to Honor W.E.B. DuBois at Historic-Landmark Ceremony Saturday," *Berkshire Eagle*, October 22, 1979.

49. "Ghanaian Official to Attend," *Berkshire Eagle*, September 28, 1979; "Senegal's Ambassador to the UN Will Attend Ceremony," *Berkshire Eagle*, October 15, 1979; Moore, "900 Turn Out." It is interesting to note that while

he was chancellor, Bromery, who has served as the president of Springfield College, Westfield State College, and Roxbury Community College—all in Massachusetts—led the lengthy effort to rename the University of Massachusetts Library the W. E. B. Du Bois Library.

50. Jean Caldwell, "DuBois Homesite Dedicated as US Site," *Boston Sunday Globe*, October 28, 1979. Bond was announced as keynote speaker on September 13, 1979, in the *Berkshire Eagle*.

51. Julian Bond, quoted in ibid.

52. Moore, "900 Turn Out."

53. Ibid.

54. Rule, "Two Pioneering Black Scholars."

55. W. E. B. Du Bois, "What Great Barrington Means to Me," quoted in *Writings by W.E.B. Du Bois in Periodicals Edited by Others*, vol. 2, *1910–1934*, ed. Herbert Aptheker (New York: Kraus-Thomson, 1982), 260.

56. Quoted in Drew, *Great Barrington*, 376.

57. Florence Logan, quoted in Steve Moore, "DuBois Remembered: 'Elegant, Handsome,'" *Berkshire Eagle*, October 19, 1979.

58. One such photograph ran in the *Berkshire Eagle*, October 20, 1979.

59. *Berkshire Eagle*, November 3, 1979.

60. "NY Architect Firm of Bond-Ryder Offers to Design Du Bois Memorial," *Berkshire Eagle*, November 1, 1979. The firm was founded by renowned black architect J. Max Bond Jr., whose many designs include the Bolgatanga Library, in Ghana; the Martin Luther King Jr. Center for Nonviolent Social Change, in Atlanta; and the Birmingham Civil Rights Museum.

61. *Berkshire Eagle*, July 12, 1980.

62. Richard T. Delmasto, "Du Bois's Hometown Legacy Remains Mostly Ignorance," *Berkshire Eagle*, February 17, 1983.

63. Horace Smith, quoted in ibid.

64. Delmasto, "Du Bois's Hometown Legacy."

65. Stephen Fay, "Du Bois, Harassed in Own Country."

66. Homer Meade, quoted in ibid.

67. Fay, "Du Bois, Harassed in Own Country."

6. AN UNCERTAIN LEGACY

1. Du Bois, *Autobiography*, 39–40.

2. "Film on Du Bois Is Being Made," *Berkshire Eagle*, March 29, 1978. Carlton Moss, a writer, director, producer, and actor, is perhaps best known as

the writer of *The Negro Soldier* (1944), a film about Joe Louis that was used in army orientations during World War II. See Lauren Rebecca Sklaroff, "Constructing G.I. Joe Louis: Cultural Solutions to the 'Negro Problem' during World War II," *Journal of American History* 89, no. 3 (December 2002), http://www. historycooperative.org/journals/jah/89.3/sklaroff.html.

3. Nordstrom, "Truth Shall Make You Free."

4. University of Massachusetts Board of Trustees, Trustee Document T94-096, http://www.library.umass.edu/spcoll/manuscripts/dubois_papers/dbnaming.html (accessed June 21, 2004).

5. "Rep. Conte, Mrs. Du Bois to Be Honored," *Berkshire Eagle*, May 14, 1973.

6. "UMass Scholars Eagerly Await Acquisition by University of W.E.B. Du Bois Homesite," *Berkshire Eagle*, June 14, 1982. The deed transferring ownership to the University of Massachusetts was received at the Great Barrington Registry of Deeds on July 20, 1988; University of Massachusetts, Special Collections and Archives, W. E. B. Du Bois Collection, bk. 676, p. 232. Many thanks to the head of special collections, William Thompson, for help with finding the deed.

7. For more on the UMass anthropology department's work, see http://www.library.umass.edu/spcoll/manuscripts/dubois_papers/dbanthro.html (accessed June 21, 2004).

8. Delmasto, "Du Bois's Vision for Future."

9. Claudette Callahan, "UMass Dig Under Way at Du Bois Site," *Berkshire Eagle*, July 25, 1984.

10. Robert Paynter, quoted in Stephen Fay, "W.E.B. Du Bois Birthday Observances Set," *Berkshire Eagle*, February 21, 1989.

11. Stephen Fay, "Tax Collector Targets Du Bois Site for Taking," *Berkshire Eagle*, August 2, 1985.

12. Robert G. Guidi, quoted in "Dubois Site Needs Waiver on Tax Bill," *Berkshire Eagle*, August 8, 1985.

13. "Dubois Site Needs Waiver."

14. Fay, "Du Bois Birthday Observances Set"; Daniel O. Bellow, "Du Bois' Birthday Is Celebrated," *Berkshire Eagle*, February 27, 1989; Cooper, "Du Bois Memorial Planned."

15. Susanna Cooper, "In His Home County, Du Bois Remains an Unsung Hero," *Berkshire Eagle*, October 1, 1989.

16. Ibid.

17. "Greylock Senior Obtains Exhibit on Du Bois for School Gallery," *Berkshire Eagle*, January 12, 1989.

18. Esther Dozier, quoted in Lyrysa Smith, "Local Hero," *Albany Times Union*, February 2, 2003. A difficult note to add: as I was in the final editing stages of this book, Rev. Dozier was found dead—stabbed to death—in her home, on June 11, 2007. Police charged her husband with the crime, and Great Barrington mourned the loss of the historic church's first female minister.

19. Smith, "Local Hero."

20. See Great Barrington Land Conservancy, "Welcome to Great Barrington Housatonic River Walk," http://www.gbriverwalk.org/index.html#home.

21. W. E. B. Du Bois, "The Housatonic River" (address, annual meeting of the alumni of Searles High School, July 30, 1930). For the full text of the speech, see http://www.gbriverwalk.org/riverwkDuBoisCourier.html.

22. "Du Bois Homesite Dedication," Great Barrington, Mass, 1969, W. E. B. Du Bois Library, University of Massachusetts Amherst, http://www.library .umass.edu/spcoll/collections/dubois/index.htm.

23. "Upper Housatonic Valley African American Heritage Trail," Upper Housatonic Valley National Heritage Area, http://www.uhvafamtrail.org/default .html.

24. Ellen G. Lahr, "For Name of New Schools, Historian Suggests Du Bois," *Berkshire Eagle*, June 23, 2004.

25. Julian Bond, quoted in "Confederate School Names Spur Debate," CNN.com, December 26, 2003, http://www.cnn.com/ (accessed October 12, 2004). Harrison, a psychologist, later withdrew her request, claiming that she had rethought the issue of "southern heritage."

26. Lloyd Hamlin, quoted in "Confederate School Names."

27. Sally Harris, letter to the editor, *Berkshire Eagle*, July 6, 2004.

28. Rachel Fletcher, letter to the editor, *Berkshire Eagle*, July 15, 2004.

29. Barbara Bartle, letter to the editor, *Berkshire Eagle*, July 6, 2004.

30. Lynnmarie Reilly, letter to the editor, *Berkshire Eagle*, July 6, 2004.

31. Katharine Bambery and Daniel Allentuck, letter to the editor, *Berkshire Eagle*, July 15, 2004.

32. Karen Johnson and Gary Johnson, letter to the editor, *Berkshire Eagle*, July 15, 2004.

33. Jean Tomich, letter to the editor, *Berkshire Eagle*, August 11, 2004.

34. J. Alan Turner, letter to the editor, *Berkshire Eagle*, August 16, 2004.

35. Katharine Bambery and Daniel Allentuck, letter to the editor, *Berkshire Eagle*, September 5, 2004.

36. "Cop-out in BHRSD," *Berkshire Eagle*, October 11, 2004.

37. Kathy Duhon, letter to the editor, *Berkshire Eagle*, October 16, 2004.

38. Gary Leveille, letter to the editor, *Berkshire Eagle,* October 20, 2004.

39. Ellen G. Lahr, "Accusations Fly over School Naming," *Berkshire Eagle,* October 22, 2004.

40. John Grogan, quoted in ibid.

41. Stephen Bannon, quoted in Derek Gentile, "What's in a Name? Appellations for Schools on Agenda," *Berkshire Eagle,* January 17, 2005.

42. Rachel Fletcher, letter to the editor, *Berkshire Eagle,* January 19, 2005.

43. Stephen Bannon and Richard Coons, quoted in Derek Gentile, "Berkshire Hills Names New Schools: 'Media Circus' Ends with Muddy Brook, Monument Valley," *Berkshire Eagle,* January 19, 2005.

44. Alan Wilkins, quoted in Gentile, "Berkshire Hills Names New Schools."

45. "Inanimate Objects," *Berkshire Eagle,* January 20, 2005.

46. Laurie Lane-Zucker, letter to the editor, *Berkshire Eagle,* January 21, 2005.

47. Joseph I. Cohen and Rebecca Patt, letter to the editor, *Berkshire Eagle,* January 21, 2005.

48. David W. Blight, *Race and Reunion: The Civil War in American Memory* (Cambridge, Mass.: Harvard University Press, 2001), 2–3.

49. Judith Keefner and Anthony Blair, quoted in Derek Gentile, "Du Bois Signs Put on Ballot," *Berkshire Eagle,* February 15, 2005.

50. Editorial, *Berkshire Eagle,* February 15, 2005.

51. "David Du Bois, Journalist and Educator, Dies at 79," *Berkshire Eagle,* February 2, 2005. The *Eagle* also ran an op-ed piece about David Graham Du Bois by Bernard A. Drew, "Lunch with an Aging Panther," *Berkshire Eagle,* February 12, 2005.

52. Meta Ukena, letter to the editor, *Berkshire Eagle,* February 20, 2005; David Levinson, letter to the editor, *Berkshire Eagle,* February 20, 2005.

53. Esther Dozier, quoted in Derek Gentile, "Du Bois Sign Backers Seek to Clarify Record," *Berkshire Eagle,* April 21, 2005.

54. Rachel Fletcher, quoted in Gentile, "Du Bois Sign Backers."

55. Derek Gentile, "The Myth and the Man," *Berkshire Eagle,* May 4, 2005.

56. Derek Gentile, "Fish Wins Race: Voters OK Du Bois Signs," *Berkshire Eagle,* May 24, 2005.

57. Derek Gentile, "Board OKs Du Bois Signs in Great Barrington," *Berkshire Eagle,* June 7, 2005.

58. Ed Dartford, letter to the editor, *The Berkshire Eagle,* June 19, 2006.

59. Simpson, *9/11: The Culture of Commemoration,* 77.

60. Randy F. Weinstein, letter to the editor, *Berkshire Eagle*, January 26, 2006.

61. Ethan Kelley, "Civil Rights Awareness Rising in Days before Du Bois Birthday Celebrations," *Berkshire Record*, February 23, 2006; Derek Gentile, "'Brilliant Essayist' Honored: W.E.B. Du Bois Center Opens," *Berkshire Eagle*, February 13, 2006; Du Bois Center for American History, "W.E.B. Du Bois and the Promise of America: The Color Line since 1865," event program, February 11, 2006. Many thanks to Cecily Mills for saving her copy of the evening's program for me.

62. Again, thanks to Cecily Mills for saving her copies of the program of the birthday celebration at the church.

63. Jessica Willis, "Du Bois Site Gets Boost," *Berkshire Eagle*, July 4, 2008; *Friends of the Du Bois Homesite* (newsletter), no. 1 (Summer 2008).

64. Paul Boyer, "Whose History Is It Anyway? Memory, Politics, and Historical Scholarship," in Linethal and Engelhardt, *History Wars*, 137.

65. Blight, *Race and Reunion*, 397.

Index

American Civil Liberties Union
(ACLU). *See* Wilson, Walter
American Legion, xvii, 47, 66–67, 75,
91–92, 93, 95, 97, 109, 113,
121–22
Aptheker, Herbert, 111–12, 128, 140
Arnold, Benedict, 65, 70, 71–73, 74,
92, 156, 178n57
Ashley, Col. John, xvi, 7. *See also*
Freeman, Elizabeth "Mum Bett"
Attucks, Crispus, 72, 75

Barbers, Philip and Stephanie, 51,
102–3, 174–75n15, 176n28
Belafonte, Harry, xvii, 47
Berkshire County Historical Society,
2, 61, 115
Berkshire Courier, 5, 13, 18;
opposition to Du Bois memorial,
61, 63, 64, 65, 77, 83, 90, 117,
155; support for young Du Bois, 19,
61, 131
Berkshire Eagle, x, 55, 61, 65, 98,
101, 105, 107, 120–24, 128, 134,
135, 154; letters to the editor about
Du Bois in, 63, 64–65, 66, 70,
70–76, 78–79, 90, 106, 118–19,
120–21, 125, 146–49, 150,
151–52, 153, 156, 157; school

naming controversy coverage,
146–52; support for Du Bois in,
xvii, 64, 69–70, 89, 90, 115,
116–18, 125, 130, 132–33, 139,
142, 143, 153, 154–55; Walter
Wilson and, 48, 50, 51, 52, 115
Berkshire Hills Regional School
Committee. *See* school namings
Berkshire Record, xvii
Berkshires, the, ix, x, xvi, xxiv, 1–5,
11, 25, 26, 48, 50–51, 57, 58,
60–61, 65, 69, 78, 80, 85, 92, 101,
126–28, 135, 137, 147
Black Panthers, 34, 66, 81, 90, 98
Blight, David, 152, 157, 159
Bond, Horace Mann, 87, 99, 100, 130
Bond, Jean Carrey, 130, 133
Bond, Julian, xvii, 34, 87, 90,
99–100, 101, 129–30, 146
Bond, Max, 133, 188n60
Bonneville, Raymond, 68–69, 75,
85–86
Brent, Phillip, 51, 58, 84–85, 111
Brooke, Edward W. (Sen.), 67–68,
114, 179n66
Brown v. Board of Education (1954),
29, 129, 146. *See also* segregation
Burghardt, Mary, 5, 9, 11, 12–14, 16,
18, 19, 20, 106, 116